AF659302

NATURE TOURISM

NATURE TOURISM

Atul Shrivastava

CENTRUM PRESS
NEW DELHI-110002 (INDIA)

CENTRUM PRESS
H.O.: 4360/4, Ansari Road, Daryaganj,
New Delhi-110002 (India)
Tel: 23278000, 23261597, 23255577, 23286875
B.O.: No. 1015, Ist Main Road, BSK IIIrd Stage,
IIIrd Phase, IIIrd Block, Bangalore-560085 (INDIA)
Tel: 080-41723429
Email: centrumpress@gmail.com
Visit us at: www.centrumpress.com

Nature Tourism

© Reserved

First Edition, 2010

ISBN 978-93-80540-01-6

PRINTED IN INDIA

Printed at Mehra Offset Press, Delhi

Contents

Preface

Nature Tourism, often referred to as Ecotourism, was introduced to the tourist industry in the early 1980s. Ecotourism was initially connected with outdoor travel to remote, unique, and/or scenic areas. Though early Ecotourism involved an educational aspect, this was not a crucial or required element to the industry or the consumer. However, as the demand for Ecotourism has increased, the inclusion of educational elements has become increasingly important. Since its conception, Ecotourism has grown to include an entire methodology of planning, management, and economics. It is a robust and encompassing process that not only includes site information, but also considers the environment, conservation, education, equitable social benefits, and community responsibility.

Nature tourism responsible travel to natural areas, which conserves the environment and improves the welfare of local people. It is tourism based on the natural attractions of an area. Examples include birdwatching, photography, stargazing, camping, hiking, hunting, fishing, and visiting parks. These experiential tourists are interested in a diversity of natural and cultural resources. They want what is real, and they want to be immersed in a rich natural, cultural, or historical experience.

From the standpoint of conservation, nature-based tourism provides incentives for local communities and landowners to conserve wildlife habitats upon which the industry depends – it promotes conservation by placing an increased value on remaining natural areas. As nature tourism becomes more important to the local economy, communities have additional incentive to conserve their remaining natural areas for wildlife and wildlife enthusiasts.

The nature-based tourism efforts in Texas will continue to focus on achieving habitat conservation by providing information and assistance to private landowners, communities, businesses, and local community leaders wishing to make nature-based tourism an integral part of their business and community. By empowering people at the local level, we hope to build and provide guidance to a growing industry that holds great promise for sustainable economic development and conservation of wildlife habitat. Nature Tourism is one of the fastest growing segments of the tourism industry. Over 21 million United States residents regularly travel to view wildlife and enjoy nature, and spend $40 billion each year on trip related costs.

Tourism has qualified as the world's largest industry, with travel becoming easier and faster people are taking the opportunity to visit other countries. At the end of the century the worldwide tourist trade will grew. The very nature of tourism being wildlife particularly to encounter wildlife, in its natural Domain. In addition wildlife tourism benefits communities of the area. Thus tourist advertising as ecotravel, ecotour, tourism and nature tourism. The concept of development is its infancy yet.

—*Atul Shrivastava*

1

Introduction

Nature Based Tourism

Nature based tourism is reported to be one of the fastest growing tourism market. It accounts for a small fraction of overall global tourist industry. A lack of relevant knowledge and experience, inability to compete with well establish commercial operations and lack of access to capital for investment are some of the factors inhabiting its development. This book aims at providing material on concepts, structure, motivation and sources of finance methods of organising and monitoring the nature based industry.

'Nature Tourism': Meaning, Value and Boundaries

'Nature tourism' is not a term commonly used by visitors. It is not seen to be a holiday type in its own right – almost no-one speaks of taking a "nature-based holiday" or trip, just as few people would describe themselves as cultural tourists! Instead it is a term of value to the tourism industry in the context of visitor desires, experiences and activities.

Nature in Tourism

In its broadest sense, nature in tourism involves experiencing natural places, typically through outdoor activities that are sustainable in terms of their impact on the environment.

These can range from active to passive and include everything from bush walking and adventure tourism experiences to sightseeing, scenic driving, beach experiences and wildlife viewing. In many instances a visitor may combine several of these in the one trip. For keen outdoor enthusiasts, and there are many, the great majority of adventure activities directly depend on nature and natural environments for their successful conduct. Fundamentally, the role of nature can vary from 'crucial to the visitor experience' to 'enhances the visitor experience'-particularly in relation to such variables as active or passive measures of the activity involved. For passive and active visitors alike, nature is also playing an increasingly important role in giving something back to people relaxing, enriching the spirit, getting back to basics).

By doing so, it is able to enhance their broader experience of a destination. And for mainstream domestic visitors, these benefits tap more accurately into nature's deeper meaning. Nature-based experiences are intimately linked to all other aspects of the visitor's total experience of a destination, such as food, culture, relaxation, health, escape, family needs, accommodation, transport, etc. All serve to complement each other and together form the basis of a visitor's overall satisfaction with their holiday.

Nature tourism–responsible travel to natural areas, which conserves the environment and improves the welfare of local people. It is tourism based on the natural attractions of an area. Examples include bird watching, photography, stargazing, camping, hiking, hunting, fishing, and visiting parks. These experiential tourists are interested in a diversity of natural and cultural resources. They want what is real, and they want to be immersed in a rich natural, cultural, or historical experience.

From the standpoint of conservation, nature-based tourism provides incentives for local communities and landowners to conserve wildlife habitats upon which the industry depends – it promotes conservation by placing an increased value on remaining natural areas. As nature tourism becomes more important to the local economy, communities have additional incentive to conserve their remaining natural areas for wildlife and wildlife enthusiasts.

The nature-based tourism efforts in Texas will continue to focus on achieving habitat conservation by providing information and assistance to private landowners, communities, businesses, and local community leaders wishing to make nature-based tourism an integral part of their business and community. By empowering people at the local level, we hope to build and provide guidance to a growing industry that holds great promise for sustainable economic development and conservation of wildlife habitat.

Ecotourism

Ecotourism is ecologically sustainable tourism, with a primary focus on experiencing natural areas, that fosters environmental and cultural understanding, appreciation and conservation.

Ecotourists, with their strong focus on learning about the natural environment, minimising negative impacts and contributing to its care, lie at one specialist end of the nature in tourism spectrum, albeit an important one. They are in effect ambassadors (or early adopters) for a set of personal values towards which it now appears many other market segments, potentially comprising much larger visitor numbers, are moving.

Conserved and protected areas (including Marine and National Parks), the Earth's biodiversity, and respect for local culture and those who have been traditional guardians of our natural environments, can be central to their interests.

Ecotourists are also characterised by knowing what they want and being strongly self-active in accessing it. They will often plan and book their experiences and travel needs themselves, leaving tourism operators with more time and the broader opportunity to pursue tourists with more mainstream nature-based interests, and those seeking adventure activity.

Soft and Hard Adventure Tourism

Soft and hard adventure tourism activities also comprise a subset of activities strongly associated with the natural environment and nature-based tourism. Related market segments include 'adventure sports' such as mountain biking.

Anecdotal evidence from Australian tourism operators suggests that demand for both soft and hard adventure tourism is growing. Research suggests that spending by nature-based tourists (particularly those with an interest in adventure activities and visiting significant nature destinations including national parks) is often substantially above average, per visitor and per night.

It is important to recognise that international source markets can culturally differ over which activities they will describe as 'soft' and which as 'hard' (e.g. snorkelling, surfing, ballooning and orienteering may be viewed as soft by one market and hard by another). Similarly, differences in outlook can arise between younger and older visitors from the same source market. For many major international markets, soft activities rather than hard are more frequently preferred by those interested in adventure-based experiences in natural areas.

Soft adventure activities commonly require a moderate level of physical involvement by participants and are less physically challenging than hard activities. They can include –hiking/bush walking, mountain biking/bicycling, camping, horseback riding, orienteering, walking tours, wildlife spotting, whale watching, river and lake canoeing and fishing.

The numbers undertaking such activities can be substantial – e.g. the NSW Fisheries estimates that recreational fishing is enjoyed by over 1 million New South Wales residents each year, as well as around 300,000 visiting anglers. There is evidence from leading natural destinations that bush walking activity rates are also significantly increasing, particularly when support facilities are good, with highest participation rates in the 'under 2 hours' and '2 hours to a full day' categories.

Wildlife viewing also achieves high levels of participation. Hard adventure activities commonly involve a higher level of physical or rugged involvement or a potentially greater personal challenge for participants. The risk factor can also increase. Hard adventure activities with a nature basis or need include – caving, scuba diving, trekking, white water rafting, kayaking, rock and mountain climbing, cross-country skiing, safaris, surfing, wind surfing, ballooning and ocean sailing.

By contrast, bungy jumping does not depend on a nature setting. At the more challenging end of the hard adventure scale, support equipment can be involved or be absolutely necessary-e.g. climbing gear, oxygen tanks, ocean-going kayaks.

Special Interest Tourism

Nature-based tourism and its various subsets can also encompass some particularly challenging, but potentially high spending, special interest market segments. These often comprise socially and environmentally aware, highly educated and potentially demanding visitors who travel both to learn and to achieve personal and social goals. Most of these visitors are serviced and targeted by specialist tourism operators and suppliers who often provide highly expert guides as part of the service. Examples include the 'not for profit' travel sector in the United States whose interests can range widely, encompassing anything from wildlife expeditions to scientific and cultural tours. The major non-profit institutions of North America, such as natural history museums, zoos, universities and botanical societies, commonly promote their own worldwide travel programs to membership, alumni and donor bases that can run into the millions. Accessing and converting their small groups (approximately 5 to 20 people) travel market can be difficult. It takes time, effort and a great commitment to high quality standards and delivery.

An equally dedicated nature-based special interest visitor segment exists with bird-watching. Enthusiasts will travel long distances (and often at short notice) to sometimes remote and hard-to-access destinations, in order to sight new and rare species. In addition, readily identifiable communication channels (such as the ornithologists' special interest newsletters) can exist for accessing such market segments.

Wildlife Tourism

Wildlife tourism involves travel to observe wildlife in natural environments and preferably their native habitat. It is a further subset of nature tourism and one in which significantly high levels of domestic and international interest exist. Wildlife tourism involves wild and non domesticated animals and can encompass free-ranging and captive circumstances. Given the unique character and special appeal of most of Australia's wildlife, this suggests it may represent a tourism opportunity area for some destinations. The Blue Mountains, Barrington Tops, North and South Coast areas and Outback New South Wales possess great potential in this regard given their species diversity and relative convenience as destinations from major source markets and ports of entry.

Wildlife tourism encompasses the chance to encounter fauna (and flora) in terrestrial, aquatic/marine and aerial settings and to gain some further understanding of a wide variety of species (including viewing kangaroos, koalas, whales, dolphins, seals, fish and birds). Undertaking this activity in a manner that is environmentally responsible is important to ensure less disturbance to wildlife and habitats.

In terms of major visitor trends, 'appreciative tourism' involving observation, photography and interaction with wild animals is large scale, prominent and growing. Consumptive tourism involving such activities as hunting and (non-catch and release) fishing is also large scale, but declining.

Ideally, wildlife tourism should include some element of education and an increased appreciation of nature and conservation issues. Potential new models for wildlife tourism in Australia are being developed. These involve wildlife sanctuaries with feral free habitats attempting to use tourism and other enterprise based revenue sources as a means to help protect endangered native species and develop recovery plans for the species. Activities directly related to wildlife viewing, such as scuba diving and whale watching, are experiencing rapid worldwide growth in popularity and it is clear that the concept of wildlife viewing itself is gaining global currency with visitors. It has been estimated to generate $30 billion worldwide in revenues each year.

Alaska has experienced strong tourism growth in recent years, particularly in wildlife tourism, with more than 46% of its visitors engaging in this activity Nationally in the USA, wildlife viewing is the third highest purpose for trips each year (671 million) after sightseeing (1037 million) and family gatherings (778 million). It is expected that wildlife activities will increase 61% nationally over the next 52 years to Year 2050 43% of Canadians are involved in outdoor recreation each year and 18.6% have a wildlife component to their trip. 74.5% watch wildlife on the media and this is a major influence on driving wildlife tourism.

The worldwide value of whale watching is estimated at over $2 billion. In Australia it has been estimated to generate $100 million with almost one million people watching each year. In New South Wales alone, more than 200,000 people annually pay for whale watching tours – double the number of 10 years ago.

Wildlife tourism should also seek to maximise the benefits to local communities, while avoiding problems such as disturbance to wildlife and pollution. Types and magnitudes of environmental impacts associated with wildlife tourism vary with the type of tourist activity pursued – some impacts are obvious and easily identifiable while others are indirect and difficult to quantify. The impacts on particular animals should not be considered in isolation from the broader environmental settings and wider animal population.

The conservation benefits of wildlife tourism can include – its financial contribution; practical (in kind) contribution; socioeconomic incentive for conservation; and education.

Sustainable Tourism

Sustainable tourism is envisaged by the World Tourism Organisation (WTO) as "leading to management of all resources in such a way that economic, social and aesthetic needs can be fulfilled while maintaining cultural integrity, essential ecological processes, biological diversity and life support systems".

Sustainable tourism might also be defined as "tourism which is economically viable but does not destroy the resources on which the future of tourism will depend, notably the physical environment and the social fabric of the host community".

Furthermore, "A clear distinction should be made between the concepts of ecotourism and sustainable tourism: the term ecotourism itself refers to a segment within the tourism sector, while the sustainability principles should apply to all types of tourism activities, operations, establishments and projects, including conventional and alternative forms".

The goal of 'ecologically sustainable development' is to improve the total quality of life, both now and in the future, in a way that maintains the ecological processes on which life depends.

Soft Adventure

- Moderate level of physical involvement.
- Less physically challenging Hard Adventure.
- Physical, challenging, risky Ecotourism.
- Committed niche.
- Learning/caring.

Nature Tourism

Including the benefits of nature in tourism embraces what is commonly termed 'nature tourism' and its various subsets, plus the wider visitor benefits provided by nature.

Nature may be crucial to the experience or it may enhance the experience.

Supplementary Definitions with Significant Relevance to Nature in Tourism

Geotourism

Geotourism is concerned with sustaining or enhancing a destination's geographic character – the entire combination of natural and human attributes that make one place distinct from another. Geotourism encompasses both cultural and environmental concerns regarding travel, as well as the local impact tourism has upon communities and their individual economies and lifestyles. Aesthetics, heritage and the wellbeing of residents are included as some of its concerns.

Geotourism has also been summarised as restorative and reconstructive forms of tourism that enhance a destination's natural and cultural distinctiveness, as well as provide a high-quality visitor experience. Geotourism is obviously closely related to sustainable tourism, even though it has its own refined concerns and focus.

Ecologically Sustainable Development

"Using, conserving and enhancing the community's resources so that ecological processes, on which life depends, are maintained and the total quality of life, now and in the future, can be increased."

Conservation

"The management of human use of the biosphere so that it may yield the greatest sustainable benefit to present generations while maintaining its potential to meet the needs and aspirations of future generations."

"The protection, presentation, maintenance, management, sustainable use and restoration of the natural environment (and its ecosystems)."

The issue of management is vital in relation to tourism. The environmental impacts of tourism as a service industry must be recognised and never dismissed, but they also need to be placed in perspective. Ecological sustainability will never be achieved through a focus on environment and biodiversity alone. Social and economic values and needs must become integral concerns of nature conservation management. Likewise the tourism industry must address the concerns of natural area managers and recognise them as important partners in delivering sustainable experiences to visitors. Managed protected areas and other conservation sites now provide accessible means by which all visitors can experience at first hand nature in its wider diversity (and come to appreciate its values). Effectively planned and managed, this can foster conservation benefits – the basic challenge is to deliver good management, planning, education and resourcing.

Interpretation (Directed at Visitors)

1. "A special process of stimulating and encouraging an appreciation of the natural and cultural heritage of a region, as well as a means of communicating nature conservation ideals and practices."
2. "A means of communicating ideas and feelings which helps people enrich their understanding and appreciation of their world, and their role within it."

The first definition sees interpretation from a visitor's perspective as a means of value-adding to their experience because of the added interest it creates when more is known about an attraction or experience.

The second definition places the responsibility back with the visitor to arrive at their own understanding based on their collective experiences.

3. "An educational activity which aims to reveal meanings and relationships through the use of original objects, first hand experience and illustrative media, rather than simply by communicating factual information."

Principles for successful interpretation People learn better when they are actively involved in the learning process. People learn better when they are using as many senses as appropriate. It is generally recognised that people retain approximately 10% of what they hear, 30% of what they read, 50% of what they see and 90% of what they do.

Insights that people discover for themselves are the most memorable as they stimulate a sense of excitement and growth. Learning requires activity on the part of the learner. Being aware of the usefulness of the knowledge being acquired makes the learning process more effective.

Enhancing the quality of interpretation at visitor centres, attractions, on tours, along trails/drives and 'in the field' or on site, is a major opportunity area for 'nature in tourism' in New South Wales. As far as possible, interpretation needs to capture a visitor's imagination, intellect or emotions (even momentarily) and in so doing grab their interest. Differences such as age, and cultural background are also obvious considerations. When pursuing excellence in interpretation, there are as many paths of possibility open to visitor managers as there are creative ideas in the world. To fail to explore these is to risk having an audience label the interpretive approach adopted as too dull, tired, serious, patronising, over-complicated, overwhelming, superficial, cautious, etc.

Great creative ideas resulting in exciting interpretation outcomes are often achieved more successfully if more innovative creative development processes are applied, and the creative net cast more widely. Building wider creative alliances by involving other people with different 'skill sets' (e.g. who are known for their innovative & 'wildcard' thinking capacities as well as essential sense of humour & fun) can often prove of value-particularly if they are properly rewarded for the business significance of their personal contribution to the results. A capacity for simple but effective delivery coupled with good commonsense and *empathy* also helps. Summarising its benefits, interpretation is an effective way of adding value to the experience, employing more locals, creating a cultural connection for visitors, building understanding and differentiating an operator's product in the market.

Nature Tourism

In industrial countries, mass tourism and recreation are now fast overtaking the extractive industries as the largest threat to indigenous communities, and 'pristine' environments. These are destinations that tourists now want to visit. Attractive landscape sites, such as sandy beaches, lakes, riversides, and mountaintops and slopes, are often transitional zones, characterized by species-rich ecosystems. Typical physical impacts include the degradation of such ecosystems. The ecosystems most threatened with degradation are ecologically fragile areas such as alpine regions, rain forests, wetlands, mangroves, coral reefs and sea grass beds. The threats to, and pressures on, these ecosystems are often severe because such places are very attractive to both tourists and developers. Since 1945, visits to the 10 most popular mountainous national parks in the United States have increased twelvefold. In the European Alps, tourism now exceeds 100 million visitor-days. Every year in the Indian Himalaya, more than 250,000

Hindu pilgrims, 25,000 trekkers, and 75 mountaineering expeditions climb to the sacred source of the Ganges River, the Gangotri Glacier. They deplete local forests for firewood, trample riparian vegetation, and strew litter. Even worse, this tourism frequently induces poorly planned, land-intensive development.

Negative impacts from tourism occur when the level of visitor use is greater than the environment's ability to cope with this use within the acceptable limits of change. Uncontrolled conventional tourism poses potential threats to many natural areas around the world. It can put enormous pressure on an area and lead to impacts such as soil erosion, increased pollution, discharges into the sea, natural habitat loss, increased pressure on endangered species and heightened vulnerability to forest fires. It often forces local populations to compete for the use of other critical resources. Tourism development can put pressure on natural resources when it increases consumption in areas where resources are already scarce. Water, and especially fresh water, is one of the most critical natural resources. Tourism can also create great pressure on other local resources like energy, food, and other raw materials that may already be in short supply.

Greater extraction and transport of these resources exacerbates the physical impacts associated with their exploitation. Because of the seasonal character of the industry, many destinations have ten times more inhabitants in the high season as in the low season. A high demand is placed upon these resources to meet the high expectations tourists often have. Important land resources include minerals, fossil fuels, fertile soil, forests, wetland and wildlife. Increased construction of facilities for tourism and recreational has increased the pressure on these resources and on scenic landscapes. Direct impact on natural resources, both renewable and non-renewable, in the provision of tourist facilities can be caused by the use of land for accommodation and other infrastructure provision, and the use of building materials.

Tourism can cause the same forms of pollution as any other industry: air emissions, noise, solid waste and littering, releases of sewage, oil and chemicals, even architectural/visual pollution. Transport by air, road, and rail is continuously increasing in response to the rising number of tourists and their greater mobility. To give an indication, the number of international air passengers worldwide rose from 88 million in 1972 to 344 million in 1994.

One consequence of this continuing increase in air transport is that tourism now accounts for more than 60% of air travel and is therefore responsible for an important share of air emissions. One study estimated that a single transatlantic return flight emits almost half the CO_2 emissions produced by all other sources (lighting, heating, car use, etc.) consumed by an average person yearly. Transport emissions and emissions from energy production and use are linked to acid rain, global warming and photochemical pollution. Air pollution from tourist transportation has impacts on the global level, especially from carbon dioxide emissions related to transportation energy use. And it can contribute to severe local air pollution. Some of these impacts are quite specific to tourist activities. For example, especially in very hot or cold countries, tour buses often leave their motors running for hours while the tourists go out for an excursion because they want to return to a comfortably air-conditioned bus.

In areas with high concentrations of tourist activities and appealing natural attractions, waste disposal is a serious problem and improper disposal can be a major despoiler of the natural environment-rivers, scenic areas, and roadsides. For example, cruise ships in the Caribbean are estimated to produce more than 70,000 tons of waste each year. Today some cruise lines are actively working to reduce waste-related impacts. Solid waste and littering can degrade the physical appearance of the water and shoreline and cause the death of marine animals.

Construction of hotels, recreation and other facilities often leads to increased sewage pollution. Wastewater has polluted seas and lakes surrounding tourist attractions, damaging the flora and fauna. Sewage runoff causes serious damage to coral reefs because it stimulates the growth of algae, which cover the filter-feeding corals, hindering their ability to survive. Changes in salinity and siltation can have wide-ranging impacts on coastal environments. And sewage pollution can threaten the health of humans and animals.

Often tourism fails to integrate its structures with the natural features and indigenous architectural of the destination. Large, dominating resorts of disparate design can look out of place in any natural environment and may clash with the indigenous structural design. A lack of land-use planning and building regulations in many destinations has facilitated sprawling developments along coastlines, valleys and scenic routes. The sprawl includes tourism facilities themselves and supporting infrastructure such as roads, employee housing, parking, service areas, and waste disposal.

Tourists using the same off road trail over and over again trample the vegetation and soil, eventually causing damage that can lead to loss of biodiversity. Such damage can be even more extensive when visitors frequently stray off established trails. Wildlife viewing can bring about stress for the animals and alter their natural behaviour when tourists come too close. Safaris and wildlife watching activities have a degrading effect on habitat as they often are accompanied by the noise and commotion created by tourists as they chase wild animals in their trucks and aircraft. This puts high pressure on animal habits and behaviours and tends to bring about behavioural changes. In some cases, as in Kenya, it has led to animals becoming so disturbed that at times they neglect their young or fail to mate.

After decades of sustained growth in volume and visibility, tourism is now one of the leading global industries (11% of global GDP) and one of the major migratory movements in modern society (about 700 million international travellers in 2001), producing significant impacts on resource consumption, pollution, and social systems. It can be compared in its deleterious impacts and environmental risks to any other major industry. On the other hand, tourism is a unique tool for awareness building and learning for guests and hosts alike. Sound natural and cultural environments are its basic assets, while peace is one of its basic requirements. Fortunately there is an encouraging 'greening' of mainstream tourism. Greater sustainability in the industry as a whole will have the largest impact on overall wildlife protection, and on communities and individuals. But 'nature-based tourism' will play a crucial role in the communities and natural environments under the greatest pressure from the development of tourism.

Nature Tourism, often referred to as Ecotourism, was introduced to the tourist industry in the early 1980s. Nature tourism attracts tourists with an interest in temporarily living in, and coming to better understand a specific, novel, relatively natural ecosystem. Its primary focus is on experiencing natural areas that fosters environmental and cultural understanding, appreciation and conservation. Nature tourism was initially connected with outdoor travel to remote, unique, and/or scenic areas. Although in its early stages there was a strong educational aspect, this was not a crucial or required element to the industry or the consumer. However, as the demand has increased, the inclusion of ecology as an integral educational element has become increasingly important. This is why nature tourism is an important topic in applied ecology.

Since its conception, nature tourism has grown to include an entire methodology of planning, conservation management, and economics. It is becoming a robust and encompassing process that not only includes site information, but also considers the sustainability of the ecosystem, conservation management, education, equitable social benefits, and community responsibility. Nature Tourism now includes several major principles:

- Education about the area.
- Sustainable use of resources, and avoidance of degradation.
- Enhancement of local community and assistance in development.
- Respect for cultural/social/political aspects of local people.
- Profit from the tourism industry providing a boost to the local economy.

Nature-based tourism attracts people interested in visiting natural areas for the purpose of enjoying the scenery, including plant and animal wildlife. Examples of on-site activities include hunting, fishing, photography, bird watching, and visiting parks and studying information about the ecosystem. An example is visiting, photographing, and learning about organgatuangs in Borneo. The returns to an individual from the experience have been described as potentially life-changing or at least memorable, and the development of new skills and knowledge. Since the mid-1990's nature tourism has emerged as a human activity distinct from adventure travel. Packages tend to be marketed as a more politically correct, environmentally and culturally aware" form of tourism, e.g., responsible travel to natural areas that conserve the environment and improve the wellbeing of local people. In this sense nature tourism is being increasingly recognized as a tool for sustainable development. Achieving this aim is a challenge, because high standards have to be met. But when it is achieved, communities and natural environments are the immediate beneficiaries.

However, despite their "green image", few nature tourism packages contribute a positive benefit to the global environment. A major contradiction comes from considering the environmental impact of the energy consumed in transportation to the exotic location. One study estimated that a single transatlantic return flight emits almost half the CO_2 emissions produced by all other sources consumed by an average person yearly. Arrival also introduces its own set of problems. As in any tourist activity, adverse impacts are ever present, such as cultural erosion and atmospheric pollution, and the drain on local natural resources to provide Western living standards as enclaves in Third World countries. Problems of sustainability are also evident in the developed countries.

For example in winter 2000, 76,271 people entered Yellow stone National Park on snow mobiles, outnumbering the 40,727 visitors who came in cars, 10,779 in snow coaches and 512 on skis. A survey of snow mobile impacts on natural sounds at Yellow stone found that snow mobile noise could be heard 70% of the time at 11 of 13 sample sites, and 90% of the time at 8 sites. At the Old Faithful geyser, snow mobiles could be heard 100% of the time during the daytime period studied. Snow mobile noise drowned out even the sound of the geyser erupting. In Yosemite National Park, the number of roads and facilities have been increased to keep pace with the growing visitor numbers and to supply amenities, infrastructure and parking lots for tourists.

These actions have caused habitat loss in the park and are accompanied by various forms of pollution including air pollution from automobile emissions; the Sierra Club has reported "smog so thick that Yosemite Valley could not be seen from airplanes". This occasional smog is harmful to all species and vegetation inside the Park. Such issues are being addressed by planning and managing destinations, setting up institutional partnerships and the continued development of environmentally friendly technology.

The concept of ecotourism has come into common use in the last decade. It describes a goal towards which tourism entrepreneurs, government agencies, non-governmental organizations (NGOs) and communities have been aiming at for much longer. A definition put forward by The Ecotourism Society in 1991 describes it as 'responsible travel to natural areas that conserves the environment and sustains the wellbeing of local people.' Professionals working within the field of ecotourism generally agree that 'ecotourism' stands out within the area of nature tourism by:

- Travel to a natural area.

- Travel that supports the conservation of biodiversity.
- Travel that brings benefits to local host communities.
- Travel that leads to greater understanding of the natural or cultural environment visited.

Including these four components in a travel package significantly restricts the number of tourism products that can genuinely be labelled ecotourism. To some people, ecotourism is regarded as one niche market within the larger, and rapidly expanding market of nature tourism. Here it has been estimated that nature-based tourism now comprises 20 per cent of the world travel market, and ecotourism 7 per cent. A package labelled ecotourism has some inbuilt constraints; the main one being that participants are responsible and benefit conservation efforts and local communities, and the visitor has participated in some learning experience. One example might be camping at a national park, paying an entry fee, following park rules of conduct, buying supplies at a gateway community outside the park, and participating in a natural history lesson. However, these kinds of constraints are what all kinds of nature tourism are aiming for. In this respect, it is perhaps better to retain the term nature tourism as an umbrella for all packages that involve the softer interaction of people with habitats and species as a primary objective of the holiday.

Nature tourism requires interactions and partnerships with conservation NGOs, government tourism and resource management agencies, community groups and the private sector. Above all it requires the management of the many impacts of massed humans introduced into species rich ecosystems. Even better would be the integration of nature tourism into international strategies for sustainable development. In this context, the United Nations Environment Programme (UNEP) has been appointed by the Commission on Sustainable Development (CSD) as the Interagency Coordinator or lead agency responsible for implementation of Agenda 21 issues on tourism. Together with the World Tourism Organization (WTO/OMT), UNEP is the main focal point on sustainable tourism for CSD and the Convention on Biological Diversity for devising global strategies for tourism can contribute to environmental conservation.

2

Nature Based Tourism in the World

A new study out today found that many nations throughout the world, including the United Kingdom, are seeing an annual increase in visitors to their conservation areas. The research, published today (29 June) in the journal PLoS Biology, found that in 15 of the 20 countries for which information was available there was an increase in the number of visitors to their nature reserves. This has important implications for nations who are reliant on nature-related tourism to generate funds for conservation, as well as for engaging the public about the importance of conserving biodiversity.

Professor Andrew Balmford, Professor of Conservation Science at the University of Cambridge and lead author of the study said: "Nature-based tourism is one of the most tangible benefits that people derive from conserving biodiversity. Unfortunately it is often remarkably poorly quantified. When a study based on visit rates to American and Japanese nature reserves last year showed these were declining, it prompted widespread concerns that the public was falling out of love with nature. However, this report refutes this contention."

For the study, the researchers compiled and then analysed a database with far broader geographical coverage than previous ones. Their findings show that since the 1990s, while visitor numbers have been falling slightly in the US and Japan, these results are exceptional: in three-quarters of the 20 countries analysed, visitation to nature reserves is increasing-in some countries by as much as 7 or 8 per cent per year. In Africa, Europe, Asia and Latin America the increases were on average positive and the United Kingdom saw an average 3 per cent annual increase.

It is believed that the previous results for the US and Japan arose because the growth in nature-based tourism is linked with wealth, with visit rates increasing fastest in the poorest countries (such as Ghana, Madagascar and India), and growing more slowly in richer ones, eventually falling below zero in the richest nations. Professor Balmford explains: "We don't yet have the data to understand why this link with wealth arises. It could be because affluence leads to a rise in sedentary alternatives to nature-based pastimes, such as TV or the Internet, but other explanations-such as a shift from increasingly overcrowded reserves to quieter nature areas nearby where visitors are not counted, or even to overseas reserves-are equally plausible."

Professor Balmford concludes: "The trends demonstrated in the paper underscore the point that nature-based tourism generally remains extremely popular and is in most places still growing quickly.

"There are many places where large-scale nature tourism is not feasible, and there are important concerns to be addressed about the potential negative impacts of tourism on local people and on the environment. But despite these caveats, we believe nature-based tourism continues to offer an important route to linking conservation with sustainable development." Nature-based tourism has grown in importance in recent decades, and strong links have been established between it and ecotourism. This reflects rising incomes, greater levels of educational attainment and changing values, especially in the Western world. Nature-based tourism is quite varied. Different types of such tourism are identified and their consequences for sustainability of their resource-base are briefly considered. The development and management of nature-based tourism involves many economic aspects, several of which are discussed. For example, one must consider the economics of reserving or protecting land for this type of tourism. What economic factors should be taken into account?

Economists stress the importance of taking into account the opportunity costs involved in such a decision. This concept is explained. However, determining the net economic value of an area used for tourism is not straightforward. Techniques for doing this, such as the travel cost method and stated value methods, are introduced. Natural areas reserved for tourism may have economic value not only for tourism but also jointly for other purposes, such as conserving wildlife, maintaining hydrological cycles and so on. These other purposes, should be taken into account when considering the use of land for nature-based tourism. According to one economic point of view, land should be used in a way that maximises its total economic value. While this approach has its merits, it does not take into account the distribution of benefits from land use and its local impacts on income and employment. These can be quite important politically and for nature conservation, and are discussed. Finally, there is some discussion of whether fees charged to tourists for access to environmental resources should discriminate between domestic tourists and foreigners.

Economic Squeeze or Prosperity Ian Yeoman

With oil prices heading towards US $150 a barrel (July 2008) and will probably reach $200 by the end of the year, demand for air travel is faltering as consumer spending is squeezed and stagflation sets in, all reminiscing the oil shock of 1974, when oil prices rose from $2 to $8 overnight. Combined with falling house prices, tension in the Middle East, food inflation and increased demand for consumerism in China, the world is on a course of meltdown (some would say) or is this just another recession. So, what are the prospects for world tourism to 2030? Dr. Ian Yeoman, Victoria University's resident travel and tourism futurologist explains.

The strong growth in world tourism over the last decade correlates to economic well being. When economies grow, personal income rises which results in the discretionary income being spent on tourism. According to the UN World Tourism Organisation, the growth in international arrivals significantly outpaces economic output. In the recent years when world economic growth has exceeded 4% per annum, the growth of tourism volume tends to be higher at 6.5% per annum. At the same time world economics have always been doom and burst, therefore the present situation is nothing new.

Is it all about Oil?

With West Texas Intermediate Crude Oil hovering at $150 a barrel, the tourism industry is seeing a series of energy surcharges being added to the price of air tickets and business complaining that oil is driving up costs. In 1956, the Shell Oil geologist, M King Hubbert, predicted that US oil production (barrels pumped per year) would peak in the early 1970's. Most geologists at the time rejected Hubbert's analysis, until 1970 when oil production peaked within the lower US 48 states. Since then, numerous respected geologists have refined Hubbert's methodology and applied it to worldwide oil production, country by country. They concluded that world production of oil will peak between 2004 and 2008 (today's time zone). Most geologists estimate that 2 trillion barrels of oil were formed in the earth over millions of years.

To date we have pumped out half of this supply. British Petroleum (BP) predicts there are forty years left of oil supplies. But the implications of this forecast are not straightforward. As world demand grows and supply diminishes, prices will soar. Some 30 years ago, we had a taste of what can happen with soaring oil prices. But then there was plenty of oil. In the Autumn of 1973, the Organization of Petroleum Exporting countries (OPEC) imposed oil restrictions and increased the price by 70% to $7 a barrel. Protesting US support of the Yom Kippur War, OPEC raised the price again to $7 per barrel in 1974 (a 130% increase within 12 months). With the overthrow of Shah of Iran and the Iran-Iraq war, oil prices escalated to $40 per barrel in 1981. This is the equivalent to $70 per barrel in current dollars.

The effect of this rise meant that drivers all over the world had to adhere to a reduced speed limit on roads. There were restrictions on heating systems and the use of electricity for outdoor displays and advertising. In the USA, long queues appeared at gasoline stations, something that was unheard of in those days. The oil crisis led to a recession in 1975, the first of four worldwide economic downturns that were triggered by oil prices and Middle Eastern events. Over the next five years, governments developed non-OPEC sources of oil, expanded nuclear power installations and implemented intensive conservation measures.

Oil Shocks – What Happened in 1974!

The impact of rising prices in 1974 on international tourism according to the UN World Tourism Organisation was;

1st Year (1975): Continued Growth in International Tourism: The first year following the oil shock of 1974, the impact on tourism was not generally perceptible. International tourism demand continued to grow rapidly, at a rate of 8.1%, from 1974 to 1975. This growth was even stronger than that recorded in previous years (3.4% in 1974 and 5.2% in 1973).

2nd Year (1976): Slowdown in Tourist Flows: By the second year, adjustment policies introduced in late 1975 had led to a decline in purchasing power in many oil importing countries, which in 1976 triggered a steep slowdown in tourism demand, with growth of only 2.3% worldwide, 1.5% in Europe and-4.9% in Africa.

3rd Year (1977): Strong Recovery in Tourism Activity: During the third year, 1977, tourism growth resumed its earlier pace and even regained some lost ground, with a rate of 8.2%.

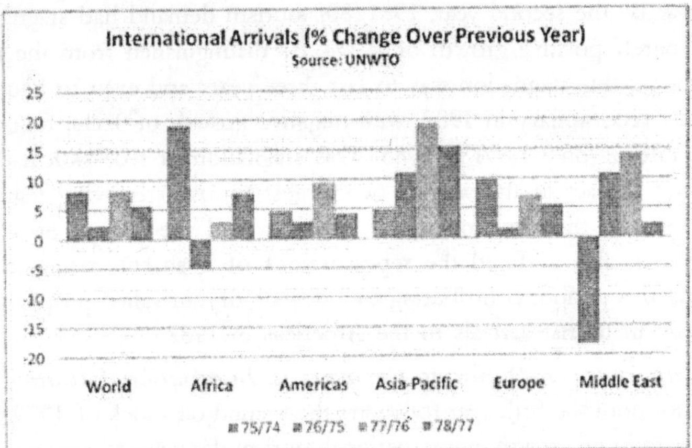

International Arrivals 1974-1977 (m) (Source UNWTO)

Region	1974	1975	1976	1977
World	*205.7*	*222.3*	*227.4*	*246.1*
Africa	3.9	4.7	4.4	4.6
Americas	47.7	50	51.5	56.4
Asia-Pacific	9.7	10.2	11.3	13.6
Europe	140	153.9	156.2	167.2
Middle East	4.3	3.5	3.9	4.5

As a result, world economic growth (GDP) in 1975 fell to 1.9%, and then subsequently rose to 5.1% in 1976 and 4.4% in 1977. Therefore, the impact of the oil shock in 1974 was only limited to one year, with recovery across all markets in subsequent years.

Oil shocks-What happened in 1979

The oil shock of 1979 was a result of the Iranian revolution; this crisis came at a time when the world was still recovering from the first crisis in 1974, so the second impact was more adverse. The effect of the crisis was a slowdown in economic growth and disposable income across most western economies.

1st Year (1980): Continued Growth in Tourism Activity: During the first year following the oil shock of 1979, international tourism demand continued to increase at a sustained pace, with 2% growth in world tourism in 1980.

2nd, 3rd, 4th Years (1981, 1982, 1983): Stagnation in Tourism Flows: By the second year, 1981/80, tourism demand had stagnated, with barely positive growth of 0.2%. As distinguished from the first oil shock, this stagnation was to last three years and even to become slightly recessionary in 1982, with negative growth of-0.5%, followed by a rate of only 1.8% in 1983. This stagnation or recession had its primary impact in the world's two largest tourism receiving regions: Europe and the Americas. The Americas, and the United States in particular, also suffered the repercussions of a sharply rising dollar during this period, contributing to a decline of unrivalled proportions (-4.5%) in tourist arrivals to the Americas in 1982.

5th Year (1984): Strong Recovery in International Tourism: It was not until the fifth year following the second oil shock of 1979 that earlier rates of growth in international tourism demand were recovered. As during the first oil shock, growth rates in world tourism even caught up to their earlier pace, with positive growth of 8.8% in 1984, and continuing sustained growth of 4.3% in 1985 and 3.2% in 1986.

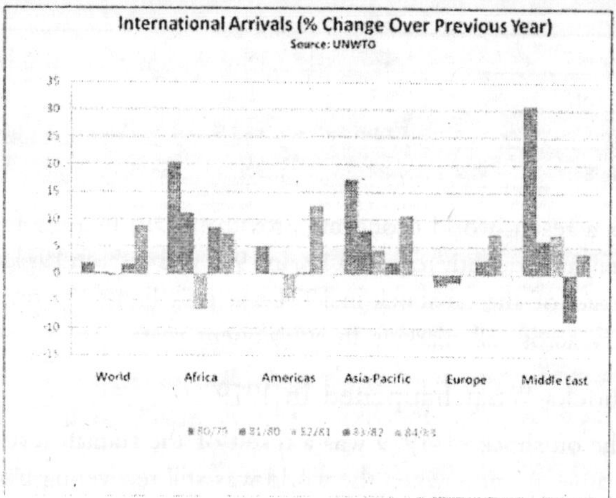

As a consequence, the second oil shock of 1979 resulted in Europe entering a prolonged period of stagflation, with international arrivals falling by 2.2% in 1980. Europe did not recover until 1984. In the Americas, the high exchange rate for the US $ had lasting effects, prolonging recession for international demand to the region at a time when growth was returning to the rest of the world. In 1985, when the US $ peaked, tourist arrivals to the Americas declined by 3.4%.

The impact of the second oil shock on international tourism was therefore greater than the first, as between 1980 and 1983, growth in the international arrivals was limited with an increase of only 1.4%.

It Might Not seem like it, but we are in a better position than in 1974 and 1979: But it is not all doom and gloom. There are good reasons to believe that the economic consequences of a jump in oil prices will be less severe now than they were in the 1970s and early 1980s. Energy conservation is stronger than in the 1970s, due to government taxation policies. Additionally, a shift to other fuels and a decline in heavy industries has made rich economies much less dependent on oil than they used to be. Since the early 1970s, the amount of oil consumed per real dollar has fallen by almost half in rich countries. In addition, high oil prices encourage innovation and conservation. This means the development of better aircraft that are more fuel efficient and the use of alternation energy sources. The problem is, transport is an oil based system combined with the factors that demand is increasing and refinery capacity is constrained. The world didn't come to an end when we moved from a wood to a coal economy or from a coal to an oil economy. Today, we are in a transformation process from oil to a hydrogen economy therefore it is going to hurt.

So, What are the Prospects?

Forecasting, by its very nature, is a hazardous exercise. Projecting future international tourism flows has become more difficult over time, because, on the one hand, events such as 9/11 cause a temporary disruption but, on the other hand, climate changes causes more permanent change to tourist flows. Therefore, two scenarios have been prepared based upon different economic growth rates, oil prices, climate change, transport flows and personal disposal incomes. The scenarios are called Best Case and Middle Class Squeeze.

Scenario One – The best Case

Over the next two decades, international arrivals will grow by 3.4% per annum and receipts by 4.4%, based upon oil prices averaging $80-$90 a barrel, new energy innovations, world GDP rising by 129% by 2030 but falling levels of disposal incomes amongst an aging population most significantly between 2015-2030. In these economic circumstances, Europe will remain the worlds dominant region. However, a shift will take place, with Europe losing market share to Asia and the Middle East by 2030. Europe's share of international arrivals will fall from 54.6% to 41.1%, whereas the Asia and Pacific region will enjoy a rise in market share of 19.3% to 28.8%, with a similar increase in receipts. The Americas' market share will remain stable and Africa will experience a significant growth but from a small base. The changes in market share reflect different growth rates for different regions. Europe will grow at 2.3% per annum, whereas Asia will grow at 5%.

Scenario One - Best Case

Arrivals	Base Year (m)	Forecast (m)	Average Annual Growth Rate %	Market Share (%)	
	2005	2030	2005-2030	2005	2030
Total	802.9	1897	3.4	100	100
Europe	438.7	779.9	2.3	54.6	41.1
Asia and the Pacific	155.3	546.5	5	19.3	28.8
Americas	133.2	309.8	3.4	16.6	16.3
Africa	37.3	101.8	4	4.6	5.4
Middle East	38.4	158.9	5.7	4.8	8.4

Receipts	Base Year (US $ Bn)	Forecast (US $ Bn)	Average Annual Growth Rate (%)	Market Share (%)	
	2005	2030	2005-2030	2005	2030
Total	677.5	2016.2	4.4	100	100
Europe	349.7	787.1	3.2	51.6	39
Asia and the Pacific	134.6	568.5	5.8	19.9	28.2
Americas	145.2	412.7	4.2	21.4	20.5
Africa	21.8	98.2	6	3.2	4.9
Middle East	26.3	149.7	7	3.9	7.4

Source: Tomorrow's Tourist 2008.

From an analysis of expenditure, it seems that receipts in the Middle East will rise from US $26.3 billion to US $149.7 billion, a staggering growth rate of 7% per annum, capturing 7.4% of all tourism expenditure. Africa will follow a similar pattern, with receipts rising from US $21 billion in 2005 to US $98 billion by 2030, a growth rate of 6% per annum. Growth in world tourism will be slower than the decades prior to 2005 as a result of shrinking and ageing populations therefore, the average growth rate will be 3.4% to 2030, compared to the historic average of 6.5%. By 2030, more than US $5 billion will be spent by international tourists every day across the world, from US $2 billion in Europe to US $1.5 billion in Asia. By 2030, international arrivals will reach 1.9 billion international arrivals, spending US $2 trillion.

Scenario Two – Middle Class Squeeze

The middle classes of the world are facing rising prices and less monies for out of home expenditure, all shaped by the economic disease of stagflation where inflation is higher than GDP growth. In this scenario, oil production peaks in 2009 with prices averaging over $200 a barrel over the next decade in real terms but then falling as demand falters. In this scenario, the world hasn't been able to adjust to the transformation between oil and hydrogen economy until 2020, and in the meantime transport and travel has become more expensive. The scenario presumes mass belief in the plenitude of available oil reserves, limited intervention of supply and failure to respond quickly enough to alter demand, triggers a sudden and prolonged period of economic shocks, political instability and environmental disasters. The low priced oil economy has ended. This difficult transformation squeezes economic growth amongst the middle classes of the world and leads to economic demise.

In this scenario, a growth rate of 1.4% per annum is assumed representing 1.1 billion international arrivals and $979bn in receipts. The short term impact of this scenario sees the end of low cost carriers- in many destinations and long haul travel becomes more characterised by travel for the rich, exclusive and necessary. Intercontinental travel subsequently slows down, whereas interregional travel is supplemented by alternative public transport systems. In this scenario city based tourism with good connectivity fares better than rural destinations where connectivity is poor. In the Middle Class Squeeze scenario, Europe market share falls from 54.6% to 49.8% but the Asia and Pacific region don't see the rapid rises as seen in the Best Case scenario due to slowdown in economic development. In fact Europe's compactness, an increase in inter regional travel, along with a slowdown in outbound travel to other world regions buffer tourism in Europe.

Scenario 1 – Middle Class Squeeze

Arrivals	Base Year (m)	Forecast (m)	Average Annual Growth Rate %	Market Share (%)	
	2005	2030	2005-2030	2005	2030
Total	802.9	1129.7	1.4	100	100
Europe	438.7	562.7	1.0	54.6	49.8
Asia and the Pacific	155.3	254.9	2.0	19.3	22.6
Americas	133.2	193.3	1.5	16.6	17.1
Africa	37.3	47.8	1.0	4.6	4.2
Middle East	38.4	71.1	2.5	4.8	6.3

Receipts	Base Year (US $ Bn)	Forecast (US $ Bn)	Average Annual Growth Rate (%)	Market Share (%)	
	2005	2030	2005-2030	2005	2030
Total	677.5	979.4	1.5	100	100
Europe	349.7	471.2	1.2	51.6	51.6
Asia and the Pacific	134.6	237.6	2.3	19.9	19.9
Americas	145.2	186.3	1.0	21.4	21.4
Africa	21.8	35.7	2.0	3.2	3.2
Middle East	26.3	48.7	2.5	3.9	3.9

Source: Tomorrow's Tourist 2008.

Concluding Remarks

One can never forecast an exact future, the role of scenarios is to ask what if questions. It is now certain that the world is entering a phase of stagflation fuelled by high oil prices, but the key uncertainty is how long it will last. As we can see from this analysis, the world has been here before, but the length of the stagnation could be 1, 2, 5 or 10 years, who knows? The two scenarios, Best Case and Middle Class Squeeze represent different growth rates under different economic conditions, the difference being nearly 900 million holidays. So, can the world meet the challenges of the 'end of oil' and massive impact on world tourism, economic development, prosperity – if not, we will see significant increases in poverty and war.

Reports of rapid growth in nature-based tourism and recreation add significant weight to the economic case for biodiversity conservation but seem to contradict widely voiced concerns that people are becoming increasingly isolated from nature. This apparent paradox has been highlighted by a recent study showing that on a per capita basis, visits to natural areas in the United States and Japan have declined over the last two decades.

These results have been cited as evidence of "a fundamental and pervasive shift away from nature-based recreation"—but how widespread is this phenomenon? We address this question by looking at temporal trends in visitor numbers at 280 protected areas (PAs) from 20 countries. This more geographically representative dataset shows that while PA visitation (whether measured as total or per capita visit numbers) is indeed declining in the United States and Japan, it is generally increasing elsewhere. Total visit numbers are growing in 15 of the 20 countries for which we could get data, with the median national rate of change unrelated to the national rate of population growth but negatively associated with wealth. Reasons for this reversal of growth in the richest countries are difficult to pin down with existing data, but the pattern is mirrored by trends in international tourist arrivals as a whole and so may not necessarily be caused by disaffection with nature. Irrespective of the explanation, it is clear that despite important downturns in some countries, nature-related tourism is far from declining everywhere, and may still have considerable potential both to generate funds for conservation and to shape people's attitudes to the environment.

Across southern Africa, nature-based tourism reportedly now generates roughly the same revenue as farming, forestry, and fisheries combined. Worldwide, tourism as a whole has been estimated to account for roughly 10% of gross domestic product (GDP), with wildlife viewing and outdoor recreation (much of it centred on protected areas) reportedly making up one of its fastest growing sectors. Though statistics like these are rarely supported by detailed data, they underpin widespread recognition that nature-based tourism is an important ecosystem service, capable of generating substantial resources for both conservation and local economic development. This is particularly significant given that PAs are under increasing pressure to provide economic justification for their existence.

This positive perspective stands in sharp contrast to growing concerns about an emerging disconnect between people and their natural environments. Increasing urbanisation and the rise of sedentary, indoor pastimes (such as television, the Internet, and video games) have been linked to a reduction in informal, outdoor recreation (Pyle's "Extinction of Experience"), with potentially serious consequences for childhood development, mental and physical wellbeing, and environmental knowledge and concern. Many see this as a major challenge for biodiversity conservation: if people no longer experience and know their natural environments, how can they be expected to care about them?

These worries have been further fuelled by a recent and widely publicised paper examining trends in 16 measures of outdoor recreation (14 from the United States, plus one each from Japan and Spain). This analysis showed that, expressed per head of population, visits to natural areas in the United States and Japan (as well as participation in duck-hunting and fishing in the United States, but not hiking, camping, or other hunting) have declined since the late 1980s From these per capita trends the authors conclude there has been "...a fundamental and pervasive shift away from nature-based recreation". However, the paper produced no evidence of declines outside the United States and Japan (and per capita national park attendance in Spain, the only other country sampled, has not declined), raising the possibility that the reported shift may not be universal.

To date, lack of data has meant no study has looked at trends in nature-based tourism across more than a handful of countries. Here, we use newly compiled information on visitor numbers to 280 PAs in 20 countries (Australia, Canada, Chile, China, Ecuador, Ghana, India, Indonesia, Japan, Korea, Madagascar, Peru, Philippines, Rwanda, South Africa, Sri Lanka, Tanzania, Uganda, UK, United States) between 1992 and 2006 to explore the generality of the United States and Japan results and to understand the apparent mismatch with the claim that globally, nature-based tourism is on the rise.

Importantly, because we are interested in trends in nature tourism as a whole as well as individual interest in nature, we analyse changes in both total visit numbers and visit numbers corrected for national population size. The latter are a better reflection of per capita interest in a country's PAs, but the former are a more sensible proxy for trends in the overall benefit derived from nature tourism as an ecosystem service.

Results

Our analysis of standardised rates of change in PA visit numbers provides limited support for the previously reported declines in nature-based activities in the United States. Using total visit numbers, only 14 out of 51 US PAs for which we could get data showed significant decreases in visit number (at $p<0.05$), while 11 exhibited significant increases. Adjusting for changes in national population size, the number of US PAs experiencing significant declines rose to 27 and the number with increasing attendance fell to just 6. Clearly, the decline in per capita visitation to US PAs we could sample is real, but arises largely because absolute attendance has been almost static despite a growing national population. In Japan, the only PA for which we had data showed a nonsignificant decline in visits, whether expressed in terms of total or per capita visit numbers.

More interestingly, these weak declines in two countries are far from globally typical: instead, visitor trends show marked geographical variation. When we pooled standardised rates of change within continents, rather than being negative we found that trends in total visit numbers were not significantly different from zero in North America or Australasia, and were on average positive in Africa, Europe, Asia, and Latin America (Figure 1A; $F_{5,274} = 10.2$, $p<0.001$; in post hoc tests only Australasia and North America had rates of changes not significantly different from zero at $p<0.05$).

There was similar broad-scale variation when we compared trends in per capita visit numbers across continents (Figure 1B: $F_{5,274} = 10.4$, $p<0.001$, with significant positive trends again everywhere apart from Australasia and North America). These patterns of spatial heterogeneity were confirmed when data were analysed by country. Total visit numbers to PAs on average grew in 15 out of the 20 countries sampled and fell in four (with Uganda showing no change). Even allowing for population growth, per capita visit numbers rose in 14 countries (with Uganda and Australia added to the list of countries showing falling visitation). The only country we sampled outside the Organisation for Economic and Co-Operation Development (OECD) with consistently falling PA visitation was Indonesia.

National rates of change are closely associated with wealth. In contrast to the United States and Japan, poorer countries typically had increasing numbers of PA visits, with median standardised rates of growth in total visit numbers showing a clear negative relationship with per capita GDP. This result was not due to correlated variation in population growth, because the negative link with rising wealth held when visit numbers were adjusted for changes in population size. As a further check for any confounding effects of population growth, we compared changes in total visit numbers with national population growth rates, but found no association between the two. The tendency for PA visitation to be increasing in poorer countries appears to be independent of population growth.

Discussion

Our dataset on PA visits has far broader geographical coverage than any others we are aware of, yet yielded no evidence to support the idea of a consistent global decline in nature-based recreation. Instead it appears that falling visitation is mostly restricted to a few well-off countries. When we adjusted visit numbers for population growth to examine individual participation in nature recreation we were able to replicate previously reported declines in per capita visit number in the United States and Japan, but also found that in most other countries population-adjusted visit numbers have been increasing.

These patterns were more marked when we looked at trends in PA visitation as a whole, using total numbers of PA visits. We found these are growing on four out of six continents and in 15 of the 20 countries for which we could get data. These changes in average visit rates are quite well predicted by wealth, but are unrelated to national population growth—confirming the finding from the per capita analysis that it is not the case that visitation is increasing simply where populations are growing rapidly. Instead, it appears that PA visitation is generally growing, but at a progressively lower rate with rising affluence.

We do not have a ready explanation for this negative link between visit growth and wealth, and believe this will be hard to unravel from correlational analyses alone. It could be related to the emergence of "videophilia", or to other aspects of growing urbanisation or increasingly sedentary lifestyles. These ideas are plausible, but direct evidence for them is sparse. Given that very many potential drivers co-vary with one another and with time, causality may be difficult to establish until more detailed data become available, or an experimental approach is adopted. One nonexclusive alternative explanation for the patterns of changing PA visitation that we see could be that many formal protected areas in richer countries are becoming increasingly crowded and thus less attractive to nature enthusiasts. Overcrowding and the perception of overcrowding have been noted as a concern of visitors to many larger US National Parks for over a decade. If would-be visitors are instead switching to less publicised sites where visitors are not counted, overall visit rates to natural areas in these countries could be stable or even growing, yet still recorded as declining.

One other explanation for the pattern we see could be that there is a shift in preference away from domestic destinations as nature-focused tourists become wealthier and alternative wildlife attractions in less costly developing countries become more accessible. Strikingly, the patterns we uncovered for PA visitor trends are echoed by those for international tourism more generally: standardised national rates of change in all foreign arrivals (from) co-vary positively with median changes in total and per capita PA visit numbers. Changes in foreign arrivals also show a negative relationship with per capita GDP, falling to zero growth in the United States. These results suggest that trends in nature-based recreation might be less driven by attitudes to nature per se and more to do with how rising wealth and the emergence of new destinations influence the dynamics of recreation as a whole. To resolve this, more data would be needed than we were able to obtain on the nationalities and motivations of visitors to individual PAs.

Regardless of the underlying drivers, our analyses indicate that it is premature to conclude that PA visit data indicate a general and pervasive shift away from nature tourism. This is apparently occurring in a few developed countries, where it is worrying, and where it certainly demands more attention. But in contrast, in most developing countries visits to protected areas are growing at rates that mirror general increases in tourism and travel—in many cases by more than 4%. This is especially significant for conservation, given that, unlike other nonconsumptive uses of ecosystems, nature-based tourism produces tangible financial flows that can, if carefully developed, be of direct benefit to local decision makers.

Tourism can often provide a strong incentive for protection in biodiversity-rich areas, and formal designation of such sites can raise their profile and influence tourism visitation. However, increasing visitor numbers alone is no guarantee that tourism revenues will be reinvested in conservation. Equally, recording visitor numbers does not equate with the much less common practices of monitoring or managing tourism impacts. International nature tourism raises other important worries—about CO_2 emissions, about its vulnerability to changing fashions, about disturbance to wildlife and nearby people, and about how far its revenues filter down to local communities. Nature-based tourism is only likely to be sustainable under certain conditions of effective planning, management, and local participation. However, to the extent that these concerns can be addressed, our results argue that far from having a diminishing role, nature-based recreation has the potential in many parts of the world to make a growing contribution to both conservation and sustainable development.

Materials and Methods

Somewhat surprisingly, there is no global database or consistent set of national statistics summarising trends in nature-based tourism. Instead, like previous authors we infer changes in the sector as a whole from visits to PAs. We compiled information on annual visitor numbers to terrestrial PAs (including any listed in). PA visits are among the most frequent forms of nature-based recreation recorded in the United States, and we suggest they are likely to account for an even greater proportion of nature recreation in other countries, where alternatives are less developed. We collected data from as many sources as possible: the grey and published literature, personal contacts, and especially the World Wide Web. The methods used to record visitors were rarely reported in detail, but varied widely, including dedicated studies, gate receipts, and traffic counts. There are also likely to be biases in some datasets, with corruption, for example, perhaps leading to systematic under-(and in some cases, maybe over-) reporting of visitor numbers. These problems may confound estimation of absolute visitor numbers, but will have less impact on within-PA changes in visitor numbers over time, and so here we used all available information.

In total we were able to collate ≤ 6y of data (between 1992 and 2006) for 280 PAs from 20 countries. We then expressed visitation trends at each PA in two ways—using total visit number, as a measure of the overall tourism benefit provided by the PA; and (as in) using visit number divided by national population size in that year (from), as a measure of per capita use of the PA. For PAs with large numbers of nondomestic visitors, tracking per capita use by dividing by national population size is imperfect (and data on visitor origins are too patchy for any more sophisticated adjustment by population size). However, data we obtained for 190 PAs (many lacking time series information and so excluded from our core analysis) indicate that, for all except one continent, a mean of >70% of visitors are nationals, so that errors caused through adjusting by national population size are relatively limited. The exception is Africa, where on average only ~30% visitors are nationals. For this continent, adjustment by national population growth (which is also generally higher than elsewhere) is probably excessive and so negatively biases estimates of trends in per capita visit rates.

For each PA we next performed linear regressions of total visit number and per capita visit number on year, and derived standardised measures of rates of change (ranging from +1 to "1) as (slope/ maximum total or per capita] visit number predicted by the regression during the 15-y range). We explored geographical variation in trends in our two measures of visit numbers by calculating median standardised rates of change across continents, and across countries. We compared the latter with per capita GDP adjusted for purchasing power parity (PPP) (for 2005, from), using linear regression weighted by the number of PAs sampled in each country. As an additional check to see whether our results for total visit number were confounded by changes in national population size, we performed an equivalent weighted regression of national median change in total visit number versus annual population growth (for 1990–2006, from). Last, to see whether our findings were specific to nature-related tourism, we also obtained data on trends in all foreign arrivals between 1995 and 2005 (again from), and compared standardised national rates of change (calculated in the same way as for PA visits) with per capita GDP and with median standardised rates of change in total visit numbers.

Heritage and Nature-Based Tourism in the Northern Forest Region

The Northern Forest Region (NFR) contains hundreds of thousands of acres of forestlands. Ensuring a successful, sustainable environment for future generations will necessitate utilizing natural and human resources in ways that will enhance, not undermine the region's characteristics. One of the tools for achieving sustainability is the region's tourism industry. The success of the NFR's tourism industry is greatly dependent upon four factors—the weather, the changeable demands of the travelling public, the Northeast's economic health, and gasoline prices. The first two are difficult to predict long term, the third is recovering from a lengthy downturn, and forecasts for the fourth are not encouraging at present.

Given its quaint villages, beautiful woodlands, scenic byways, recreation facilities, and rural workscapes, the NFR possesses a product mix that appeals to travel preferences of millions of Americans as evidenced by the following

- 48 percent of U.S. travellers are interested in visiting remote or untouched paces.
- 57 percent are attracted by culture.
- 76 percent want to visit a place they have never visited before.

With domestic travel increasing by 3.5 percent in 2005, and with another 1.8 percent increase projected during 2006, there is potential for gradually increasing the flow of dollars and revenue into the NFR. A breakout of 2002 traveller spending and tax revenues generated in the four states housing the NFR follows. Note that in Maine, New Hampshire and Vermont, visitor spending engenders important levels of revenue for those states, ranging between 11-20%.

To be objective, increasing nature and heritage recreation and tourism in the NFR will produce both positive and negative impacts upon host areas. On the positive side, such activity has helped to diversify local and regional economies, generate economic growth, and expand public services. Tourism performs as an export activity, bringing money from outside the area to be spent on local goods, services and activities. At the same time, it stimulates the development of new infrastructure and superstructure. These actions influence other non-tourism activities to locate in the area, thereby creating new jobs, wages, other forms of spending, and tax revenues. However, there are potential drawbacks. There is no guarantee that new businesses will be locally owned, or staffed by area residents. Wage and other forms of money leakage have occurred in other, largely rural locales when a large proportion of ownership, employees, as well as goods and services is imported from outside the geographic area.

This is a very real threat within the NFR, wherein communities that are already fiscally overextended must finance infrastructure needed to support new tourism activities, with no guarantee about the length of their tenure. It is further exacerbated by the fact that different skill sets are required by the hospitality and tourism industry than the traditional primary and secondary sector jobs being displaced. While New Hampshire has provided a training mechanism for tourism employees, and Vermont's is in the beginning stages, these are model programs not yet available elsewhere in the U.S. To date, anecdotal support for the New Hampshire program is very strong, but there is no corroborating research.

Employment

There are 5.4 million direct and 2.5 million indirect U.S. tourism employees. Employment growth offers residents more job opportunities, enabling other local residents to benefit form the trickling-down of jobs formerly performed by new tourism employees. One needs to be careful to take into account whether new jobs are filled by locals or others who are lured into the community by new employment opportunities. The following table depicts the availability of full and part-time tourism jobs within the states comprising the NFR, during 2002-03. During this period, New Hampshire experienced the greatest percentage of tourism employment growth, with Maine and Vermont each experiencing substantially lower rates of job growth; New England as a whole received a 2.3 percent increase in tourism job growth, while the U.S. rate was 2.2 percent.

Leisure and Hospitality Employment Of concern to NFR economic planners should be the tourism industry's reputation for providing substandard, seasonal jobs, and straining the local infrastructure. Despite this commonly shared belief, rural recreation counties as a whole experienced 24 percent employment growth during the 1990s, which was approximately double the rate of other non-metropolitan counties. Nationally, the average earning per job in "recreation counties" was $22,234 in 2000, or about $450 less than in other rural counties. While this is consistent with the prevailing attitude about low paying tourism jobs, the USDA found that earnings per job increased faster in recreation counties than in non-recreation ones, possibly in response to spin-off economic opportunities in areas where tourism is thriving. As a result, according to a USDA study of 311 rural recreation counties, recreation and tourism "resulted in lower local poverty rates" as well as improvements in educational attainment and health measures.

Further, tourism helped to increase job diversity by creating or supporting 51 different types of private sector jobs and an additional 51 indirect private sector jobs. Tourism had a slightly positive impact upon earnings for multiple job workers, as earnings were approximately $29.6 thousand per capita or about two thousand higher than in other, non-recreation rural counties. Traditionally, tourism has been more important to the economic wellbeing of states with substantial rural regions than predominantly urban states. During 2005, the three northern New England states provided 25 percent of New England's direct and indirect leisure and hospitality employment, despite having only 22 percent of New England's 2000 population and 23 percent of its total employment.

One of the benefits derived from tourism actually may prove to be a significant threat to the NFR, as new jobs mean more employees, and their families may move into the area. This resulting population growth provides what geographers term an increase in market *threshold.* As more service market thresholds—*def.* the minimum population required to support specific services—are met, there will be even greater growth.Not all development that may occur in the NFR will be deemed desirable by residents. This is where tourism, like any other form of economic activity, can threaten the natural and cultural character of the NFR, making sustainability a problematical goal to achieve. Avoiding these pitfalls is dependent upon a pro-active policy consisting of master planning, zoning, capital improvements programs, and other tools.

Tourism Markets

Travel and tourism is an enormous economic engine. During 2004, there were an estimated 1.2 billion person trips in the U.S., or 6.5 billion visitor person-days. 43% of these trips were taken for various marketable occasions, 41% were to visit friends and relatives, and 16% were for business-related purposes. Within the NFR, an estimated 22.5 million visitors spent approximately $7.4 billion and generated more than 200,000 jobs. While there are no data for total overnight versus one-day trips in the region, based upon Maine's experience, it is estimated that the ratio of day-to-overnight visitation is approximately 4-to-1. Tourism DMOs would like to increase the relative proportion of overnight visitors. Tourism futurists believe the travel markets that are most likely to increase in coming years are those seeking enrichment, health, revitalization, enhancement, ecotourism, and soft adventure.

This reflects growing interest in environmental and cultural/heritage forms of travel. During the last six months of 2005, one-third of Americans visited an art museum, historic museum, zoo, botanical garden, science centre, or similar facility. Opportunities such as these abound within the NFR, but the travelling public must be made aware of them first. Visitors to the NFR are significantly more likely to engage in outdoor recreation, winter sports and activities, and camping than the national average—all important reasons that people have visited the area traditionally. "Geotourism" and "enrichment tourism" are target audiences for NFR tourism businesses. These travellers have relatively large disposable incomes. NFR destinations must market to such travellers by convincing them that new and different enrichment opportunities are available. Educational programs with a cultural, heritage, or environmental theme appeal to such people. Between 2000 and 2004, there was a 30 percent nationwide increase in people who said they observe or photograph wildlife (to 125 million), and a 17 percent increase in people who observe scenery (to 151 million). According to the Travel Industry Association, 49 percent of travellers have indicated that they prefer to experience local culture, and 41 percent prefer to see and do things that are "authentic" while on vacation.

It must be noted that shopping ranks as a very important activity in all three states. Unfortunately, comparable data were not available for northern New York state. Culture and heritage tourism remains one of the fastest growing segments of the travel industry. There is a strong indication that visits to a cultural or heritage attraction enhance visitors' enjoyment of a place and cause them to return. In 2004, 146.4 million U.S. adults took a trip of 50 or more miles to engage in this type of travel. As the following table shows, the impact of greater lengths of stay and spending will have a positive impact upon the travel businesses within the NFR. No form of tourism within the NFR has been more controversial than motorized, recreation activities, which have had an impact upon the economy and ecology of the area. In Maine and elsewhere within the region, ATV owners have faced accusations about damage to the environment.

In 2004, there were more that 59 thousand registrations of ATVs in Maine; the majority of these were state residents. ATV activities generated $200 million in net spending. The problem is that the most popular ATV areas—the Maine Highlands as well as the Lakes and Mountains—are also popular settings for other, lower-impact forms of outdoor recreation. Conservationists oppose the proliferation of ATV usage. Others disagree, arguing that the economic benefits outweigh the environmental costs. In New Hampshire, during 2002-03, ATV and trail bike travel parties contributed $162 million in direct and indirect spending, and the total impact on the state's economy (direct, indirect and induced impacts) was about $264 million.

Snow mobiling is a form of winter recreation whose overall impact on the economy is frequently overlooked because it comes into conflict with cross country skiers and snowshoeing. The total impact of snowmobiling in New Hampshire was $350 million; in Vermont it was $165,252,700.

During the last ten years, recreation vehicles have been displacing traditional forms of camping. In 2005, 7.2 million US households owned at least one recreation vehicle. Sales of RVs have gone flat, however, it is projected that 8 million household will own an RV in 2010.

There has been a 22 percent growth in RV rentals during 2005 relative to 2004. RV travellers spend an average of $91 per day at local businesses, for meals, groceries, and/or gifts.

Trends

a. Recent Travel Increases. During 2005, domestic travel increased by 6 percent compared to 2004, and leisure travel was up 9 percent. This growth reflects a steady rise in the Consumer Confidence Index, rising employment, falling unemployment, and growing disposable incomes since November 2005. Overall, a 1.8 percent growth in domestic travel is projected for 2006. With a projected larger number of travellers, visitation to the NFR should increase, provided the area is prepared to take steps necessary to maintain or increase its market share.

b. Marketing on the Internet. This is a very good time for non-mainstream tourism destinations to market to potential travellers. For the first time in history, the marketing "playing field" has been levelled substantially by the Internet. During 2004, nearly 64 million people, 30 percent of the U.S. adult population, used the Internet to obtain travel information; by 2005, 79 million Americans were utilizing it. In 2004, 44.6 million booked services online.

   Recognizing this, the region's travel industry has dramatically increased its use of the Internet to promote sustainable forms of tourism; this includes everything from promoting ecotourism to increasing mindfulness of cultural and heritage attributes. Therefore, it will be essential that Internet connectivity be made available throughout the NFR. State and national parks and forests as well as other systems serving outdoor recreationists should be prepared to provide highly functional electronic reservations systems and email services.

c. Gasoline Prices and Tourism. Tourism in the NFR is very vulnerable to rising transportation costs, given that 1) an overwhelming proportion [75-80%] of NFR visitors arrive by automobile, and 2) much of the NFR is situated a full day's drive from its principal marketplaces. The price of gasoline will be a key factor in the region's success a destination. Regular-unleaded gasoline rose from a regional average of $1.60 during 2003, to $1.87 during 2004, to $2.25 during 2005. The national average was $2.92 per gallon in late April of 2006.

   This represents a nearly 85 percent increase during a period of less than 36 months. If this trend continues, Regular-unleaded gasoline may sell for more than $4.00 per gallon by 2010, an event that would be extremely detrimental to the NFR's tourism industry and overall economic wellbeing. Should the price of gasoline continue to rise, there will be increasing demand for outdoor recreation opportunities that are geographically convenient to markets, i.e., within or adjacent to urban areas, offered at comparatively low cost.

d. Travel Party Composition. The average U.S. travel party contains 3.8 members; however the region's travel parties tend to be smaller than the U.S. mean: Maine's average part size is 3.4, while New Hampshire's is 2.7, and Vermont's is 2.3 persons. Northern New England's visitors also tend to be older than the U.S. average: Percentage of Visitors Who are Less Than 35 Years of Age

This is an indication that the NFR is becoming increasingly dependent upon couples without any children living at home, particularly those households in the 45-and-older age cohorts. The leading generator of visits to Maine and New Hampshire is Massachusetts, with New York serving as Vermont's principal market. The Middle Atlantic states are northern New York state's leading sources of visitors. Other important markets are in-state residents and visits from the remaining New England

and Middle Atlantic states. California and Florida contribute a small but measurable number of visitors. Following a period of several years when their levels of visitation had been spiraling downward, the number of visitors from eastern and central Canada has been increasing since 2002, largely in response to a more favourable currency exchange rate for Canadians. Much emphasis has been placed upon marketing to the Baby Boomer generation.

This segment will continue to travel farther a field, stay away longer, and demand more services than earlier generations such as the Matures. As Baby Boomers retire, they will be looking for upscale conveyances and conveniences—including larger campsites, better access roads, improved recreation and fitness facilities, food services, and WiF—to take them to out-of-the-way areas and serve them while away from home.

Other generations that warrant the attention of marketers are the "Gen-Xers" and "Millennials". The former is a generation of knowledgeable travellers with much more experience with the Internet than their parents. Millennials are a large market segment (28%) that is confident, knowledgeable, independent and demanding of travel options that may never have been considered by prior generations.

While the topic of this report is Tourism, its fundamental concerns are rural jobs and protection of the region's environment. As one examines the potential for growth of the travel industry in the Northern Forest Region, the following tourism-related axioms must be considered:

Opportunities

- tourism has a generally positive impact upon local and regional economies (spending, revenues, tourism multipliers, purchases of services, creation of new services and commercial enterprises) that will be difficult for regional leaders to ignore.
- sustainability (of the environment, economy and sociocultural character) is the desired end of well-designed tourism enterprises, necessitating that a pro-active stance be adopted by government and commercial interests, one that permits tourism development while addressing the long-term ramifications of introducing new populations and landscape change and into the NFR.
- More than ever before, visitors are seeking quality, authentic

experiences and products, and are willing to pay for these, as long as value is provided; the presence of numerous, comparatively unspoiled natural areas and not-yet-gentrified communities bodes well for the future of tourism in the NFR.

- Partnerships/strategic alliances among former rival areas and businesses are essential in order to provide a competitive tourism product mix—a combination of accommodations, attractions and services. This is particularly true for rural areas and communities that lack a single, significant travel-generator.
- Geotourism and enrichment tourism strategies are sustainable, market-driven approaches that maintain or enhance the geographical character of a place—its environment, heritage, aesthetics, culture, and the wellbeing of its residents. Geotourism can be employed to leverage NFR's competitive advantages in the Northeast's tourism market place.
- Efforts to build interest in visitation to the Northern Forest Region should occur in cooperation with initiatives to build brand loyalties for souvenirs consisting of local products. This is a win-win situation.
- There are natural links between leisure travel and business travel, using the popularity of a place as a visitor destination to lure business, conferences and other meetings into the NFR.
- The Internet will be a key component in getting out the word about all that the NFR has to offer potential visitors. Efforts to link the various components (states, sub-state travel regions, communities) together have the greatest likelihood for success.

Challenges

- Tourism represents a potential threat to the natural environment and cultural character of the region because it engenders change.
- With the exception of New Hampshire (and recently in Vermont), the lack of centralized training in the operation of tourism businesses is a problem. Because of the competition for tourism dollars, and the growing sophistication of service providers and consumers in neighbouring areas, proper education and training of hospitality and tourism personnel must be coordinated.

- Long term rural residents are known for their avoidance of change; this attitude can prove detrimental to critical vocational retraining as well as planning and zoning efforts
- Few rural communities will be able to attract visitors alone; therefore, it is essential that people and agencies work within and among communities to develop, promote, and provide sustainable forms of tourism in the NFR. Towns within the region need to work together to implement legislative coalitions in order to expand awareness, on the part of lawmakers, of rural concerns and the prospects and threats presented by tourism growth within the NFR.
- It will be difficult to convince local people in some areas that visitation is really a viable option, as many have grown up with the awareness that their town was considered "undesirable." Only by changing attitudes will a stronger sense of stakeholder participation in tourism planning and development initiatives be accomplished.
- Second homes are a major component of the NRF's development and its quality of life; yet data about this industry are nearly non-existent in this region.
- There continues to be no uniform method for collecting, disseminating and applying regional tourism data. Prior to the federal government's decision to disband the U.S. Travel and Tourism Administration in 1995, the individual states had already eschewed efforts to standardize tourism data collection. Now, with the absence of this central domestic tourism research entity, state and local tourism research has become increasingly self-regulating, making state-to-state comparison impractical. Within most states, data are collected then aggregated at state (and perhaps county and/or sub-state tourism region) level. Only in exceptional instances are local level data sets available. As a result, existing sample sizes are too small to have validity at the local scale. This situation makes the process of conducting issue-specific research very difficult.

3

Maine Nature-Based Tourism

Background

The nature-based tourism discussion in the state of Maine was prompted by issues raised at the November 2003 Blaine House Conference on Maine's Natural Resource-based Industries. In September 2004, the Department of Economic and Community Development (DECD) retained FERMATA, Inc., a nationally-known experiential tourism development consulting firm, to assess Maine's opportunities in nature-based tourism; one of the fastest growing niches in the travel industry. Governor John Baldacci has provided leadership for the Maine Nature Tourism Initiative throughout the entire project.

Fermata, Inc. worked with state agency representatives, members of various state level organizations with interests in tourism and natural resources, and stakeholders in three rural pilot project areas: the Western Mountains, the Highlands, and Downeast.

Project Goals

1. Demonstrate how nature-based tourism development can be planned and implemented across the entire state.
2. Establish the Maine Nature Tourism Initiative as one of the administration's key strategies for rural economic development through job creation and tax revenue generation.
3. Provide a framework to support and compliment local and regional experiential tourism development efforts.
4. Furnish Maine visitors with accurate and comprehensive information on opportunities to experience the state's unique natural, historical, and cultural resources.

Vision

Experiential tourism enables rural communities to take advantage of their region's heritage, culture, and natural resources in new ways while also supporting traditional resource-based activities. It also enhances and diversifies traditional natural resource-based industries. Given the array of marketable travel and recreational experiences available throughout the Maine Woods, efforts to support experiential tourism service providers should result in net new dollars coming in to support rural, local economies.

Coordination and implementation of the Maine Nature Tourism Initiative actions is expected to be led largely by local coalitions of tourism promotion agencies and other stakeholders with support and local capacity development assistance from appropriate state agencies and others as needed.

Experiential Tourism: An Evolving Sector

At once recreational and educational, experiential tourism revolves around venues and activities that allow tourists to be active participants in (rather than only passive beneficiaries of) their travel experiences. Experiential tourism relies on *in situ* natural, cultural, and historical resources, and helps people learn not only about the world around them but about themselves as well. It includes activities that draw people outdoors such as birding and other wildlife viewing, hiking, camping, learning about the history of a region, and nature photography, in addition to other cultural, historical, or nature-based activities.

While individual travel interests may differ, experiential tourists are all bound together by the shared goal of engaging in activities from which they can develop a deeper understanding of a region, its unique natural attributes, and its local history and culture.

In recent years, a variety of tourism market studies have documented the travelling public's increasing desire for experiences that allow them to learn first-hand the lifestyle, culture, and history of rural areas. For example, according to the Travel Industry Association of America (TIA), 48% of U.S. travellers are interested in visiting a place that is "remote and untouched." Moreover, 57% are attracted by an area's "culture," and 76% of U.S. travellers state that they "would like to visit some place they have never visited before" (TIA 2002).

TIA research also shows that cultural and historic tourists, as well as tourists whose main purpose is to learn about new places, constitute a significant portion of the American travel market. For example, recent TIA studies demonstrate that 81 percent of U.S. adults who travelled in the past year, or 118 million tourists, are considered historical/cultural travellers. These travellers included historical or cultural activities on almost 217 million person-trips last year, up 13 percent from 192 million in 1996. At the same time, 30.2 million adults have taken an educational trip in the past three years, and 18% of travellers in the past year said that taking such a trip was the main purpose of their travel (TIA 2003).

What Experiential Tourists Do

Numerous market segments or niches come under the experiential tourism umbrella, many of which are among those most rapidly expanding within the general tourism market. For example, wildlife-associated recreation, as opposed to outdoor recreation in general, now involves millions of Americans in hunting, fishing and a variety of non-consumptive activities such as birding, bird feeding, and wildlife photography. In 2000, the National Survey of Recreation and the Environment compiled data indicating that in the previous year "an estimated 129 million people took the time to stop and observe the natural scenery around them and an estimated 96 million people also took the time to view wildlife or wild flowers, while 71.2 million people viewed birds."

In 2004, these numbers rose to 151 million people viewing natural scenery, 125 million viewing or photographing wildlife, and 122 million viewing/photographing wild flowers. Moreover, Fermata's own research indicates that experiential tourists look for five primary opportunities when choosing a destination: to enjoy the sights, smells, and sounds of nature; to be outdoors; to see wildlife species not seen before; to get away from the demands of everyday life; and for family recreation.

In addition to the sights and sounds of nature, the TIA report, *Geotourism: The New Trend in Travel* (2003), points out that "authenticity is a primary theme when examining travellers wants and needs". Four in ten (41%) travellers say their experience is better when they can see and do something authentic (as opposed to those travel experiences that are constructed). In addition, half of all travellers prefer to experience the local culture (49%) and support local businesses (49%) at their destinations. Finally, the TIA also reports that, in general terms, enrichment, health/revitalization/enhancement, and eco-tourism/soft adventure are among the tourism areas most likely to grow in the U.S. market (TIA 1998).

Nature Based Tourism In India

India is one of the most unique countries in the world. The physical, economical, cultural and religious diversity of India has always been an enigma for the rest of the world. Hence, people from all over the world have been attracted to this huge and mysterious land in the east. With India rapidly emerging as a major economic stronghold, every sector in the nation is witnessing tremendous growth and development. One such rapidly growing sector in India is tourism and one of its offshoots that is drawing tourists from across the globe is ecotourism in India.

Tourism with a Difference

Ecotourism in India is a niche industry that has mainly developed in the past few years. Ecotourism is largely based on the concept of sustained tourism or eco-friendly tourism. It has often been the case with the tourist destinations in India where the ecological balance of a fragile area has degraded drastically due to the pressure of tourism. Hence, the country is trying to promote tourism in a manner in which it generates considerable revenue without disturbing the delicate ecosystem in the region. This type of tourism is extremely essential for India considering that it has one of the richest biodiversities in the world. The nation is blessed with the massive Himalayan barricade in the north, an extensive peninsula with a rich coastal line on both sides and rich forests and landscapes that are unique to the nation of India. Hence, the government is trying to push the concept of ecotourism so that these rich habitats do not get affected even after the influx of tourists.

Forms of Ecotourism in India

There are various forms of ecotourism in India that attract an increasing number of tourists each year. Some of the most prominent forms include Wildlife tourism, Agro tourism, Village tourism and even Religious tourism. Of these, wildlife tourism is emerging as one of the most popular forms of ecotourism in India. India has an unbelievable diversity with respect to flora and fauna and has some of the most renowned national parks and tiger reserves like Kanha, Ranthambore, Kaziranga, Corbett and Sunderbans. Apart from this, agro tourism is making its own mark and tourists are flocking to India to get a taste of the rustic rural life of the countryside. These are some of the aspects that have promoted ecotourism in India to a great extent. However, India's full potential is yet to be realized and in the future years the country can expect to reap some great rewards.

Tourism in India

Tourism is the largest service industry in India, with a contribution of 6.23% to the national GDP and 8.78% of the total employment in India. India witnesses more than 5 million annual foreign tourist arrivals and 527 million domestic tourism visits. The tourism industry in India generated about US$100 billion in 2008 and that is expected to increase to US$275.5 billion by 2018 at a 9.4% annual growth rate. The Ministry of Tourism is the nodal agency for the development and promotion of tourism in India. It maintains the "Incredible India" campaign.

According to *World Travel and Tourism Council*, India will be the world's leading tourism hotspot, having the highest 10-year growth potential. The *Travel & Tourism Competitiveness Report 2007* ranked tourism in India 6th in terms of price competitiveness and 39th in terms of safety and security.

However, India's tourism sector currently lags behind less endowed countries and faces serious challenges including shortage of hotel rooms. In 2007, there were only 25,000 tourist-class hotel rooms in the whole of India. Among other factors hindering the growth of the tourism industry in India are stringent visa requirements and congested airports. Despite short-and medium-term setbacks, tourism revenues are expected to surge by 42% from 2007 to 2017. India has a growing medical tourism sector. The 2010 Commonwealth Games in Delhi are expected to significantly boost tourism in India.

Tourism by State

Andhra Pradesh has a rich cultural heritage and a variety of tourist attractions. The state of Andhra Pradesh comprises scenic hills, forests, beaches and temples. Andhra Pradesh is the home of many religious pilgrimage centres, one of them being 'Tirupati,' the abode of Lord Venkateswara, which is the richest and most visited Hindu temple in India. Hyderabad is known for its rich history, culture and architecture representing its unique character as a meeting point for North and South India, and also its multilingual culture, both geographically and culturally.

Also known as The City of Nizams and The City of Pearls, Hyderabad is today one of the most developed cities in the country and a modern hub of information technology, ITES, and biotechnology. Hyderabad offers many attraction to the tourists. It is famous for its delicious Hyderabadi Biryani. It is India's second largest metropolitan.

Andhra Pradesh is the home of many religious pilgrim centres. Tirupati, the abode of Lord Venkateswara, is the richest and most visited religious centre (of any faith) in the world. Srisailam, the abode of Sri Mallikarjuna, is one of twelve Jyothirlingalu in India, Amaravati's Siva temple is one of the Pancharamams, and Yadagirigutta, the abode of an avatara of Vishnu, Sri Lakshmi Narasimha. The Ramappa temple and Thousand Pillars temple in Warangal are famous for some fine temple carvings. The state has numerous Buddhist centres at Amaravati, Nagarjuna Konda, Bhattiprolu, Ghantasala, Nelakondapalli, Dhulikatta, Bavikonda, Thotlakonda, Shalihundam, Pavuralakonda, Sankaram, Phanigiri and Kolanpaka.

The golden beaches at Visakhapatnam, the one-million-year old limestone caves at Borra, picturesque Araku Valley, hill resorts of Horsley Hills, river Godavari racing through a narrow gorge at Papi Kondalu, waterfalls at Ettipotala, Kuntala and rich biodiversity at Talakona, are some of the natural attractions of the state. Kailashagiri is situated adjacent to sea in Visakhapatnam, it is one of the beautiful sight which shows the entire beauty of Visakhapatnam having other side sea. A beautiful park is developed on the hill top of Kailashagiri, the city boasts of having a park on hill top that has a luxurious toy train, ropeway and beautiful view of beach front into which Eastern Ghats merge into the sea. Further, Visakhapatnam is home to many tourist attactions like INS Karasura Submarine museum (The only one of its kind in India), the most beautiful and the longest Beach Road in India, Yarada Beach, Araku Valley (Known as poorman's Ooty, a lot of movies are shooted here), VUDA Park, Indira Gandhi Zoological

Gardens, etc. The weather in Andhra Pradesh is mostly tropical and the best time to visit is in November through to January. The monsoon season commences in June and ends in September, so travel would not be advisable during this period.

Places to Visit

- Hyderabad: The capital of AP, it is a melting pot of various cultures, known for its historical monuments as well as modern marvels. The places to visit are-Charminar, Mecca Masjid, Salarjung Museum, Hussain Sagar, Lumbini Park, Snow world, Ramoji Film city, Water world, Hitech city, Golconda, Paigah tombs, Falaknuma palace.
- Visakhapatnam: A beautiful city on the east coast, it boasts of natural and man-made beauties. The places to visit are-Kailashagiri, R.K.Beach, Rushikonda beach, Simhachalam temple, Vizag-Bhimili Beach Road, Bojjannakonda, Thatlakonda, Appikonda Beach, Yarada Beach, Bhimili Beach, Gangavaram Beach, Borra Caves, Araku valley, Tenneti Beach Park, Ross hill church, Dolphin's nose mountain, Submarine Museum, Aquarium, Indira Gandhi Zoological Gardens, Duduma waterfalls and Red sand hills.
- Tirupati: India's most famous and richest temple. Lord venkateshwara temple, Tirumala, Deer Sanctury, Horsely Hills, Sri Kalahasti Temple, Lepakshi.
- Vijayawada: Commercial hub of AP. Places to visit are-Kanakadurga Temple, Gandhi hill, Prakasham Barrage, Krishna River bank, Mangalagiri Temple.

Assam

Assam is the central state in the North-East Region of India and serves as the gateway to the rest of the Seven Sister States. Assam boasts of famous wildlife preserves – the Kaziranga National Park (*pictured*) and the Manas National Park, largest river island Majuli and tea-estates dating back to time of British Raj. The weather is mostly sub-tropical. Assam experiences the Indian monsoon and has one of the highest forest densities in India. The winter months (October to April) are the best time to visit.

It has a rich cultural heritage going back to the Ahom Dynasty which governed the region for many centuries before the British occupation. Other notable features include the Brahmaputra River, the mystery of the bird suicides in Jatinga, numerous temples including Kamakhya of Tantric sect, ruins of palaces, etc.

Bihar

Bihar is one of the oldest inhabited places in the world with history of 3000 years. The rich culture and heritage of Bihar is evident from the innumerable ancient monuments that are dotted all over the state in eastern India. Bihar is home of many tourist attractions. Bihar is visited by scores of tourists from all over the World all the year round. Around total 6,000,000 (6 million) tourist visits Bihar every year.

In the earliest day, tourism in region was purely based Educational tourism as Bihar was home of some prominent ancient universities like Nalanda University & Vikramaúîla University.

Bihar one of the most sacred place of various religions like Hinduism, Buddhism, Jainism, Sikhism & Islam, Many tourist travel to Bihar to visit their pilgrimage. Mahabodhi Temple, a Buddhist shrine and UNESCO World Heritage Site is also situated in Bihar. Mahatma Gandhi Setu, Patna, is one of the longest bridge in the world.

Delhi

Delhi is the capital of India. A fine blend of old and new, ancient and modern in every stream of life is the soul of Delhi. A melting pot of cultures, religions and castes makes Delhi a diverse place. Delhi has been the capital of India from the mythological days. The rulers left behind their trade marks in the architecture. Delhi currently has many renowned monuments and landmarks such as the Tughlaqabad fort, Qutub Minar, Purana Quila, Lodhi Gardens, Jama Masjid, Humayun's tomb, Red Fort, Safdarjung's Tomb, Jantar Mantar, India Gate, Rashtrapati Bhavan, Laxminarayan Temple, Lotus temple and Akshardham Temple.

Delhi is famous for its wide roads and crisp winters. It is one of the few places in India where colours of nature changes with the seasons. From Kerala to Kashmir and from Gujarat to Assam all the mouth watering delicacies and shopping goods are found in Delhi. The cosmopolitan nature of the city has only added to the beauty and glory of it. Big gardens, wide roads, ancient structures, and power of politics is what Delhi is all about.

Goa

The state of Goa is situated on the West Coast of India, between the borders of Maharashtra and Karnataka and is better known to the world as the former Portuguese enclave on Indian soil. Goa presents a somewhat different picture to the foreign visitor than any other part of India. The state of Goa is famous for its excellent beaches, churches, and Hindu temples. The Bom Jesus cathedral, Mangueshi Temple and Shantadurga are famous attractions in Goa. Recently a Wax Museum (Wax World) has also opened in Old Goa housing a number of wax personalities of Indian history, culture and heritage.

Himachal Pradesh

A summer view of Khajjiar, a hill station in Himachal Pradesh. Home to the some of the most popular Hill Stations, and home also to some exquisite alpine & Trans-Himalayan destinations, the Indian state of Himachal Pradesh is a major product in the Indian tourism market. Himachal is famous for its sweet apples. Among the major crowd pullers in Himachal Pradesh are: Shimla, the state's capital, Manali, Dharamshala, Dalhousie and Kasauli.

Jammu and Kashmir

Jammu is noted for its landscape, ancient temples, Hindu shrines, castles, gardens and forts. Hindu holy shrines of Amarnath and Vaishno Devi attracts tens of thousands of Hindu devotees every year. Jammu's natural landscape has made it one of the most popular destinations for adventure tourism in south Asia. Jammu's historic monuments feature a unique blend of Islamic and Hindu architecture styles.

Tourism forms an integral part of the Kashmiri economy. Often dubbed "Paradise on Earth", Kashmir's mountainous landscape has attracted tourists for centuries. Notable places are Dal Lake, Srinagar Phalagam, Gulmarg, Yeusmarg and Mughal Gardens etc. However, the tourism industry is severely affected by the insurgency. In recent years, Laddakh has emerged as a major hub for adventure tourism. This part of Greater Himalaya interpreted as "moon on earth" comprising of naked peaks and deep gorges was once known for the silk route to High Asia with the sub continent.

Tamil Nadu

Tamil Nadu or "the land of Tamil" is a beautiful state nestled in the southern Indian peninsula, on the shores of the Bay of Bengal and the deep blue Indian Ocean. Many great rulers including the Cholas, Pallavas, Pandyas and the Vijayanagara Empire ruled over parts of Tamil Nadu. The state is known for its cultural heritage and temple architecture. Tamil literature is amongst the oldest in India. Much of the ancient culture of Tamil Nadu is still alive. We have Carnatic music, an Indian classical tradition. Bharatha Natyam is its twin dance form, always accompanied by this music and the rich tradition of folk music continues to inspire people.

Attractions

- Chennai-Capital of Tamil Nadu and also India's fourth largest metropolitan.
- Madurai-Madurai Meenakshi Amman Temple. Oldest city in southern India.
- Coimbatore-Industrial centre, Temples, Kovai kutralam waterfalls.
- Mahabalipuram-World famous for its Shore Temples.
- Chidambaram-Lord Shiva in the enthralling form of a Cosmic Dance.
- Kanchipuram-The Golden City of a thousand temples, Handloom Silk.
- Kanyakumari-Southernmost tip of India, where the Arabian Sea, the Indian Ocean and the Bay of Bengal meet.
- Ootacamund-Queen of southern hill resorts of India.
- Rameswaram-Well-known pilgrimage in India.
- Thanjavur-The rice bowl of Tamil Nadu.
- Tiruchirapalli-City on the banks of river Cauvery.
- Auroville-International Utopian city being built, Aurobindo Ashram Associations.
- Mudumalai Wildlife Sanctuary-Wildlife sanctuary.
- Kodaikanal-Princess of hill stations in southern India.
- Kolli Hills-Herbal Hills/Quiet Hills/Medium budget.

Ponducherry

The Union Territory of Pondicherry comprises four coastal regions viz-Pondicherry, Karaikal, Mahe and Yanam. Pondicherry, Karaikal and

Yanam are situated on the East Coasts and Mahe on the West Coast. Pondicherry is the Capital of this Union Territory and one of the most popular tourist destinations in South India. The city has many beautiful colonial buildings, churches, temples, and statues, which, combined with the systematic town planning and the well planned French style avenues, still preserve much of the colonial ambience. Pondicherry is also a popular weekend destination. It is a blend of spiritual aura, French colonial heritage, Tamil culture, Virgin beaches and the cosmopolitan flair of many nationalities in a small but varied town.

The popular tourist destinatins are the four beaches in Pondicherry, they are Promenade Beach, Paradise Beach, The Auroville Beach and Serinity Beach. Sri Aurobindo Ashram located on rue de la Marine, is one of the most well known and wealthiest ashrams in India. Auroville (City of Dawn) is an "experimental" township located 8 km North-West of Pondicherry. Auroville is meant to be a universal town where men and women of all countries are able to live in peace and progressive harmony, above all creeds, all politics and all nationalities.

There are a number of old and large churches in Pondicherry some of which have been built in eighteenth and nineteenth century. A number of heritage buildings and monuments are present around the Promenade beach such as the Children's Park & Dupleix Statue, Gandhi statue, Nehru Statue, Le Café, French War Memorial, 19th Century Light House, Bharathi Park, Governors Palace, French War Memorial, Romain Rolland Library, Legislative Assembly, Pondicherry Museum, French Institute of Pondicherry at Saint-Louis Street etc. Pondicherry Botanical Gardens is located south of the New Bus Stand. Chunnambar Backwater resort is situated 8 kms from Pondicherry, along the Cuddalore Main Road. This tropical paradise is flanked by a quiet-flowing creek on one side. Boating and tree house here are very popular.

Karnataka

Karnataka, the eighth largest state in India, is a veritable treasure trove of tourist delights. By virtue of its varied geography and long and rich history, Karnataka boasts of numerous spots of interest for tourists. Karnataka has been ranked as fourth most popular destination for tourism among states of India. With its 507 out of the 3600 centrally protected monuments, Karnataka has the second highest number of protected monuments in India, next only to Uttar Pradesh.

The Kannada dynasties like Kadamba, Chalukya, Rashtrakuta, Vijayanagara Empire, Hoysala, Ganga, Ratta and many more they ruled Karnataka perticularly North Karnataka and other parts of India. They built great monuments related to Buddhism, Jainism, Shaivism. The monuments are still present at Badami, Aihole, Pattadakal, Hampi, Lakshmeshwar, Sudi, Hooli, Mahadeva Temple (Itagi), Dambal, Lakkundi, Gadag, Hangal, Halasi, Galaganatha, Chaudayyadanapura, Banavasi, Belur, Halebidu, Shravanabelagola, Sannati and many more. The great Islamic monuments are present at Bijapur, Bidar, Gulbarga, Raichur and other part of the state. Karnataka is famous for its waterfalls. Jog falls of Shimoga District is one of the highest waterfalls in Asia. This state has 21 wildlife sanctuaries and five National parks and is home to more than 500 species of birds.

Karnataka is a rock climbers paradise. Yana in Uttara Kannada, Fort in Chitradurga, Ramnagara near Bangalore district, Shivagange in Tumkur district and tekal in Kolar district are a rock climbers heaven. Gol Gumbaz at Bijapur, has the second largest pre-modern dome in the world after the Byzantine Hagia Sophia. Karnataka has two World heritage sites, at Hampi and Pattadakal, both are in North Karnataka. Karnataka has many beaches at Karwar, Gokarna, Murdeshwara, Surathkal and many more

Kerala

Kerala is a state on the tropical Malabar Coast of southwestern India. Nicknamed as one of the "10 paradises of the world" by the National Geographic traveller, Kerala is famous especially for its ecotourism initiatives.

Its unique culture and traditions, coupled with its varied demography, has made it one of the most popular tourist destinations in India. Growing at a rate of 13.31%, the tourism industry significantly contributes to the state's economy. The Kerala Tourism Development Corporation, the government agency that oversees the tourism prospects of the state, has adopted the brand "God's Own Country" for its campaigns.

The slogan holds global Superbrand status. Kerala is gifted with 42 rivers running as the life stream of the culture. This state has a variety of land scapes which can attract the tourists such as coastal regions, backwaters, Nilgiri mountaing on one side, malabar highlands, and so on.

Madhya Pradesh

Madhya Pradesh is called the "*Heart of India*" because of its location in the centre of the country. It has been home to the cultural heritage of Hinduism, Islam, Buddhism, Sikhism, Jainism and Persian. Innumerable monuments, exquisitely carved temples, stupas, forts and palaces are dotted all over the State. Madhya Pradesh is also known as Tiger State because of tiger population in MP (Madhya Pradesh). Many Famous national parks like Kanha, Bandhavgadh, Shivpuri, Sanjay, Pench are located in MP.

The natural beauty of Madhya Pradesh is equally varied. Consisting largely of a plateau, the State has everything. Spectacular mountain ranges, meandering rivers and miles and miles of dense forests offering a unique and exciting panorama of wildlife in sylvan surroundings.

Attractions

- Bhopal-The Capital City of Madhya Pradesh also known as 'The City Of Lakes' with many large and small lakes. It is also known as The City of Mosques. Bhopal is surrounded by small and large infrastructure towers. It is also has many other important places for tourism such as :
- Indore-The city of queen Ahilyabai Holkar famous for Temples and Largest Infrastructures in Central India. It is also known as "The Commercial Capital Of Madhya Pradesh". Besides this it is famous for Rajwada, Petroleum Refinary and Regional Hub Of Telecommunication.
- Gwalior-The Royal City of Madhya Pradesh, famous for its forts, Tomb of Rani Lakshmibai, Palace of Tansen.
- Jabalpur-Also referred as Sanskardhani is the city of marbles. It is famous for Marble Hills, Bheraghat, Madan Mahal, Narmada Water Fall, Dhuadhar, Shahi Minar, Tals and many forts.
- Ujjain-The City of Temples famous for many tourist spots such as Mahakali Temple, Vinayak Temple, Shipra River, Vikramaditya Palace.
- Pachmarhi-The Queen of Hills. It is the most important point of interest. It is famous for Handi Khoh, Jata Shankari Caves.

- Panna-Referred as The Diamond City. It is famous for Diamond Mines, Water Falls, Panna Tiger Reserve, Bundel Forts.
- Mandavgarh-It is Famous for Temples and Beaches.
- Khajuraho-A very important tourist Spot in Madhya Pradesh famous for the infamous Shiv Temples and Chandela Structures.
- Omkareshwar-An Important Hindu Pilgrim Spot.
- Mandla-The Capital of Rani Durgavati. It is famous for Kanha National Park, Durgavati Forts.
- Shivpuri-It is famous for National Parks.
- Singrauli-It is famous for Giant Coal Mines.

Maharashtra

Unlike most other states in India, Maharashtra boasts of a large number of popular and revered religious venues that are heavily frequented by locals as well as out-of-state visitors. It also boasts of the City of Mumbai with its Bollywood fame, ancient cave temples at Ajanta and Ellora, the Bibi Ka Maqbara at Aurangabad, the Mahalakshmi temple in Kolhapur, the city of Pune the seat of the Maratha Empire, the fantastic Ganesh Chaturthi celebrations.

Orissa

Orissa has been a preferred destination from ancient days for people who have an interest in spirituality, religion, culture, art and natural beauty. Ancient and medieval architecture, pristine sea beaches, the classical and ethnic dance forms and a variety of festivals. Orissa has kept the religion of Buddhism alive. Rock-edicts that have challenged time stand huge and over-powering by the banks of the river Daya. The torch of Buddhism is still ablaze in the sublime triangle at Udayagiri and Khandagiri Caves, on the banks of river Birupa. Precious fragments of a glorious past come alive in the shape of stupas, rock-cut caves, rock-edicts, excavated monasteries, viharas, chaityas and sacred relics in caskets and the Rock-edicts of Ashoka. Orissa is also famous for its well-preserved Hindu Temples, especially the Konark Sun Temple. Orissa is the home for various tribal communities who have contributed uniquely to the multicultural and multilingual character of the state. Their handicrafts, different dance forms, jungle products and their unique life style blended with their healing practices have got world wide attention.

Punjab

Punjab is one of India's most beautiful states. The state of Punjab is renowned for its cuisine, culture and history. Punjab has a vast public transportation and communication network.

Some of the main cities in Punjab are Amritsar, Chandigarh, and Ludhiana. Punjab also has a rich religious history incorporating Sikhism and Hinduism. Tourism in Punjab is principally suited for the tourists interested in culture, ancient civilization, spirituality and epic history. Some of the villages in Punjab are also a must see for the person who wants to see the true Punjab, with their beautiful traditional Indian homes, farms and temples, this is a must see for any visitor that goes to Punjab.

Rajasthan

Rajasthan, literally meaning "*Land of the Kings*", is one of the most attractive tourist destinations in Northern India. The vast sand dunes of the Than Desert attract millions of tourists from around the globe every year.

Attractions

- Jaipur-The capital of Rajasthan, famous for its rich history and royal architecture.
- Jodhpur-Fortress-city at the edge of the Than Desert, famous for its blue homes and architecture.
- Udaipur-Known as the "Venice" of India.
- Jaisalmer-Famous for its golden fortress.
- Barmer-Barmer and surrounding areas offer perfect picture of typical Rajasthani villages.
- Bikaner-Famous for its medieval history as a trade route outpost.
- Mount Abu-Is the highest peak in the Aravalli Range of Rajasthan
- Pushkar-It has the first and one of the very Brahma temples in the world.
- Nathdwara-This town near Udaipur hosts the famous temple of Shrinathji.
- Ranthambore-Situated near Sawai Madhopur, this town has one of the largest and most famous national parks in India.

Sikkim

Originally known as Suk-Heem, which in the local language means "peaceful home", Sikkim was an independent kingdom till the year 1974, when it became a part of the Republic of India. The capital of Sikkim is Gangtok, located approximately 185 kilometres from New Jalpaiguri, the nearest railway station to Sikkim. Although, an airport is under construction at Dekiling in East Sikkim, the nearest airport to Sikkim would be Bagdogra. Sikkim is considered as the land of Orchids and mystic cultures and colourful traditions. Sikkim is well known among trekkers and adventure lovers, as West Sikkim has a lot to give them. Places near Sikkim include Darjeeling also known as the Queen of hills and Kalimpong. Darjeeling, other than its world famous "Darjeeling tea" is also famous for its refined "Prep schools" founded during the British Raj. Kalimpong is also famous for its flora cultivation and is home to many internationally known Nurseries.

Uttarakhand

Uttaranchal is the 27th state of the Republic of India. Blessed with magnificent glaciers, majestic snow-clad mountains, gigantic and ecstatic peaks, valley of flowers, skiing slopes and dense forests, this Abode of Gods includes many shrines and places of pilgrimage. *Char-dhams*, the four most sacred and revered Hindu temples: Badrinath, Kedarnath, Gangotri and Yamunotri are nestled in the Mighty Himalayas. Haridwar which means *Gateway to God* is the only place on the plains.

A picturesque state, with a breathtaking panoramic view of Himalayas, Uttarakhand promises its tourists a visit full of fun and unforgettable moments. It contains the most fascinating and beautiful part of the Himalayas and provide watershed for Gangetic River System spanning 300 km from Satluj in the west to Kali river in the east. Nanda Devi (25640 Ft) is the second highest peak in India after Kanchenjunga (28160 Ft).

Dunagiri, Neelkanth, Chukhamba, Panchachuli, Trisul are other peaks above 23000 Ft. It is considered abode of *Devtas, Yakashyas, Kinners*, Fairies and Sages. They all are present here on glittering peaks, roaring rivers, beautiful hills slopes and valleys in one or another form. It boasts of some old hill-stations developed during British era like Mussoorie, Almora and Nainital. Serenity, divinity and eternity comes alive at charming Nature Retreats such as Dunagiri.

Uttar Pradesh

Situated in the northern part of India, Uttar Pradesh is important with its wealth of monuments and religious fervour. Geographically, Uttar Pradesh is very diverse, with Himalayan foothills in the extreme north, the Gangetic Plain in the centre, and the Vindhya Mountain Range towards the South. It is also home of India's most visited site, the Taj Mahal, and Hinduism's holiest city, Varanasi. The most populous state of the Indian Union also has a rich cultural heritage, and at the heart of North India, Uttar Pradesh has much to offer. Places of interest include Varanasi, Agra, Mathura, Jhansi, Prayag, Sarnath, Ayodhya, Dudhwa National Park and Fatehpur Sikri.

West Bengal

Kolkata, one of the many cities in the state of West Bengal has been nicknamed the City of Palaces. This comes from the numerous palatial mansions built all over the city. Unlike many north Indian cities, whose construction stresses minimalism, the layout of much of the architectural variety in Kolkata owes its origins to European styles and tastes imported by the British and, to a much lesser extent, the Portuguese and French. The buildings were designed and inspired by the tastes of the English gentleman around and the aspiring Bengali Babu (literally, a *nouveau riche* Bengali who aspired to cultivation of English etiquette, manners and custom, as such practices were favourable to monetary gains from the British). Today, many of these structures are in various stages of decay. Some of the major buildings of this period are well maintained and several buildings have been declared as heritage structures.

From historical point of view, the story of West Bengal begins from Gour and Pandua situated close to the present district town of Malda. The twin medieval cities had been sacked at least once by changing powers in the 15th century. However, ruins from the period still remain, and several architectural specimens still retain the glory and shin of those times. The Hindu architecture of Bishnupur in terracotta and laterite sandstone are renowned world over. Towards the British Colonial Period came the architecture of Murshidabad and Coochbehar.

Historic Monuments

The Taj Mahal is one of India's best-known sites and one of the best architectural achievements in India. Located in Agra, it was built between 1631 and 1653 by Emperor Shah Jahan in honour of his wife, Arjumand Banu, more popularly known as Mumtaz Mahal. The Taj Mahal serves as her tomb. The Golden Temple is one of the most respected temples in India and the most sacred place for Sikhs. The Golden Temple is located in Amritsar, Punjab, India. The Bahá'í temple in Delhi, was completed in 1986 and serves as the Mother Temple of the Indian Subcontinent. It has won numerous architectural awards and been featured in hundreds of newspaper and magazine articles. The Victoria Terminus in Mumbai was built by the British and is a UNESCO World Heritage Site. The Taj Mahal Palace is an icon of Mumbai.

Rural Tourism

India is a country of rich culture and heritage. With above 70% population residing in around 6 million plus villages, real India has its roots right inside this simplistic structure.

Nature Tourism

India has geographical diversity, which resulted in varieties of nature tourism;

- Water falls in Western Ghats including Jog falls (highest in India).
- Western Ghats.
- Kerala backwaters.
- Hill Stations.
- Wildlife reserves.

Wildlife in India

India is home to several well known large mammals including the Asian Elephant, Bengal Tiger, Asiatic Lion, Leopard and Indian Rhinoceros, often engrained culturally and religiously often being associated with deities. Other well known large Indian mammals include ungulates such as the domestic Asian Water buffalo, wild Asian Water buffalo, Nilgai, Gaur and several species of deer and antelope. Some members of the dog family such as the Indian Wolf, Bengal Fox, Golden Jackal and the Dhole or Wild Dogs are also widely distributed. It is also home to the Striped Hyaena, Macaques, Langurs and Mongoose species. India also has a large variety of protected wildlife. The country's protected wilderness consists of 75 National parks of India and 421

Sanctuaries, of which 19 fall under the purview of Project Tiger. Its climatic and geographic diversity makes it the home of over 350 mammals and 1200 bird species, many of which are unique to the subcontinent.

Some well known national wildlife sanctuaries include Bharatpur, Corbett, Kanha, Kaziranga, Periyar, Ranthambore and Sariska. The world's largest mangrove forest Sundarbans is located in southern West Bengal. The *Sundarbans* is UNESCO World Heritage Site.

Hill Stations

Several hill stations served as summer capitals of Indian provinces, princely states, or, in the case of Shimla, of British India itself. Since Indian Independence, the role of these hill stations as summer capitals has largely ended, but many hill stations remain popular summer resorts. Most famous hill stations are:

- Pachmarhi, Madhya Pradesh-It is also known as The Queen of Satpura.
- Araku, Andhra Pradesh.
- Gulmarg, Srinagar and Laddakh in Jammu and Kashmir.
- Darjeeling in West Bengal.
- Munnar in Kerala.
- Ooty and Kodaikanal in Tamil Nadu.
- Shillong in Meghalaya.
- Shimla, Kullu in Himachal Pradesh.
- Nainital in Uttarakhand.
- Gangtok in Sikkim.
- Mussoorie in Uttarakhand.

In addition to the bustling hill stations and summer capitals of yore, there are several serene and peaceful nature retreats and places of interest to visit for a nature lover. These range from the stunning moonscapes of Leh and Ladhak, to small, exclusive nature retreats such as Dunagiri, Binsar, Mukteshwar in the Himalayas, to rolling vistas of Western Ghats to numerous private retreats in the rolling hills of Kerala.

Beaches

Elephants and camels rides are common on Indian beaches. Shown here is Havelock Island, part of the Andaman and Nicobar Islands.

India offers a wide range of tropical beaches with silver/golden sand to coral beaches of Lakshadweep. States like Kerala and Goa have exploited the potential of beaches to the fullest. However, there are a lot many unexploited beaches in states like Andhra Pradesh, Gujarat, Maharashtra, Tamil Nadu and Karnataka. These states have very high potential to be develop them as future destinations for prospective tourists. Tourist beaches are:

- Beaches of Vizag, Andhra Pradesh.
- Beaches of Puri, Orissa.
- Beaches of Digha, West Bengal.
- Beaches of Goa.
- Kovalam Beach in Kerala.
- Marina Beach, Chennai.
- Beach Temples of Mahabalipuram.
- Andaman and Nicobar Islands.
- Beaches in Mumbai.
- Lakshadweep.
- Beaches of Diu.
- Beaches of Midnapore, West Bengal.

Adventure Tourism

- River rafting and kayaking in Himalayas.
- Mountain climbing in Himalayas.
- Rock climbing in Madhya Pradesh.
- Skiing in Gulmarg or Auli.
- Boat racing in Bhopal.
- Paragliding in Maharashtra.
- Medical tourism in India.

Remote Sensing and GIS Based Ecotourism Planning: A Case Study for Western Midnapore, West Bengal, India

Ecotourism has attracted increasing attention in recent years, not only as an alternative to mass tourism, but also as a means of economic development and environmental conservation. Being a nature based tourism; it takes into account the natural ecological attraction, their conservation and development. Its main aim is to safeguard the environment, making it beneficial to the local people by generating revenue and education and pleasure for the tourist.

Ecotourism is one of the fastest growing sectors in the tourism industry at present. The market for nature holidays is certainly a growing one. In 1993, the World Tourism Organization (WTO) has estimated that nature tourism generates 7 per cent of all international travel expenditure, where the total annual global earning from tourism is nearly $3 trillion and 212 million people are employed. Year 2002 has been declared as an International Year of Ecotourism (IYE) by the United Nations. This reflects its global importance.

Its evolution took place in western society to experience wild nature. It started in 1872 in the United States with Yellow stone Park, in 1879 in Australia with Royal Park and in 1885 in Canada with Banff Park and Niagara Falls to set aside natural areas for protection and recreation in the form of national parks. There is a worldwide system of thousands of protected areas in all parts of the globe now. Since 1970, globally the number of protected areas has increased by 185%. The present area, is 926,349,646 square kilometres, in parks which is an increase of 51.5% since 1970.

India has vast natural resources ranging from snowcapped mountains, blooming valleys, sea resorts, rolling rivers, dense forest, priceless mountains, temples and other places of heritages to vast desert areas, which can be important destinations for tourists (domestic and foreign). In spite of such bounties of nature and varieties of religion, culture and ethnicity, India accounts for only 0.4 % of the global tourism market and similar insignificant fraction of the world tourism revenue. There is a need to develop tourist destination that can be managed scientifically to attract large number of international as well as domestic tourists.

Present study is an attempt to identify potential ecotourism sites in eastern India using Remote Sensing and GIS techniques in forest dominated area of western Midnapore, West Bengal. After identifying the potential sites, a demonstrative plan has been made for Ecotourism development based on locally available natural resources.

Study Area

Study area includes five complete ranges (Chandrakona, Arabari, Nayabasat, Pirakata and Godapiyasal Forest Range), and two partial ranges (Midnapore range and Lalgarh range) of East Midnapore Forest Division of Midnapore District of West Bengal. From the administrative point of view, these area cover five blocks of northern Midnapore i.e., Chandrakona I, Chandrakona II, Garbeta III, Salbani and Keshpur. The Midnapore, district lies in north of the Kasai River and is an agricultural-trade centre on the Grand Trunk Road from Calcutta to Amritsar. Kharagpur Railway Junction, across the river, provides major rail connections. The topography, soil, vegetation, drainage pattern, climate have played important role in growth of the region.

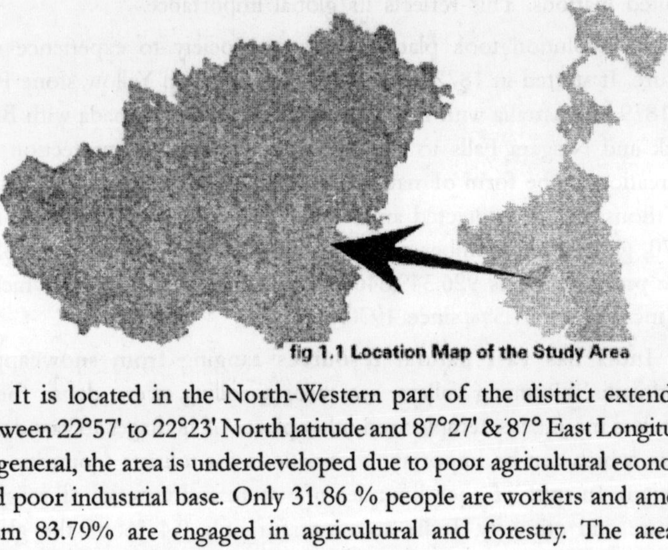

fig 1.1 Location Map of the Study Area

It is located in the North-Western part of the district extending between 22°57' to 22°23' North latitude and 87°27' & 87° East Longitude. In general, the area is underdeveloped due to poor agricultural economy and poor industrial base. Only 31.86 % people are workers and among them 83.79% are engaged in agricultural and forestry. The area is dominated by rural population, which is about 92.15%, and the percentage of urban population is only 6.85% living in three urban centres viz., Chandrakona Town, Khirpai and Ramjibanpur the north eastern part of the block.

The Western half of the study area is dominated by thick forest mainly of North Indian moist deciduous and North Eastern Tropical Dry deciduous forest consisting of dry peninsular sal.

The significant forest resources with memorable historical past make it ideal place for Ecotourism development. This will contribute significantly to economic development if Ecotourism is developed by Forest Department by involving the local population as well as NGO and private organization.

Methodology

Ecotourism planning requires exploring diverse types of natural and cultural attractions along with demographic characteristics, to provide the base for designing the travel industry different from the mass tourism standard. To fulfil this purpose Remote Sensing and GIS approach has been used. The methodology is given in the Fig. IRS 1D LISS III Data has been used for the study. The study area was then extracted using the block map generated from the census data. The extracted digital data was further analysed to generate vegetation density map, land use/land cover map and soil productivity map.

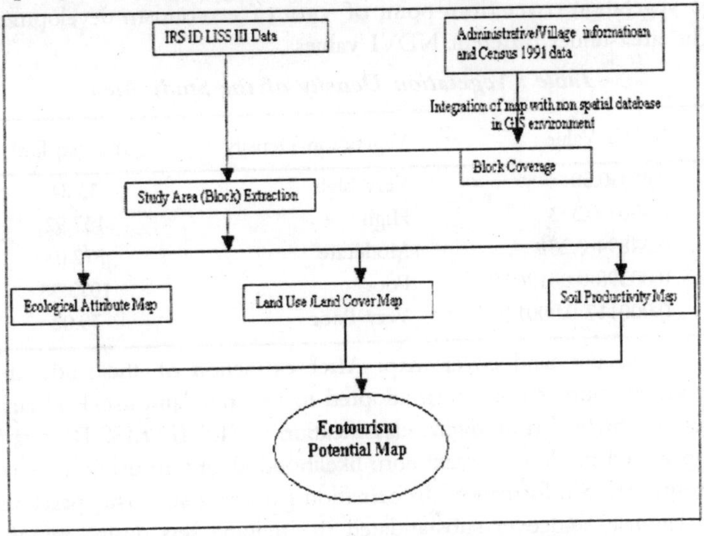

Vegetation Density Map: The information regarding the vegetation density can be of great help to identify and declare ecotourism potential site. In order to get these informations, NDVI approach has been used, which is highly correlated with vegetation parameter such as green leaf, biomass, leaf area and is indicator of photosynthetic activity and hence is of considerable value for vegetation discrimination and monitoring. NDVI values ranges between-1 to +1 and except vegetation, other features show either negative or zero NDVI values, using informations derived from NDVI, the study area is broadly classified into five categories among which the higher values show agricultural region while the most of the forest area fall under moderate value and lowest value reflect no vegetation, most of them are fallow or waste land.

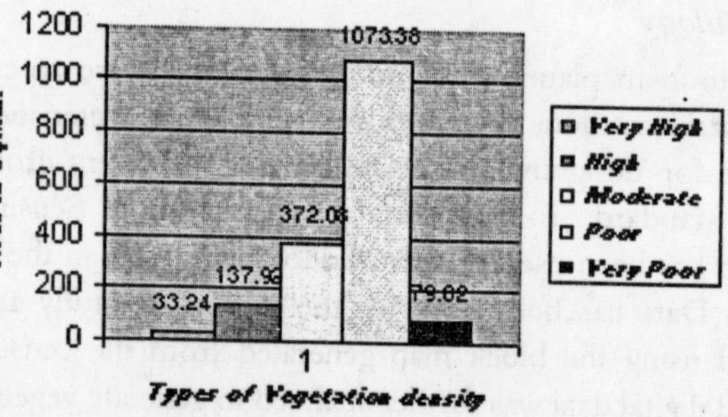

The weightage has been given on the basis of the relative importance of vegetation cover from point of view of ecotourism development. The area under different NDVI values.

Table : Vegetation Density of the Study Area

NDVI Value	Vegetation Density	Area (sq km)
0.624-0.50	Very high	33.24
0.4967-0.353	High	137.92
0.34894-0.201	Moderate	372.08
0.00398-0.0019697	Poor	1073.38
0.000117-0.000126	Very Poor	79.02

Land use land cover map: After extraction of the study area, stratified approach has been adopted to generate land use/land cover output obtained from digital classification of IRS 1D LISS III data by supervised mode with maximum likelihood algorithm using necessary ground truth information. Information gathering site visits pertaining to landuse/landcover substantiated the training sets during remotely sensed image classification by MXL classifier.

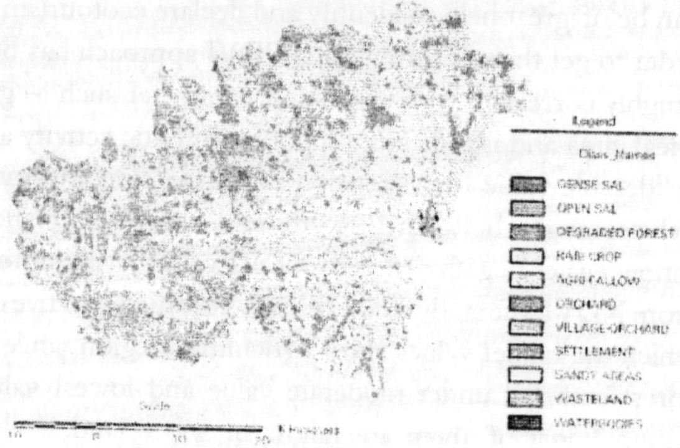

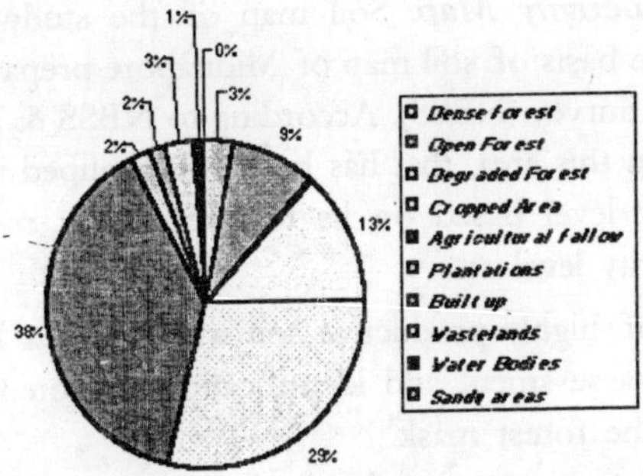

Table : Land Use/Land Cover Statistics Of The Study Area

S. N.	*Landuse CLASS*	*Area (Sq Km)*	*Landuse Suitability*
1	Dense forest	49.57	Highly important for ecotourism, can serve as main ecotourism attraction, area need to be conserved.
2	Open Forest	148.47	Very important for ecotourism, area needs to be managed and conserved properly to attract ecotourist as well as general tourist.
3	Degraded Forest	227.89	Need to be managed, properly with possibilities of new plantations. Important from point of view of medicinal plantations and agro-forestry scheme.
4	Cropped Area	487.69	Area under agriculture should not be converted to other schemes. Any infrastructure development should be restricted.
5	Agricultural fallow	657.33	It can be used fore agro-forestry scheme, land reclamation, for agricultural use or used for urban development.
6	Plantations	33.57	Plantation areas should be properly monitored and protected form and any encroachment.
7	Built up	27.91	Suitable for ecotourist Infrastructure development.
8	Wastelands	47.72	-do-
9	Water Bodies	15.02	Active Recreation as boating, park and natural zoological park.
10	Sandy areas	1.98	Not suitable.
	Total	1697.15	

Soil Productivity Map: Soil map of the study area has been prepared on the basis of soil map of Midnapore prepared by National Bureau of Soil Survey (NBSS). According to NBSS & LUP nine types of soil found in this area, that has been sub grouped into three types of productivity level based on its texture, depth, moisture holding capacity, erodivity level etc.

The area of highly productive soil within forest land have been considered for assessment and identification of potential ecotourism area by using the forest mask.

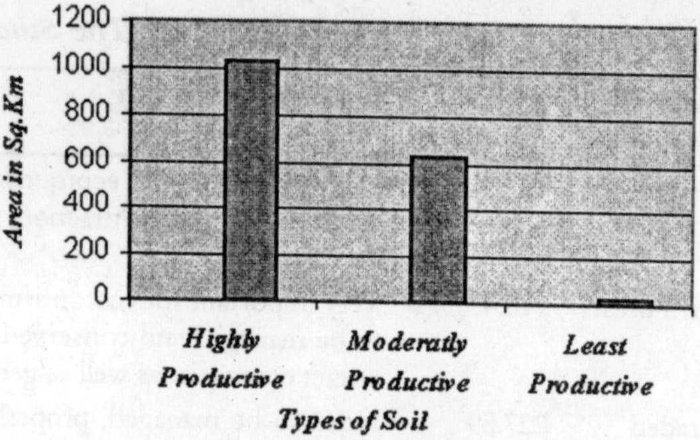

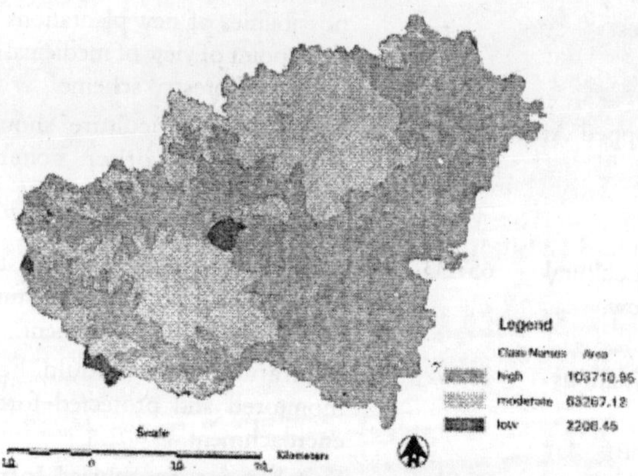

Table : Soil Productivity of the Study Area

Soil Characteristics	Area (sq km)
Highly productive	1037.10
Moderately productive	632.67
Least productive	22.08

Generation of The Ecotourism Potential Map

These maps are taken as the parameters to evaluate the area of high ecological importance. For this purpose a weighted approach was adopted to identify the areas having Ecotourism potential. The input in the form of ARC/INFO coverages were assigned relative weightage in accordance to its influence/importance in decision making based on expert opinion, and each other class in the individual coverage was ranked according to its potential of being for being developed for Ecotourism. The higher the vegetation index and higher the soil productivity, higher will be the forest density, so such sites in the map can be considered for conservation. The following formula is used to identify the Ecotourism potential sites.

$$EP_i = \Sigma(VD_i + LU/LC_i + SP_i)$$

Where i = 1,2,-------n, VD = Vegetation Density, LU/LC = Land use/ Land Cover, SP = Soil Productivity

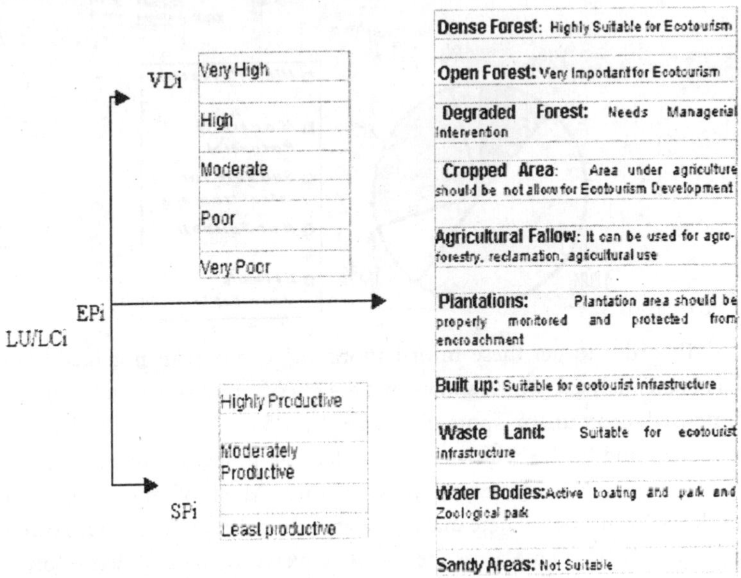

Result and Discussion

Ecotourism activities include bird watching, trekking, mountaineering, horse riding and elephant riding within the forest wilderness trail, staying in natural caves, studying about flora and fauna, simple bush walking, fishing, animal behaviour study, ecological studies. Based on the existence of the different motivations of ecotourists, the destination area and type of nature tours should be diverse, as a diversified nature of tour industry is more economically viable and stable.

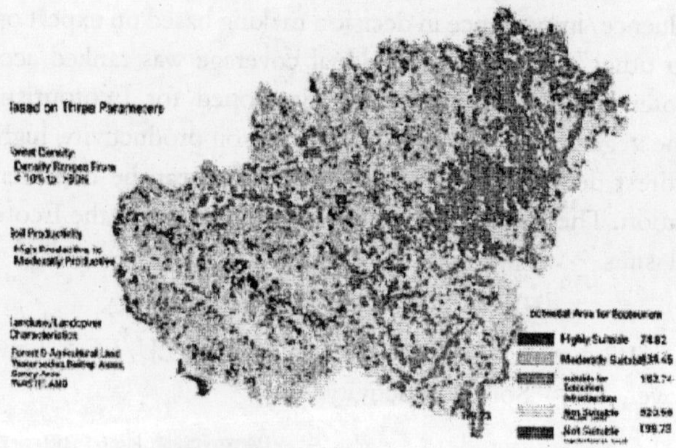

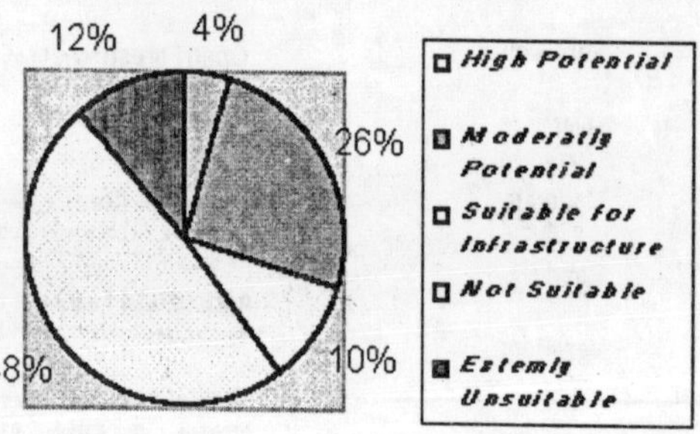

In order to get these informations the ecotourism potential map has been analysed, which shows that 4.42% of area comes under highly potential ecotourism spots followed by 25.67% under moderately potential and 9.62% which comes under low potential are suitable for development of ecotourism infrastructure. Most of these sites fall under Salbani block, where maximum area are covered by forest followed by Garbeta III. These areas are mostly covered by natural dense forest that can be considered for conservation. This forest is a part of elephant migration corridor, from Saranda forest (East Singhbhum, Jharkhand) to the forest of North Bengal. The other blocks, Keshpur and Chandrakona I and II are having less ecotourism potential site, and so it can be used for ecotourism infrastructure development.

Planning for Ecotourism Infrastructure in the Study Area

In view of the result, the ecotourism planning can be done which can bring development of this underdeveloped area by employing the local people as well as by infrastructure development. Ecotourism being truly a form of environmentally conscious tourism and not just pursuit of remote pristine locations. It can be made sustainable with continuous capacity to safeguard natural environment as the very basis of tourism attraction. It should also provide and maintain the quality of tourist experience and satisfaction as well as benefit to the local people in the area. To fulfil this purpose, there is need to follow some guidelines which are highlighted below:

1. Sustainable development of ecotourism requires the balance between three elements the tourists, the place and the host community". Therefore, at management level Government should involve local people along with NGO and private organization
2. To maintain visitor satisfaction in crowded locales and protection of natural features, and to maintain high quality of service there is need to assess the carrying capacity of the potential site at planning level.
3. Generally the ecotourism destination is developed in eco-fragile area, which has time specific attraction. The duration of visit and activity pattern of the tourist should be decided by implementing authorities to maintain natural harmony.
4. Proper ecotourism legislation and environmental measures should be framed and along with this strict enforcement measures should be imposed at eco-destination.
5. Along with this there is also need for publicity and advertisement of ecotourism destinations, Environmental group accreditation (tour operator) and adequate funding to maintain the environmental quality of the potential ecotourism destinations.

Based on the above guidelines, action area has been selected within the study area. An example of the proposed demonstrative plan is given for northwestern part of Salbani Block. The fused product of IRS 1D LISS III and PAN data has been used to get both multispectral and high resolution information, zoning plan has been proposed for ecotourism infrastructure development as well as ecotourism activities. The selection of the area for infrastructure development has been done on the basis of Minimum interference to the dense (density >60%) and open forest (density between 40-60%) site and cropped land. This will occupy mostly the land falling under degraded forest, scrubland, agricultural fallow etc.

In the action area there is lack of approach road to visit this place. For this purpose one non-metaled road has been proposed inside the action area, connected to the existing road. This road has been designed as a loop, which can be utilized by tourists as trail walk along the dense and open forest zone.

The proposal for above mentioned Ecotourism Infrastructure (physical and service oriented facilities) have been provided under some selected patches. The selection of these patches has been done on the basis of minimum interference to the natural dense and open forest and agriculturally most productive zones. Four patches have been selected for placing of ecotourism facilities.

Zone 1: Tourist cottages/rest houses, green hotels and restaurant, public convenience facilities

Zone 2: Tourist Information centre, conveyance Facilities, tourist guide map, public convenience facilities, Detail map of the ecotourism destination, tourist circuit map to show its link to other place of tourist interest Do and Don't board, medical aid facilities communication facilities etc. This has been chosen due to his location near entry point.

Zone 3: Tourist Information Centre, conveyance facilities elephant watchtower, public convenience facilities, and

Zone 4: Tourist cottages/rest houses, Tourist Information Centre, Conveyance facilities elephant watchtower public convenience facilities.

Conclusion

The study shows that the western part of the study area is highly potential for Ecotourism development, most of this part is endowed with lush green forests, wildlife as well as rich cultural heritage. Along with this it also fall under the elephant corridor of Jharkhand and West Bengal. So this area can be developed as Ecotourism destination by facilitating proper ecotourism infrastructure and services under policy guidelines. This will help to conserve and maintain the biological richness of the areas as well as economic upliftment of the local people by providing employment and opportunities in the field of ecotourism management.

What is Ecotourism?

In the 1990s, tourism received increasing attention especially in developing countries as it is has potential for generating income while creating incentives for conservation. It is argued that tourism allows for the use of areas, which are otherwise of low value, such as remote beaches, but perfectly meet the demands of the growing travel industry (WWF, 1995).

In India, for instance, there has been a large increase in international tourism in the last few years. In the year 2002, there has been a 14.6% increase in international tourist arrivals along with 22.4% growth in foreign exchange and most of this increase is due to India's system of national parks and variety of biodiversity present in these parks. Nature-based tourism a sub-sector of tourism can be an important channel for redistributing resources from countries who demand higher nature based vacation to developing countries, which comprise mega-biodiversity regions and protected parks.

This is because an overwhelming majority of species are located in developing countries. But these developing countries face more serious problems like rapid population growth, debts, over-exploitation of wild resources, agricultural expansion, deforestation etc., which result in the loss of valuable biodiversity and degradation of national parks.

Industrialized countries on the other hand are characterized by high and increasing demands for nature-based vacations, with protected areas representing first-rate attractions (WWF, 1995). Tourism could therefore be a means of redistributing economic resources, mitigating the socioeconomic situation both at local and national scale and contributing to biodiversity conservation.

For nature tourism to be sustainable – a number of environmental, economic and social requirements have to be fulfilled. This has led to the introduction of 'ecotourism', as a nature tourism eco-label. Given the important role played by nature-based tourism, the year 2002 has been declared as the International Year of Ecotourism. There have been several definitions of ecotourism:

The World Conservation Union (IUCN) and ecotourism society define ecotourism as "responsible travel to natural areas that conserves the environment and sustains the wellbeing of the local people." However for tourism to be called ecotourism, it should be fully compatible with the conservation goals of the country, while at the same time pose minimum threat to the continuation of local culture and society. Moreover, it should contribute by means of income and education to the contribution of ecosystems. Based on these definitions, the criteria for tourism to be called ecotourism employed in the literature may be summarized as follows:

1. Minimum physical and social impacts on the visited area.
2. Ecological education of the tourist at the natural site.
3. Notable economic participation by local tourists.

Ecotourism and its Impacts

There were two conflicting views about the impacts of ecotourism. The optimistic view is that tourists are an economic force that can promote the conservation of the natural attractions that entice the tourists in the first place. Under this concept, revenues from tourists, in the form of entrance fees, domestic airfares, accommodation and food, hiring charges of the guide, sale of local goods such as handicrafts and souvenirs and tax revenues levied on the above, are distributed among the population that is most likely to exploit the natural areas.

Such a transfer of revenue establishes a direct link between conservation and personal income. In addition, complex economic linkages transmit the impacts from those who sell goods and services to tourists to others in the local economy (who sells goods and services to the agents). For example, hotels, restaurants, and bars, hire local workers, pay rents to locals, and purchase local "intermediate inputs" like fruits and vegetables, fish, meat etc. Outside agents, including operators of boats also purchase locally supplied goods and hire local workers. Payments for these goods and services enter the economy, influencing the incomes of local agents who may not have any direct contact with tourists. These agents, in turn, stimulate new rounds of local expenditures that influence the incomes of still more local agents.

For example, the Campfire project in Zimbabwe (which is a community based wildlife management for safari tourism and sport hunting), generates yearly revenues of up to 4000 USD per household. In Asia, the ecotourism in Annapurna Conservation project have allowed for a basically self-sustaining financing of integrated conservation and development activities, to the benefit of the local population. In Latin America, according to a study by Groom et al. (1991) for Madre de Dios region in Peru, tourism benefits depend heavily on the type of destination. They found that easily accessible areas with already intervened natural environment provide less revenue compared to a remote rainforest reserve that caters to wealthier tourists. Drumm (1991) found for the Ecuadorian Amazon region that in spite of much higher tourism spending on tours in exclusive and pristine destinations, local income is found slightly higher in backpacker destinations. Lindberg and Enriquez (1994) concluded that the communities in Belize have profited significantly from tourism directed towards adjacent protected areas by selling handicrafts, providing accommodation and other services.

The pessimistic view has been that ecotourism cannot lead to sustainable development. Yu et al. (1997) finds the conditions under which the standard models of ecotourism can breakdown in Amazonian Peru. Taylor et al. (2003), finds that in Ecuador's Galapagos islands, by creating economic disparities between tourist destinations and the economies that surround them, the expansionary influences of tourism also create pressures for population growth through migration to fill jobs linked directly or indirectly to tourism. In addition to these due to flying, tourism causes significant environmental damage costs. For example, Gossling (2000) has estimated that a two-week package tour covering a typical return-flight distance of 7000 passenger kilometres is based on the use of 325 kg of fuel or air travel, including a national connecting flight, and another 100 kg of fuel for different purposes at the destination. This translates into a CO equivalent of about 3385 kg, including the effects of NO and H O. Viewed in terms of contribution of tourism to climate change, this can be substantial.

Some Issues and Future of Ecotourism

Tourist impacts on the environment, society, and economy are complex. As the nature-based tourism demand is mainly for the pristine undegraded areas, the pressure on such ecosystems can be quite high. The IUCN (1992) lists tourism as the second major threat to protected areas. If ecotourism grows rapidly beyond a certain extent several problems can emerge. These can be environmental problems, related cultural and social changes, disruption of the traditional economic activities etc. Even the local population may not be willing to tolerate visitor's beyond a particular limit. One way to deal with this problem is to find the carrying capacity of the region. Any tourism beyond the acceptable carrying capacity should be strictly prohibited. The carrying capacity can be physical, social and economic. Another major issue arising out of tourism is the distribution of benefits from tourism. As any conservation of protected areas for the purpose of tourism entails huge opportunity costs, if the benefits were not distributed fairly, this would result in huge welfare loss to the society. Most often as is the case, a greater proportion of tourism revenue gets concentrated in the hands of a few powerful players. This is because as the tourism linkages are often quite tenuous, local populations often cannot provide the services that foreign tourists demand which only large tourism operators can provide.

This leaves large tourism operators with almost no competition and hence the wealth is concentrated in the hands of few large operators, while the costs of tourism (say rising prices for goods and services) have to be borne by people living in that area. Another issue of concern is as more and more tourists arrive in the country, governments in developing countries often turn to ecotourism as the major option to generate economic benefits without adequate planning.

This can lead to unsustainable growth in the country, which can be avoided only through appropriate measures. Further, as mentioned before flying can cause significant damage to the environment and hence, these environmental costs must be internalized by suitable policy instruments. In addition to all these, one should consider the fact that the economic potential of ecotourism has remained unrealized so far because a major proportion of the nature-based tourism is characterized by non-use values.

These non-use values often accrue to tourists from the global community, while the developing countries face the costs for preservation. Basically, the economic value of tourism captured by developing countries is often minor. Many nature based tourist destinations in India charge a nominal fee or no fees at all. At present, most ecotourism spots do not even generate enough financial resources to cover their maintenance costs. Unless the costs of maintenance of the parks and the opportunity cost of protection of these nature-based tourist destinations are realized in the form of entrance fees, this would result in a huge burden on host countries. Thus, effective planning, management and control are a precondition for the sustainable growth of ecotourism.

4

Emerging Concepts in Effective Tourism Developments

Introduction

We have discussed in lesson 13 and 15 the emerging dimensions in Indian tourism and challenges posed due to globalization and liberalization. The new trends in the tourism markets compel all the destinations to develop new products and strengthen or re-engineer the existing products for retaining, enhancing and capturing new markets. The effective tourism development is the panacea for the success of the tourism industry.

The success of the future tourism development will depend upon how fast we are incorporating and implementing the effective tourism development techniques. This lesson discusses 3 major concepts of effective tourism development in Indian context: Destination Development, Human Resource Management and Open Sky Policy.

Objectives

This lesson is aimed at achieving the following objectives:

- Understand the importance of destination development.
- Understand evolution of destinations and sustainable Destination management.
- Understand the importance of Human Resource Management.
- Know the various human resource problems exist in Indian tourism.
- Know the various institutes provide tourism related courses.

Effective Tourism Development

The success of future tourism is intrinsically connected with the way in which the industry and the tourism system understand and incorporate the emerging critical trends that support its expansion. Tourism is undergoing major changes; aging world population (western countries) and active life style of older traveller, the emerging markets, growing disposable income of the youth and awareness about impact of tourism on environment, will decisively influence the number of tourists, motivation, destination and product choices as well as activities of future travellers.

The rapid liberalization and deregulation of markets will bring fierce competition based on price, quality and characteristics of the tourism products. These trends will bring profound changes in the management and planning of tourism business and destination While global trends push forward new managerial approach, the managers and planners must aware of the emerging tools that helps to manage and market business and destinations. Future trend points towards three strategic directions: satisfying consumers, destination development and management and territory organisations.

Destination Development: An Emerging Theme

Destinations face increasing challenges in international market place where numerous stakeholders (tourists, local people, tour operators, hotels and restaurants owners etc.) with diverse values and often divergent needs compete for scarce resources. The growing population of travellers and inhabitants increasingly make impact on natural and social environment. The success of tourism depends on the ability of the firms and destination to engage in sustainable use and conservation of vital resources. The destination development is the key to sustaining the natural and cultural resources on which tourism depends. Therefore steps have been taken up as key initiative in development of tourism destinations. The close interaction between the public sector, the destinations tourism marketing organisations, private sector and local residents in planning is the key principle of sustainable tourism. Thus the stakeholders can work most effectively together to manage local – global influences on their natural and cultural resources. Effective destination development is the important problem facing tourism managers.

Integrated Destination Management

A new concept adopts system approach where the ecological, physical, social spaces are linked by various networks and institutional structures. Traditionally, destination management tents to represent the tourism industries interests. Their mission is building and enhancing favourable destination image to attract targeted tourists and increase visitor numbers. Therefore, destinations and state and tourism agencies often focus their activities on tourism advertising campaigns. Historically, marketing focused on developing product, price, place and promotion, which ensure reasonable profit to individuals and organisations. Nowadays the marketing has been changed to an organizational function and a set of process for creating, communicating, delivering value to customers and its stakeholders. This reflects a shift away from mere profit motive towards creating value for a network of actors and environment.

The integrated destination management brings in destinations ecological– human communities as equitable and integrated members of planning and marketing and goal setting. The new approach integrates economic mobility, social equity and environmental responsibilities towards achieving the equality of life within living system.

Based on ecosystem network model a sustainable planning and marketing orientation does not just satisfy the needs and wants of individual but it strives to attain sustain ecosystem. The benefits are not just profits, but civic energy and social unity. Competition is replaced by dynamic interaction that aims at environmental, social, economic equity within the local – global network of living and physical structures.

Therefore, sustainable tourism marketing objectives are not to design product, price, place of a tourism destination or attraction, but to ensure quality of life and environments through tourism development. Achieving this will be a challenge. It involves developing an interactive product or place relationship that will give value to visitors and to diverse community stakeholders.

Destination Development

Tourism system, the destination region is perhaps one of the most important elements. Without the richness and variety of tourism environments around the world we would not have the same quality of tourist experience. In order to understand the supply of tourism, consideration has to be given to the different environmental social and economical contexts around the world within which tourism destinations are located. Destinations demonstrate number of common features.

- Destinations are cultural appraisals.
- They are perishable because tourism is consumed where it is produced.
- Destination involves multiple use of tourism with other uses.
- To be successful the components of the amalgam needs to be of equivalent quality.

It is important for the destination to deliver quality experience and product, and in this regard, careful planning and management is essential to ensure a tourism industry based on sustainable development. The destination brings together all aspects of tourism – demand, transportation, supply and marketing. It is one of the most important elements of tourism because destinations and their image attract tourist, motivates the visitor and therefore energize the whole tourism system. As the demand for the tourism has increased, pressure from the growing number of visitors has degraded some destinations. In response to this, planning and management strategies have been implemented in the busier destinations. Planning and management is the key to making existing tourist destination and resources more effective in meeting current as well as future demand.

Thus destination as the focus of facilities and services designed to meet the needs of the tourists.

Most destinations comprise a core of the following components:-

- Attractions – manmade features, natural features or events that provide motivation to visit.
- Access – local transport facilities.
- Amenities (accommodation, food, beverages, entertainment and retailing.
- Auxiliary services in the form of local organisations.

Infrastructure and Super Structure

Infrastructure represents all forms of construction above or below the ground, with extensive communication with the outside world as a basis for tourism activity in the area. Adequate infrastructure is essential for tourism development mainly in the form of transportation, utilities and other services. Generally infrastructure does not generate income and is treated as a public investment in most tourist developments. Where as a super structure is normally private sector activity, as it is the profit-generating element of the destination. It includes accommodation, built attractions, retailing and other services. In many countries public sector is actively providing financial incentives – grants, loans, and tax-holidays for private sector tourism investment. The destination development is a combined effort of public and private sectors.

Destination Evolution

The evolution of tourism has been closely linked to the evolution of destinations and in particular, resorts. The evolution of resorts has been driven by transport developments. Most of these are now touring centres rather than destinations in their own right, and in response touring circuits and clusters of attractions have developed. At the same time markets also respond to these terms of their tourist facilities and services. This evolution of tourism destination can be represented by tourist area life cycle (TALC). This states that destinations go through a cycle of evolution similar to the cycle of a product. The shape of TALC curve will vary, but for each destination it will be dependent upon factors, which can delay or accelerate progress through various stages such as the rate of development, access, government policy, market trends and competing destinations.

The development can be stunned at any stage in cycles, and only tourist developments promising considerable financial returns will mature to experience all stages of cycle itself is variable. The tourism destinations evolve from their beginning or inception stage through exploration, involvement, development, consolidation, stagnation and eventual decline or rejuvenation. Destination life cycle provides a framework for understanding how destinations and their market evolve. Understanding the life cycle aids the development of community – based and sustainable tourism strategies at the involvement stage.

The components of tourist destination can be effective only if careful planning and management deliver a sustainable tourism product. Only in recent years, that the negative impact on tourism on destination, rise of environmentalism and green consciousness have been set for a reassessment of the rolé and value of tourism to destinations. The concept of sustainability demands a long-term view of tourism and ensures that the consumption of tourism does not exceed the ability of the host destination to provide for future tourists. In other words it represents a trade-off between present and future needs. Perhaps the central issue for here is the gradual shift from short-term to longer-term thinking and planning at the destination.

Carrying Capacity

The concept of sustainability and carrying capacity we discussed in lesson 15 and 17. It is no longer acceptable for the industry to exploit and use-up destinations. The carrying capacity of a site, resort, or even a region refers to the ability to take tourism intervenes in the relationship carrying capacity is the maximum number of people who can use a site without an unacceptable alteration the physical environment and without an unacceptable decline in the quality of experience gained by visitor. Thus the carrying capacity roots in resource management, important aspect especially where finite destination resources are under growing pressure from users.

Development of Destination for Tourists

A sustainable tourism development model attempts to keep tourism in a particular place within the limits of capacity of the place. The late modern forms of tourism are based more on specialization, niche areas and highly competitive than on earning money from volume tourism. Butler's model of tourism development at destination provides more detailed picture of how to achieve the structural development of tourism. A different level of development in an area is presented below:-

Development of a specialized offering for tourists;

- Simplest service offering for tourists is placed at the bottom of service ladder. Common forms of services are cafeterias, petrol stations and dabas. Both local residents and tourists use these services.
- Next Step up the ladder is that there is some form of overnight accommodation in the area, a hotel, and motels but without any special attractions.
- Third step is specialized tourism service providing a greater range of attractions, activities, and accommodations.

- The fourth stage is tourism centres where the whole range of services has been adopted to the needs of tourism for one season or two-season destination.
- Final step on the ladder is advanced service – rich source of services and extensive specialization, in the form of theatres, concert halls, large museums etc.

This model presents the stages in the development from small-scale tourism to mass tourism.

Tourism development strategy When developing a destination, a planner works on two factors:-

- Pull factors – tourism products and attractions. Advanced tourism services Tourism Centres Specialized tourism services Overnight accommodation Temporary stopping places Clients or areas with a highly specialized service Centres where attractions for visitors are the predominant features of the service offering. A good choice of services, accommodation, attractions and activities Some choice as regards type of accommodation. Simple service offering for visitors.
- Push factors – determine demand, provide information about supply of attractions and marketing these areas tourism products.

The tourism destination can be designed structurally through appropriate development strategy. The development strategy provides broad guidelines, future vision and goals for of sustainable development. The procedure involved in the strategy is as follows:-

- Inventory of existing and potential resource for tourism.
- Description and analysis of the structure of the tourist industry – products.
- Analysis of demand.
- Development ambitions of representatives of tourism industry.
- Local community demands regarding tourism.
- Maintaining ecological, social, cultural and economic environment.
- Form of organization for tourism development.

These broad guidelines must be incorporated in the tourism destination development and consumption process.

Future Developments

Tourist destination of the future will be influenced by variety of factors, but technology and the demands of new tourist will be dominant. Technology permeates destination development in many ways such as, hotel communication system, computer reservation system which allows matching of demand with supply and computer generated imagery and use of virtual reality.

Thus the stage is set for a range of new tourist destinations to be developed and for the more effective management of existing destinations. There is no doubt that these new and existing destinations need to be better planned and managed and show more concern for their environment and host community.

Human Resource Development

The success of any industry depends to a great extend up on the quality of human resource and tourism is not an exception. We have already learnt that tourism is labour intensive industry which provides employment to skilled, semiskilled and unskilled workers directly and indirectly. The progressive labour force with dynamic management and responsive government and responsible society are the pillars of the tourism industry.

Traditionally, the employment has been seen as an area that is reactive to changes in the wide business environment. There is a widely accepted assumption that the role of people within organisations is required to change and develop in response to developments in markets, products and technology. Most of the large tourism companies recognized this assumption and has been started organising work and support human resource functions such as training and development. This is possible only when the external labour market permits employers to adapt these changing dimensions.

Globalization of business firms has a number of implications for human resources management. A major consequence in tourism industry is the issue of matching employee's skills with changing industry requirements. The traditional practice of employee's learning the majority of skills on the ;ob and gradually progressing to senior position is threatened by the rapid technological changes and the need to respond to the changing service requirements. Employees at the operational and managerial levels are now required to be more flexible and adaptive to constant change. Globalization has major Implications for work and employment in tourism and these include:-

- The need for different skills and competencies is the employees to be able deal with use of technology.
- Dealing with employment related consequences of mergers and strategic alliances.
- Issues of relocation of employees and social and cultural sensitiveness of those working away from home.
- New forms of tourism utilizing natural and cultural environment create a demand for indigenous employees, who could deliver better quality and original products and services.
- Meeting the needs of high skilled tourists who are more experienced and demand higher quality of products and services.

These pressures of globalization in tourism have significant implication for work and employment, especially for human resources development and dealing with cultural aspects.

Human Resource Development in Indian Context

In India there is a tremendous shortage of trained manpower in the hospitality sector. Tourism sector on an average requires manpower about 20,000 per year. Against such a requirement the actual trained output from govt. institution is only 5000 per year. When we consider all other private institutions, the total available trained manpower does not exceed 10,000 in a year. Thus there need to develop required human resource in various segment of the tourism industry, as a consequence of the rapid growth in tourism, changing technology and markets both national and international level.

The main problems involving human resource development is in the tourism sector are-

- Scarcity of qualified manpower.
- Shortage of tourism training infrastructure and qualified trainers.
- Bad working conditions in tourism sector.
- Bad strategies and policies for human resource development.

Tourism Industry has undergone a sea change with respect to human resources development and in response to emerging trends for successful tourism in the country. Both the governments and private sector have realized that hospitality with professional service is the core of tourism. For the industry, the tourists are the ultimate service activity and extending quality service ensures continued clientele. For providing world-class service will always require training, education, increased investment and development of work culture, change in the attitudes and new methods of motivating manpower in the industry for continued growth. Thus this type of pressure of globalization in tourism has significant implications for work and employment especially in human resources development. Hence necessity of trained manpower has become top priority in the agenda of tourism plans over the years.

The Government has recognized tourism as a vehicle for economic development and generator of employment for skilled-semiskilled and unskilled teaming millions not only in popular tourist destinations but also in remotest areas of hinder land The governments have been taking the initiative of setting up a number of institutes all over the country. The institutes of Hotel Management Catering and Technology Applied Nutrition were set up in New Delhi, Mumbai, Chennai, and Kolkata. In order to meet the training requirements at craft levels in specific disciplines, 14 Food Crafts Institutes were set up at different places in the country. In order to harness the resources the Ministry of Tourism established National Council of Hotel Management and Catering Technology in 1984. The established objectives of the Council are-

- Advise the Govt. on coordinated development of hotel management and catering education.
- Serve as a technical storehouse for use in training, affiliate institutions and prescribe course of study.
- Standardize courses and infrastructures requirements.
- Prescribe educational and other qualifications, experiences etc. for the members of staff in the affiliated institutions and introduce faculty development programme.
- To give certification and accrediting at the national level.

With the establishment of National Council on Hotel Management and Catering Technology has helped the expanding and modernizing the capabilities of hotel and catering education programmes. In the order to strengthen the existing training infrastructure, National Culinary Institute and Advanced Hotel Management Institute are proposed in 9th plan. The intake of candidates for the 3 years diploma course in

Hotel Management is about 2000 and efforts are made to increase the capacity. These diploma course Hotel Management and catering Technology has been recognized by All India Council of Technical Education.

Travel and Tourism Education Institutes All the Hotel Management & food craft Institutes are registered under countries Regis Act 1860 and have separate board of Governors consisting of representatives of the industry.

The institutes of Hotel Management & catering Technology & Applied nutrition, national council for Hotel Management are funded by central Governments through grants-in-aids.

Indian institute of Tourism & Travel Management (IITTM)-established as a registered society in New Delhi, fully funded by Ministry of Tourism, Govt. of Indian and has been set up to meet the needs of higher education & Training of travel and tourism act as a centre for excellence.

National Institutes of water sports were set up in Goa in 1990 promotes water sports active throughout the country. The institute establishes quality norms for adventure sports industry and certify water sports professional in the field of power boat handling & life saving. Indian Institute of skiing & mountaineering (IIS&M) Gulmarg, setup in 1968 for developing adventure sports activities like mountaineering, skiing, trekking etc.

Guide Training-of Guides is a very basic component of the tourism services. Inadequate number of trained guides makes a lot of problems to tourists especially for international tourists. Realizing this urgent need the quality training is provided by Ministry of Tourism through its tourism office or Indian Institutes of Travel and Tourism Management. The state Governments are also provides training programmes at state level.

The Govt. of India Tourism office assesses the requirement of fresh guides in the region from time to time. It conducts training courses in coordination Indian Institutes of Tourism Travel management, refresher courses and orientation programmes for custom, immigration offices and various other services providers like taxi-drivers. Thus strengthening of guide training at grass root level workers has been given an emphasis to improve the quality of service in respect of guides in India. The National Tourism policy emphasis the necessity of professional excellence in Human Resource Development and envisages the following programmes:

- Strengthening the Institutional set up for Human Resource Development and setting up of Advanced Institutes of Hotel Management and Culinary Institute.
- Qualitative Improvement and modernization of existing training Institutions.
- Setting up of food craft institutes in each state.
- Improve the standards through accreditation and quality control.
- Setting up National Tourism Documentation centre equipped with modern technology systems to function as a repository of research findings and publications on tourism.
- Encouraging Participation of private sector in human resource development and encourage them to setup independent training facilities. (Gaur Kanchilal).

Open Sky Policy

The passenger aviation industry had been highly regulated in the aftermath of Second World War till recently. The regulatory regime was based on restrictive international agreements on a bilateral basis and protected the national airlines against other scheduled competitors and charter carriers. The national airlines were thought to act as factors of economic modernization, which provided a stable and regular transport service, facilitated regional development promoted international tourism recognition.

However, in practice the aviation sector offers low quality service at unjustifiable high fares. The emerging customer dissatisfaction led to the 1978 deregulation of the US domestic market and triggered similar practices worldwide. Many countries signed open-sky agreement.

In India we have opened the aviation sector to the private sector and a number of private operators are operations flights in some selected routes. In International flights the central government has given green signal to the private sector to operate services. Jet Airways, King-Fisher, Spice Jet and Deccan Airways have already started their presence in the Indian aviation sector. With the privatization of aviation sector, the monopoly of the Indian Airlines and Air India ceased and even their existence is in danger. The immediate result is that the airline charges got reduced and the charges are now determined by the market forces-demand and supply. India has signed open sky agreement with many countries including South-East Asian countries under the open sky policy. The privatization of airlines sector and open sky policies in fact has given a boost to the tourism industry.

Summary

The growing population of travellers and inhabitants has been putting pressure on natural and social environment. The success of tourism depends on the ability of destinations to engage in sustainable use and conservation of vital resources. In integrated destination development adopts system approach where ecological, physical and social spaces are networked brings in destinations ecology and institutional structures. The integrated destination management brings in destinations ecological and human communities as equitable and integrated members of planning and marketing and goal setting.

The globalization of business firms has a number of implications for human resources management. In India there is a tremendous shortage of trained manpower, shortage of training infrastructures and substandard working conditions and lack of strategies to deal with the emerging trends. Recognising the shortfall the central government and state governments have taken various steps to improve the human resource development. The Institute of Hotel Management, catering and Technology, Applied Nutrition were set up in four metros and 14 Food and Craft Institutes were set up in all over India and established National Council of Hotel Management and Catering Technology.

Another new initiative taken by the government is to liberalize the airline sector by signing open sky agreements with other countries in order to boost in bound, outbound and domestic tourism.

Key Words

* Touring circuits,
* Clusters,
* Stakeholders,
* Re-engineering,
* Integrated destination management,
* Disposable income,

* Niche,
* Inhabitants,
* Ecology.

Glossary

Review Questions

1. What do you mean by tourist destination life cycle?
2 How is tourism destinations evolved?
3. What are the main human resource problems being faced by India?
4. What is the recommendation given by the National Tourism Policy.

Sources and Further Readings

1. Kanchi Lal, Indian Tourism: Through Inner Eyes Gour. Prabhat Agency, 2005.
2. Bhuhalis Dimitros, Costa Carlos, Tourism Management Dynamics, trends and management tools, Elsevier Buttorworth Heinemann, 2005.
3. Page J Stephen, Brunt Papul, Bushy Graham, Connel Jo, Tourism: A Modern Synthesis, Thompson Learning 2001.
4. Incredible India, Ministry of Tourism, Government of India.

Emerging Tourism Scenario

Any forms of Industrial development can make tremendous positive or negative impact on social and physical and economic environment in which it takes place. The tourism unlike other industries has a unique feature; the tourists have to visit the place of production in order to consume the output so that tourism is clearly responsible for such impacts. A number of researchers have attempted to bring the different approaches made to study of tourism impact on the destination into a unified frame work for analysis but none of these researches could provide a practicable frame work tourism impact for analysis. This lesson discusses the major impacts of tourism.

Objectives

This lesson is designed to achieve the following objectives for the students:-

- Knowledge about old and new objectives of tourism development.
- Understand the economic, social, cultural and ecological impacts of tourism.
- Understand how to overcome negative impacts of tourism development.
- Develop awareness among students that our culture, society and environment are unique and every individual has the duty to protect these.
- Understand the new concepts– eco-friendly tourism and sustainable tourism development in India.

Impacts of Tourism

The impact of tourism on any destination will be determined by a wide variety of factors:-

- Volume of tourism arrivals.
- Structure of the economy.
- Types of tourism activity.
- Differences in sociocultural characteristics between host and the tourists.
- The fragility of the local environment.

As tourism development in a destination takes place, the magnitude of impacts whether positive or negative will change the nature. Every destination is subject to a carrying capacity-a level of tourism activity that can be sustained into the long term without creating serious or irreversible changes to the destination. The carrying capacity is defined "as that level of tourist presence which creates impact on the host community, environment, and economy that are acceptable to both tourists and hosts and sustainable over future period of time". If the carrying capacity is exceeded, the destination will find that the negative impacts rapidly increase while the positive impacts diminish. The tourism development process will be hindered and irreversible damage may be experienced and finally the tourist dissatisfaction results in the decline of destinations. The damage may be concerned with social, environment or economic aspects but the end result will be the same. The economic impact of tourism has been discussed in lesson 4 and now we will discuss the social and environmental impacts.

Social and Cultural Impacts

For many countries tourism is considered as an easy way of economic development especially for developing and under developed countries. As the economic impacts are more really measurable, other types of impacts tend to remain more hidden, particularly social and cultural effects. However social and cultural change may in our more significant costs than economic benefits in the long term. This part discusses the nature of these social and cultural impacts of tourism.

Tourism is a social event. It is all about people and how people as tourists interact with other locations and peoples, engaging in experiences that may influence their own or host community attitudes, expectations opinions and life styles. Thus wide rang of tourism sociocultural event for the traveller and host community.

Sociocultural impact relate to change in societal values, systems, individual behaviour social relationship, life styles, modes of expression and community structure. The focus of socioculture impact is cantered on host a community person who resides in tourist destinations. Sharply states that from social and cultural perspective, the rapid expansion of tourism is important in two respects:-

Firstly, development of tourism as a vehicle for modernisation and diversification leads to changes and development in the structure of society. This may positive or negative. In positive sense, there may be society wide improvements on income, employment opportunities, education, local infrastructure and services. On the negative side there may be a threat posed to traditional social values, creation of fractions and there are peoples fascinated with western culture in the society who may take advantages of others and adaptations or weakening of cultural values. Secondly, all tourists to great extent inevitably take on holidays their own beliefs, values and behavioural models what may be termed as cultural baggages. Therefore, the scope for mixing of culture is great. This gives rise to two arguments about sociocultural effect of tourism.

- The interaction between host and guest could destroy traditional culture i.e. tourism primary as a threat to culture and people.
- The interaction between host and guest could create new opportunities for peace and greater under standing.

There is evidence to prove both of their aspects are correct and a consensus is by no means easy to generate. The study of the impact on society and culture is complicated by the nature of more general social and cultural change. The forces of change are many and varied, tourism being just one factor. Other aspects include the role of advertising and media, effect of multinational companies, the aspirations of government, education and immigration. Given the complexity of influencing factors, it is hard to extrapolate as one example of potential social cultural impact due to tourism. However there is wide spread assumption about sociocultural impact that if the tourist generating country has a stronger economy and culture than receiving country, then the sociocultural impact is likely to be higher. The greater the difference, greater is the impact.

Factors Influencing Sociocultural Impacts

The main factors influencing the nature and extent of social cultural impacts are:

- Types and number of tourists.
- Importance of tourism industry in the economy.
- Size and development of tourism industry.
- Pace of tourism development.
- Nature of guest – host interaction.
- Nature of host destination and cultural simulates.
- Community tolerance capacity.

Experts comment that cultural similarity or dissimilarity is one of the major factors in shaping sociocultural impact. Impacts tend to be greater where the host and guest relationship is both culturally and geographically different. UNESCO (1976) suggests that host guest interactions in mass tourism are characterized by four properties:-

- Transitory nature,
- Temporal and spatial constraints,
- Lack of spontaneity,
- Unequal and unbalanced experience.

These properties appear especially valid in the context of mass tourism to developing countries The primary problems associated with tourism are the demonstrations effect acculturation increase in crime and prostitution and health, displacement of community, general host irritation and commercialisation of culture.

Demonstration Effect

Demonstration effect is defined as changes in attitudes, values or behaviour which can result from merely observing and imitating tourists. This may be advantageous or disadvantageous to the host community. Tourists to developing countries especially if they come from very different societies introduce and display a very foreign way of life to the host population. This may be positive when it stimulates certain behaviours or inspires people to work for things they lack. More commonly, it is detrimental and causing discontent and resentment among local people especially in developing countries because if the lack of wealth to satisfy these desires.

The demonstration effect has also economic implication. Local people often tend to initiate the rich person that changes the pattern of consumption from local product to western products. Local people may turn illegal means to obtain the wealth they desire, this crime rate may increase as a result of tourism in a destination.

The demonstration effect has the greatest influence on young people and may create generation gaps and class difference between the young generations with those who wish to retain the traditional way of life. The young especially the educated tend to migrate. The young people want material side of modern life but fail to see the negative effects – such as stress, unemployment, and environmental degradation. This type of changes may be a disruptive force to traditional kinship overtime.

Acculturation

Many impacts of tourism appear relatively quickly while others tend to manifest themselves more gradually. Cultural changes falls into this last category and overtime, more long-term cultural change may result from tourism. The external influences and the evolution of society results change, regardless of the existence tourism. The enhanced networks of communication, technology and emergency of global market are all part of this process.

The infiltration of western culture into less developed countries is viewed as problematic. The attitudes, behaviour pattern; expenditure pattern may not be easily adapted from one culture to another. Nepal is a best example, which is becoming a mainstream tourist destination, and westernisation of Kathmandu is occurring as a result of tourism.

This type of change cocacolonization or Mc Donalisation is acculturation through tourism. International tourism is thought to influence sociocultural change through the process of acculturation. The theory of acculturation rests on the notion that contact between cultures results in sharing and adoptions of one another's values and attitudes.

A major concern is that when a culturally weak society comes into contact with a strong one, the process will be one way, that is the values and attitudes of the strong nation are transferred to the weak nation. Thus acculturation is more pronounced in less developed countries. Particularly those have had less contact with western society in the past. Tourism induced acculturation may be difficult to disentangle from wider cultural change.

There are two arguments on the cultural impact of tourism.

- Tourism results in the transformation of cultural events into commercialised products. (Commodification of culture)
- Tourism results in preservations and revitalisation of traditional culture practices by providing financial support engendering community pride contributing positively to the goals of sustainable tourism.

Anthropologists accept the increasing presence of international tourists in the third world as an important element in the process of acculturation where by people in contact borrow from each other's cultural heritage. In this instance the presence of stronger western ideas and practices introduced by tourism means that the process is largely one of assimilation of the weak host culture. This does not always happen of course as can be seen in those countries under powerful Islamic religion influence (Malaysia, Indonesia, and Mauritius) where active steps are taken to resists the forces of assimilations.

Sociocultural Effects of Tourism

Language

Language is a key indicator of acculturation because it is a social vehicle of communication. Tourism can change the language of host community and make an aversion towards regional languages and dialects take place in three ways:

- Economic changes through bring of immigrant or expatriate labour.

- Demonstration effect where the local community aspires to achieve the status of visitors.
- Direct social contact and the need to converse to make commercial transactions.

Sometimes, the host is obliged to learn the main incoming tourist languages in order to deal with their requirements.

Religion

In some tourist destination religion (churches, temples and mosques and monasteries) has been promoted as major tourism products and their sites attracts large number of visitors, who may or may not have belief of that particular religion Because of this increasing conflicts exists between local worshippers, devout visitors and sight seers. The tourists do not always recognize traditional ceremonies, rites and practice. In Bhutan, tourists are not permitted to visit Monasteries. In India, temples are not opened to non-Hindus in order to prevent tourism from disrupting religious life. In many countries particularly Islamic countries tourists clothing can cause offence. The Gambia, Maldives and some Islamic countries are best examples for this.

Displacement

It is also important to understand the wider repercussions of tourist development where economies have been placed priority before community concerns. The most widely discussed phenomenon is the displacement of local communities who have to move away from their residence to make way for tourism. Land is taken over by government or private investors for various reasons such as construction of hotels and other infrastructure. The forceful displacement not only makes the local community homeless but also loss lively hood. In the name of development, all over the world millions of poor tribal societies have been displaced and driven in to eternal poverty. Universal declaration of human rights (1948), which states, "the basic standards that must underpin contemporary global society is clearly contravened by some of the examples of tourism development".

Displacement establishes the nature of power relationship between the forces of tourism development, government and local communities and in most cases the local people are the losers. There are large numbers of non-governmental organisations that are campaigning to protect communities which are displaced by the developmental activities. The main slogan of the conservatisms is "our holidays, their homes".

Tourism and Crime

Tourism and crime is a new emerging area of study within tourism but there is no universal agreement on whether tourism development leads increased crime in a locality. Tourists are vulnerable because they are in unfamiliar surroundings may be carrying expensive consumer items, cash, credit cards and passports which are valuable commodities in the black market. Tourists may engage in crime and illicit activities such as violet, drunken behaviour, drug smuggling and sex tourism. It appears that especially in seasonal basis tourism raises the crime level as the tourist influx provides for more targets and possibly easier and wealthier targets. Some scholars have established certain relationship between crime and tourism.

Sex Tourism and Prostitution

Prostitution undeniably existed before the onset of mass tourism to developing countries. However, in many countries tourism has undoubtedly contributed to an increase in prostitution, organized gambling and various types of crimes. Although, there exists casual connection between crimes and tourism, it is very difficult to find hard evidence about the role played by tourism. Given the fact that similar effects have been experienced in countries that possessing low levels of tourism. It is thus wrong to make tourism the scope goat for changes.

In relation to prostitution, it seems that different attitude to sex in some third world countries were responsible for the growth of sex tourism and the prevalence of sex tourism which dates back to the accounts of early European adventures. This image has persisted in the marketing of some exotic destinations like Thailand and other South Eastern Countries. The demand for such services now includes almost everywhere affected by mass tourism. The tiny West African country of the Gambia has been successfully marketed in Scandinavian countries as the closest place to Europe guaranteeing a pleasant climate during the northern winter. It is also a place deeply affected by tourism impact on moral behaviour.

In additions to its major health effects on the entire population of some regions like Central Africa, sex tourism to developing countries is only one side of the coin, the other is the marriage trade towards industrialised countries from developing countries. Probably the most famous and best-documented sex tourism destinations are Thailand and Philippines and to lesser extent South Korea, Kenya, Dominican Republic and Brazil.

The scare of AIDS had dramatic affection prostitution. The very recent threat of AIDS as incurable sexually transmitted diseases will have important implications for the popularity of some tourist destination. The tourists wanted younger and younger prostitutes on the hope that there was a lower likely hood this disease. In recent years, however several industrialised countries have finally passed legislation, which prosecutes their residents for sex with minors overseas. (Germany, Sweden) it is hoped that this will serve as a disincentive.

With respect to crime and gambling, although there is plenty of evidence in the developed metropolitan countries of a positive relationship between tourism and increase in crime, there are few studies, which examine the situation from third world perspective. Matheson and Wall suggest that tourism and crime are influenced by population density during the peak seasons, the location of resort in relation to an international border and differences in per capita incomes between host society and the tourists.

Health

Tourism has the dual effect of promoting the provisions of improved health care in third world destination, but in addition, it act as a vehicle to spread some forms of diseases. There is increasing concern about spread of sexually transmitted diseases (STD) through tourism at a variety of level from minor diseases to spread of HIV and AIDS through sex tourism. Standard health care may improve in tourism destination as better facilities are introduced to cope with increased seasonal population. In some destinations, cultural differences in safety standards can create unknown levels of risk. Western visitors occasionally regards the fact that a low standard of public hygiene in parts of third world rarely provide safe drinking water supply and hospitals find it difficult to attract or retain the services of skilled personal.

Cultural Impact

There has been much studies conducted to investigate tourisms role in communication between cultures, its effect on the physical products of culture such as crafts and arts and influence on custom and ceremony in the host society.

Communication between cultures: Cross-cultural contact arising from tourism is thought to be functions at least 3 factors.

- Type of tourist the different categories of tourists in the third world are reflected on expected differences in their kind of interaction with local people.
- Context in which the contact takes place. Clearly things such as length of stay, the environment under which the contact occurs, and language ability will help to determine the depth of communication, which takes place.
- The role of cultural brokers, who are intermeddling occupational group such as interpreters and guide who are the conduct through which much of contacts occurs their activities are thought to have a considerable effect and on the manner and speed with which new ideas and influences are transmitted.

Tourism and physical culture: One of the obvious sign of cultural reawakening is to be found in the state of traditional art forms in third world society. The growth of tourists' handicrafts market has stimulated local production in both positive and negative directions. Positive influence may be found in the financial success traditional artefacts production in many places. On the other hand, the sheer pressure caused by a ready market for handicrafts has also lead to fall in the quality of workmanship and manufacture of cheap limitation known as airport art.

Effects of tourism on local customs: Tourism has the ability to market its products as a commodity, part of which consists of promoting the cultural attractions of holidaying in an exotic environment. Although this process is criticised cheeping cultural events such as religious ceremonies, it is also responsible for the flow of funds into many local activities.

Environmental Impact

Tourism development in many places has led to the deterioration in environmental quality since the onset of mass tourism. In many destinations, tourism development has taken place with little regard for natural environment. The effect of mass tourism and increasing awareness of human impact as environment led to a generalization that nature is not an in exhaustive resource. For some destinations the environmental effects of tourism have led to direct threat to the industry, as the success in attracting tourist lead to negative impact on the attraction of environment. This section discusses the major environmental impact of tourism. The environmental effect of tourism in developing countries is among least studied one.

However they have attracted considerable attention in developed countries where high intensity usage and demand by tourism has transformed many land farms.

Tourism bought economic prosperity which adversely affected environment. In search of holidays Million of tourists are crowding the popular beach resorts, mountain treks, jungles and at ancient monuments. The population of Goa is just one million but over one million visitors visit every year in Goa. Its beaches are crowded at peak season. The beautiful Dal Lake of Kashmir has been reduced to half of its size in less than 50 years by human encroachments. 30 years ago, Manali in Himachal Pradesh was a small hill resorts catering to the needs of people who loved nature. Now it is an overcrowded city with ugly multi storied buildings. Precious wild life –tigers, lions and panthers have become virtually extinct in Indian jungles due to hunting and poaching. The Laddakh in Kashmir is jammed with litter left by tourists. Too many hotels on the lovely beaches of Goa have created anti-tourism feelings among the local people.

Modern tourism involves thousands of visitors and demand massive infrastructure. Development takes many shapes and forms – roads, hotels, restaurants and transport facilities – altering ecological balances of destinations. The opening of new roads leads to the exploitation of remote forest areas, which provided green cover and timely rains for our fields. The rush to build tourist facilities at the most attractive and convenient sites changes the ecosystem and affects the natural beauty of the place.

The upsurge of world tourism has changed the situation and caused alarm all over the world. The environmentalists who want to save nature from destructions and motivate people to take care the future of this earth. Hunter and Green provide an overview of the major potential impact of tourism on the natural environment. The following Table illustrates the wide range of potential consequence of tourism development in specific habitats.

Major Impacts of Tourism on Natural Environment

* Habitat influenced by,
* Effects of tourism,
* Tourism development,
* Sea,
* Pollution from sewage outfall,
* Sea dumping of waste,
* Oil pollution from tourist boats,
* Litter and threat to marine creatures,
* Coastal Habitats,
* Habitat loss and fragmentation,
* Deterioration of ecological diversity,
* De-stabilization of sand dunes,
* Erosion of coastal landscape,
* Inland waters,
* Sewage pollution,
* Oil pollution from boats and barges,
* Upland/plateau Agriculture,
* Land,
* Erosion,
* Habitat loss and fragmentation,
* Disturbance to nesting birds,
* Loss of area of production,
* Conflict between adjacent agriculture,
* Uses and tourism,
* Forests,
* Habitat loss and fragmentation,
* Disturbances from recreational activities.

Tourism destination comprises a wide diversity of environment from purpose built resorts to remote natural areas. The broad categories of impact that may affect destinations are:-

- Inappropriate development,
- Loss of habitat,
- Extinction of species,
- Pollution,
- Loss of spirit.

According to European Environment Agency tourism crates following environmental problems:-

- Waste disposal,
- Reducing level of biodiversity,
- Pollution of inland waters,
- Pollution of marine and coastal zones.

There are two types of environmental impacts, which occur in destination development:-

- Those affecting the integrity and composition of the natural environment.
- Those affecting the tourist experiences of the environment.

The environmental impact associated with tourism can also be considered in terms of their direct, indirect and induced effects. It is not possible to develop tourism without incurring environmental impacts, but it is possible, with correct planning, to manage tourism development in order to minimize the negative impacts while encouraging positive impacts. The direct environmental impacts of tourism include following positive effects.

- Preservation ad restoration of historical buildings and sites.
- The creation of national parks and wild life parks.
- Protection of coral reefs and beaches.
- Maintenance of forests.

The following are the major environmental impacts of tourism in destinations.

Pollution

On the negative side, tourism may have direct environmental impact on the quality of water air and on noise levels. Sewage disposals into water will add to pollution problems and the use of powered boats on inland waterways and sheltered seas can make water impure and thereby destroy precious marine or water resources. Increased usage of the internal combustion engine for tourist transport and oil burning to provide the power for hotels air conditioning and refrigeration units pollute the air quality and noise level may be dramatically increased in urban areas through increased road, rail and traffic.

Inappropriate Development

Tourism development may be seen as inappropriate where it fails to consider the sensitive natural environment. Large tracts of coastal regions around the world are now covered by urban sprawl to cater mass tourism market. It had robbed the shores of natural features, displaced headlands and harbours with badly made structures. These types of development occur as a result of short term planning in environmental terms. Tourism creates pressure for development to meet visitor needs and expectations. Problems occur if facilities are not constructed in harmony with the local environment.

Loss of Natural Habitats and Wild Life

Development facilities and subsequent tourist use may result in rapid on physical deterioration of both natural and man made environments that have serious consequences. Hunting and fishing can have obvious impact on wild life environment. Sand dunes of desert can be damaged and eroded by over use; vegetation can be destroyed ancient monuments may be worn away or disfigured and damaged and the improper disposal of litter can detract the aesthetic quality of environment and harm precious wild life. These are just few examples of direct negative environmental impacts.

The economic impact associated with tourism development can be direct and indirect, and the same is true of environmental impacts. The tourism activity requires production of output from a diverse range of industries, including those that do not supply tourist goods and services directly, then the environmental impact associated with the output and production process of those industries should also be considered. Thus increase in tourism activities increases the demand for more and more hotels and restaurants and other infrastructure, put pressure on construction industry and natural resources and ecology.

Ecotourism

In search for new tourism products, travellers and supplies are today seeking to reshape the meaning of nature as a tourism attraction. New products have been developed in order to guarantee quality of a nature-experience and to protect the natural and cultural base for business and generation of visitors. The nature based tourism, which focuses on experiencing flora and fauna in natural settings, eco-tourism, which is a broader environmentally friendly concept.

The environmental movements have boosted awareness of the importance of natural resources for tourism development. Environment quality is important for all forms of nature tourism. Environmental quality management of a tourist destination involves protection environmental information ensures and environmental quality. Environment friendly tourism tries to minimize the negative impacts of tourism-social, cultural and environmental that (we have discussed in the beginning of this chapter) maximizes the positive impacts and to incorporate environmental education, ethics and log-turn social and economical benefits for the local population.

Ecotourism has grown as a consequence of the dissatisfaction with conventional forms of tourism, which have in a general sense, ignored social and ecological elements. The eco-tourism a more responsible forms of tourism needs the following characteristics.

- Minimum environmental impact.
- Minimum impact and maximum respect for host cultures.
- Maximum economic benefit to host country's grassroots and
- Maximum recreational satisfaction to participating tourists.

The concept of development ecotourism grew as a culmination of dissatisfaction with governments and society's negative approach to development especially from an ecological point of view.

Nature Tourism and Ecotourism

Modern nature based tourism focuses on experiencing flora and fauna is natural settings and occurs in such forms as whale watching, trips to rainforests and habitat of large mammals and viewing sceneries in natural parks or virgin areas. Nature tourism includes all forms of mass tourism, eco-tourism that use natural resource-including species, habitat, landscape, scenery and salt and fresh water features. Nature tourism is travel for the purpose of enjoying undeveloped natural areas or wild life.

Today the term nature tourism is often synonymously with ecotourism although it shares only some of the ecotourism requirements. While nature based tourism relates to nature, its attractiveness, and the visitor experience in natural settings, ecotourism takes unspoiled natural and sociocultural attractiveness into account, further Ecotourism is closer to sustainable tourism since it also takes care of environmental natural and social and cultural impacts.

The concept of ecotourism refers to environmentally responsible travel and visits to relatively undisturbed natural, cultural areas that promote environmental education, management and conservation, while providing for the beneficially active socioeconomic involvement of local population. Ecotourism is low impact nature tourism which contributes to the maintenance of specie and habitats either directly through a contribution and provides revenue to the local community.

Characteristics of Eco Tourism

- Eco tourism inspired primarily by natural history of an area, including its indigenous cultures.
- Eco-tourists visit relatively undeveloped area in the spirit of appreciation, participation and sensitivity.
- Eco tourist practices non-consumptive use of wild life natural resources and contributes to the visited area through financial means.
- Directly benefiting the conservation of the site.
- Economic wellbeing of the local residents.
- The visit should strengthen the tourist appreciation of and dedication to conservation issues in general, and to specific needs of the local.
- Eco tourism also implies a managed approach host community regions, which commits itself to establishing and maintaining the sites with the participation of local residents.
- And using the proceeds of the enterprise to fund the area land management as well as community development.

Thus Eco tourism is responsible travel to natural areas, which conserves the environment and improves the welfare of local people. Ecotourism is a sustainable form of natural resource-based tourism that focuses primarily as experiencing and learning about nature, and which is ethically managed to be low impact and non-consumptive, and locally oriented.

It typically occurs in natural areas, and should contribute to the conservation and or preservation of such areas. In many countries, eco tourism is policy consideration and initial stage, and a policy and related actions are increasingly required to ensure that tourism development is consistent with the needs of both local people and environment. Tourism policy and eco tourism policy covers wide spectrum of concern related to the implementation of tourism programmes. The tourism policy establishes strategies, objectives and guidelines to be followed for sustainable tourism development. A strategy for tourism development is as follows:

- Identifying objectives.
- Establishing priorities.
- Placing in a community context the rates of Government, tourist organisations, and local govt. private sector business ensure development of human resources.
- Establishing coordination and implementation of agreed programmes to.
- Monitoring and evaluation.

Eco Tourism in India

Today, Ecotourism is the fastest growing segment of the tourism industry attracts between 40-60% of all international tourists. The diversity of India is to be seen not only is its people, culture, religion, language and life style, the diversity starts from land itself, which is made up of snow peaks of Himalayas, beautiful valleys, tropical rainforests of south and north east blistering not deserts of north western India and beautiful western and eastern coastal regions. Each diverse geographical region generates different picture and exploring them provide a unique experience. Now all there are packaged for tourist to provide Eco-friendly holidays in India. We are promoting tourism but while promoting tourism to eco sensitive areas, the emphasis is to control the volume so that the fragile nature of the area is not disturbed. The whole objective of eco-tourism is to have purposeful travel to natural areas to understand culture, history of environment, taking special care not to alter the integrity of ecosystem while utilizing the economic opportunities that make conservation of natural resources beneficial to local people.

Thus travel to these areas enlightens, educates and revives the tired soul of the Eco-tourists and as the other hand provides a basis of economic upliftment of the local people, tribes or other stake holders directly dependant on the natural heritage. This strong relationship is primarily targeted through our eco tourism.

Ministry of tourism has formulated Ecotourism guidelines for regulated and sustainable tourism, which have focused on to respect the frailty of the earth and to leave behind the rich natural heritage for the future generations to enjoy. The guidelines are as follows:-

- Leave only foot points, take only photographs but do not take away from natural areas and heritage monuments.
- Encourage local culture, respect local traditions act help in their conservation efforts.
- Do not buy products from endangered plants or animal.
- Always follow designated trails so that animals plants are not.
- Try to respect natural habitat and support those products, which promote the cause of environment protection etc.

All these have been discussed in eco tourism guidelines of ministry of tourism. The tour operators who operate tours in fragile nature zones have adopted ASTA (American Society of Travel Agents) for the eco tourism businesses. (Gaur Kanchilal).

The basis objective of eco-tourism plan is to attain sustainable development of India's natural, cultural and ancient heritage without causing any adverse effect. The ecotourism development harmonies with local population skills, products as well as lively hoods and enhance the valuc of environment which will make them authority of conservation.

Ecotourism as discussed above is a joint venture which involves may stake holders: local people, tour operators, hotel restaurant owners, and government agencies, it is essential to have public private partnership with a clear cut demarcation of the responsibilities, commitments and rights of all the parties involved in the development. The local characters of these sites are to be kept in mind while planning for future development work. Thus documentation and mapping of the sites and their unique features are a prerequisite. The projects are to be prioritized and plan to be implementation with proper allocation of funds.

The eco tourism addresses all types of environmental problems: pollution—air, water, sound, soil and waste management for quality life through regulated activities to save the environment. For this purpose the industry has to organise training programmes and borrow knowledge from experts to deal with all issues, regularly monitor and measure the impact will ensure the achievement of environmental conservation.

Being latecomer in tourism we have learnt enough from the mistakes of developed countries and have imitated proper steps for sustainable eco tourism development.

Sustainable Tourism

We have discussed the meaning, the concept, and basic principles Sustainable tourism, The tourism development must be sustainable environmentally, socially, economically and culturally. Eco tourism is a form of sustainable tourism. Sustainable tourism must ensure quality of life of people, good experience to the tourists and maintain quality of environment alive to the requirements to protect the haphazard growth in sensitive areas, government has put number of legislation such as the forest conservation Act 1980, Wild Life (Protection Act) 1972, Environment Protection Act 1986, Coastal Regulatory Zone Act 1991.

The Rationale for Sustainable Tourism

- The tourism which is sustainable should stimulate awareness of tourism impacts be well planned with strategy identifying limits of acceptable change/carrying capacities.
- Generate direct and indirect local employment.
- Support viability of local enterprises.
- Provide income, which is retained in the local area as much as possible.
- Support diversification in local and regional economies.
- Support existing infrastructure and improve local services.
- Respect the integrity of local environment, culture, people, infrastructure and character of a area.
- Promote local pride.

- Assists in conservation of works in the natural and built environment.
- Be carefully monitored with strategic for minimising negative impacts in place.

Ministry of tourism in its tourism policy 1982 and it its guidelines to eco tourism have attempted to achieve sustainability in tourism activities by clearly indicating that the key player in the eco tourism business are the State Governments, Local Authorities, the developers and operators, the visitors and local community. Each of these has to be sensitive to the environment and local traditions and follow set of guidelines for successful development of sustainable tourism.

The areas of responsibilities are indicated as under;

The Government's

- The management plan for each area should be prepared through professional landscape architects and urban planners and in consultation with the local community as well as others directly concerned.
- Integrated planning should be adopted to avoid into sectoral and cross-sectoral conflicts.
- The architectural programmes for eco-tourism centres should include controlled access points and cabins, roads, self-guided nature trails, transportation options, interpretive centres, signs, observations towers and blinds, adequate but unpretentious lodging and dining facilities, docks, garbage disposal facility etc., as per requirement, living quarters and facilities for project personnel also have to be provided.
- Structures creating visual pollution, unaesthetic values and non-compatible architecture should be controlled.
- Exclude developments in geologically unstable zones and define development and buffer zones after proper environmental impact assessments.
- Establish standards, building codes and other regulations.
- Specify environmental, physical and social carrying capacities to limit development activities.
- Ensure continuous monitoring of adverse effects of tourism activities and initiate suitable corrective measures.

- Recognise and award quality labels to eco-tourism operators.
- Provide visitor information and interpretation services covering particularly (i) what to see and (ii) how to see and (iii) how to behave. It can be by way of brochures, leaflets, specialized guides, self-guided trails, wilderness trails, visitor information centres etc.
- Prepare and widely distribute codes of conduct to all visitors.
- Launch training programmes on eco tourism to administrators, planners, operators and general public.

Developers and Operators

- Respect and follow the planning restrictions, standards and codes provided by the Government and local authorities.
- Implement sound environment principle through self-regulation.
- Practice environmental impact assessment for all new projects and conduct development of environmental improvement programmes.
- Be sensitive to conservation of environmentally protected or threatened areas, species and scenic, aesthetic, achieving landscape enhancement wherever possible.
- Ensure that all structures are unobtrusive and do not interfere with the natural ecosystem to the maximum extent.

The Local Population

- Realise and respect the value of environment, flora and fauna, monuments and cultural heritage.
- Practice conservation of nature and culture as a way of life.
- Establish guidelines to protect valuable local resources and foster tourism development.
- Realise and react to the potential threat of investors who see opportunities for development but lack sensitivity to local value.
- Become effective nature guides and conservationists of nature areas by enhancing the practical and ancestral knowledge of the natural features of the area.
- Be friendly with the visitors and help them to practice eco-tourism codes.

- Recognize the optimal environment capacity and sociological use limits on the site in creating tourist facilities. They should also take into account safety and convenience of tourists.
- Buildings should be designed strictly on functional and environmental considerations and avoid over construction.
- Local materials and designs should be used in all constructions to the extent possible.
- Physical planning, architectural design and construction of tourist facilities should employ eco-techniques like solar energy, capture and re-utilization of rain water, recycling of garbage, natural cross ventilation instead of air-conditioning, a high level of self-sufficiency in food generation through orchards, ecological farms, aquaculture, etc.
- Energy and water saving practices should be employed to the extent possible. Also practice fresh water management and control sewage disposal.
- Control and diminish air emissions, pollutants and noise levels.
- Control and reduce environmentally unfriendly products such as asbestos, CFCs, pesticides and toxic, corrosive, infectious, explosive or flammable materials.
- Respect and support historic or religious objects and sites.
- Provide information and interpretive services to visitors especially on attractions and facilities, safety and security, local customers and traditions, prohibitive rules and regulations, self-conduct and behaviour, etc.
- Ensure adequate opportunities to visitors for communion with nature and native cultures.
- In marketing ecotourism products, customers should be given correct information, as the visitors who appreciate ecotourism products are also environmentally aware target groups.
- Ensure safety and security of visitors and inform them about precautions to be taken.
- Exercise due regard for the interests of local population, including their history, tradition and culture and future development.
- Involve the local community in various activities and vocations.

The Visitors

- Contribute to the conservation of any habitat of flora and of any site whether natural or cultural, which may be affected by tourism.
- Make no open fires and discourage others from doing, so. If water has to be heated with scarce firewood, use as little as possible. Where possible, use kerosene or fuel efficient wood stoves.
- Remove litter, burn or bury paper and carry back all non-detergents in streams or springs. If no toilet facilities are available, try to comfort yourself at least 30 meters away from water sources and bury or cover the waste.
- Plants should be left to flourish in their natural environment and resist from taking away cuttings, seeds and roots.
- Help the guides and porters to follow conservation measures. Do not allow the cooks or porters to throw garbage in streams or rivers.
- Respect the natural and cultural heritage of the area and follow local customs.
- Respect local etiquette and wear loose, lightweight clothes in preferences to revealing shorts, skimpy tops and tight fitting action wears. Respect privacy of individuals and ask permission and use restraint in taking photographs of others.
- Respect holy places and never touch or remove religious objects.
- Strictly follow the guidelines for personal safety and security.

Success stories of sustainable tourism achievers are to be encouraged and made known. It is the essence for improving the quality of life. In India in the Tourism Policy there is focused role of tourism in socioeconomic development of the backward areas weaker sections, women's and artisans and the goals to be pursued in tune with the goals of the enrichment of the environment and ecosystem and recognized the role of tourism as a potent global force for nature international understanding and for creating awareness for sustainable development.

Summary

Tourism development like other industries brings negative impacts on economy, society and the environment. The tourism industry generates foreign exchange, employment and contributes to the balance of payment. But these positive effects are often accompanied by disastrous implication such as inflation, leakages and dependency. The social impacts of tourism are demonstration effect, acculturation, prostitution and crime, displacement of community and commercialization of culture. Tourism development in many places has led to the deterioration of environmental quality. The loss of habitat, extinction of species, pollution, etc. will ultimately result in decline of the destination and even threatens the very existence of the community. In search for new tourism products, the suppliers are seeking to reshape the nature as a tourism attraction. Eco tourism, a broader concept, is environmental friendly concept involves protection and conservation of environment. This is based on the sustainable tourism development. The sustainable tourism development ensures the use of resources for present and future generations.

Motivation of Nature Tourism

In the following essay through a behavioural perspective, which means not considering external factors, we try to understand why nature tourism is one of the fastest growing segments of world tourism. To understand why this is happening is to comprehend the intrinsic motivation "nature tourists" have to pursue this type of tourism.

To recognize this motivation we must search for clues in the theories of travel motivation proposed throughout the travel research literature, and try to see if these diverse theories can actually help us identify the motivation of nature tourists and hence the growth of this tourism segment. The following essay is able to draw from several authors and their theories important conclusion on whether the models or frameworks presented can be useful to understand nature tourism and if so conclude why they are valuable. We firstly define what nature tourism is and from there we review several travel motivation theories that are applicable to this type of tourism.

To know what nature tourism is we must understand a broader classification of tourism that includes nature tourism, and that is alternative tourism. "Alternative tourism can be broadly defined as forms of tourism that set out to be consistent with natural, social and community values and which allow both hosts and guests to enjoy positive and worthwhile interaction and shared experiences". Under alternative tourism we can see the presence of natural, cultural, event and other types of tourism. Nature tourism, called by Newsome & et al. (2002) "natural area tourism", is in short "tourism in natural settings".

The proposed classification of Newsome, Moore and Dowling (2002) and their conception of nature tourism is confirmed by Ceballos-Lascuráin (1996) when he defines it as "all tourism directly dependent on the use of natural resources in a relatively undeveloped state, including scenery, topography, water features, vegetation and wildlife."

Newsome, Moore & Dowling (2002) include under nature tourism: adventure, nature-based, wildlife and ecotourism. Mc Kerchner (1998) expands the scope of nature tourism including: adventure tourism, ecotourism, alternative tourism, educational tourism, anti-tourism, sustainable tourism, responsible tourism and many other forms of outdoor-oriented, non-mass tourism. These two views of what nature tourism includes and overlap, agree, but also contradict themselves. To better understand, and conclude, what nature tourism is (for the purpose of this essay) we must understand the three relations that can occur between the natural setting and the visitor which are: in, about and for the environment. So any tourism based in a natural setting and experienced in, about or for the environment will be considered 'nature tourism'.

Tourist motivation can be defined "as the global integrating network of biological and cultural forces which gives value and direction to travel choices, behaviour and experience". The general motives underlined by research of why nature tourism is the fastest growing segment internationally in tourism are: widespread changing environmental attitude, development of environmental education, development of environmental mass media.

Pearce, Morrison and Rutledge (1998) present ten trends which represent important issues of content in describing tourist motives, we can mention four which are related to nature tourism motivation: motive to experience the environment, motive to rest and relax in pleasant settings, motive to pursue special interests and skills (scuba-diving, fishing), and motive to be healthy and fit. These motives are good starting points to discuss motivation of nature tourism, but some appear to be just social changes or reasons that have affected in some way the motives of the tourist. These motives do not give us clues in how to identify human motivation towards travel, for that reason it cannot be applied to further studies. So it is necessary to undertake an analysis of travel motivation theories.

When assessing a theory of tourist motivation and deciding if it is good for our purpose we must identify seven requirements: it functions as a true theory, it appeals to different users, it is easy to communicate, it suggests ways to measure motivation, it allows for many motives, it is dynamic and, it accounts for intrinsic and extrinsic motivation.

This essay will not review all theories of motivation and afterwards decide if they are pertinent to our purpose, which is to understand the motivation of nature tourism. The scope of this essay will only include theories, which have been reviewed and might have relevance to our purpose. In the reviewing process of motivation theories applied to nature tourism we searched for the seven requirements proposed by Pearce, Morrison and Rutledge (1998), and also took into consideration if they were applicable to understand nature tourism motivation.

People who live in cities, for example, are motivated to travel as tourists to wilderness areas because they need to escape from an artificial, monotonous environment. Gray's travel-motivation theory, although an oversimplification of motivation as noted by Mansfeld (1992), gives us two motives which can help explain why people go to natural settings. The first motive is the desire to go from a known to an unknown place, called in Gray's theory 'wanderlust'.

Secondly, a place "which can provide the traveller with specific facilities that do not exist in his or her own place of residence", referred in Gray's theory as 'sunlust'. It appears that the wanderlust-sunlust motives do help us understand why nature tourists search for settings which are different from the city-work-home routine and that enable the nature tourist to participate in activities in unknown territory and that are possible in those natural settings and not at home.

The problem with this theory is that it "represents a confusion between person-specific motivations and resort-specific attributes". For this same reason we will not consider 'Push & Pull' factors as relevant to the study of motivation. For this reason Gray's model only partially might help us understand what motivates a person to participate in nature tourism. Several other theories such as Crompton's nine motives and Iso-Ahola personal-interpersonal motives also work under these 'Push and Pull' factors which means that they focus not only in the intrinsic motivation to travel to natural settings, but also in the characteristics and benefits these settings might appear to offer (pull factors) to satisfy a need. For this reason of not focusing purely on the motivation of tourists, we will not consider them relevant to understand nature tourism motivation.

An interesting finding, while not considered a theory, is the one by Krippendorf after analyzing eight theories of travel motivation found in the literature on tourism. Through his research he saw a common place in these theories. "Firstly, travel is motivated by 'going *away* from' rather than 'going *towards*' something; secondly travellers' motives and behaviour are markedly self-oriented". So it seems that the pull factors are not so important, hence the benefits offered by the natural settings and their operators are of second importance in deciding to travel. There is more power in the intrinsic motive of self-indulgence and personal care, physically and psychologically, and by the so called 'escape' motive, than by pull factors considered in the mentioned motivation theories.

So if this 'Push and Pull' approach does not succeed in understanding motivation maybe we can try another approach, for example focusing in factors that influence motivation such as 'needs'. Pearce presents a hierarchy of travel motives based on Maslow's theory of motivation combined with the idea of a career ladder. "The career ladder emphasizes that people have a range of motives for seeking out holiday experiences".

The travel career ladder with its different levels allows for many motives, it is dynamic and to sum up it covers the seven requirements presented before. On the other hand analyzing the different levels, especially the relationship needs, self-esteem/development needs, and fulfilment needs presents possible clues to understand the motivation of nature tourism.

By comparing the needs described in different levels of the career ladder such as 'need for achievement', for example, and then consider nature tourism activities like hiking, tramping and mountaineering where the tourist proves its competence and if successful achieves a goal, it can be concluded that the travel career ladder is a helpful theory to understand nature tourism motivation. Another comparison can be drawn from the self-esteem needs level. The "need for mastery, control and competence" can be a motivation for a nature tourism activity such as scuba diving. Where mastery is required to undergo the activity successfully and safely, as well as competence, and control is basic in case of extreme scenarios underwater conditions.

So can the 'Travel Career Ladder' be the most appropriate theory to understand nature tourism motivation? If we consider the vast use of Maslow's Theory and sometimes overestimated usefulness considering it only concentrates in needs as the only driving forces to understand motivation, as well as its origin from a study of neurotic people, the answer is no. "Maslow's theory of needs largely ignores more recent developments in motivation theory" and only concentrates on needs it is a work considered a partial theory, which "tend to concentrate in one particular aspect of motivation".

Travel motivation cannot be understood by concentrating on one of the factors as mentioned before in the case of needs. It requires a complete knowledge of "the processes whereby these needs are transformed into motivated behaviour and, in particular, of the way in which people's expectations give motivated behaviour its direction". Witt and Wright (1992) present a very complete and interesting "Expectancy Theory" applied to tourist motivation, based on Vroom's theory of work motivation. It is a theory that finally is able to include all the concepts involved in the motivation process by creating a theoretical framework. It includes the needs which are important to understand motivation, but also the "decision making involved in choosing whether to go on holiday".

Together with this it is able to consider 'push and pull' factors, as well as reasons of travel. In conclusion the expectancy theory provides a framework for the analysis of tourist motivation. With all this good points taken into consideration the expectancy theory fails one of the requirements set by Pearce, Morrison and Rutledge (1998) when deciding on a good motivation theory and that requirement is it must be "easy to communicate". This is concluded as well by Witt and Wright when they say "the complexity of expectancy theory also makes it difficult to use the model to predict individual behaviour", and so complex that they suggest using the framework in training travel advisers to ask the proper questions to deliver the information best suited for a customer.

Taking into account the positive attributes of this framework, as well as the negative, let us use the framework to understand nature tourism motivation. Vroom proposes two equations; the first can be used to understand the motivation of travel or not to travel and the second formula to know why a tourist has chosen a certain destination. For our purpose we will concentrate on the first equation, which states that an individual's behaviour is determined by his/her belief that the attractiveness and valence of an outcome (a type of holiday taken) is useful to attain another outcome with greater attractiveness and valence. In other words the need of a person will be searched for depending on the value attached to that need, maybe Maslow's hierarchy of needs is useful here, and its attractiveness, through the lived experience of the instrumental outcome considered as a chosen holiday. The belief that going to a natural setting to experience the environment is seen as an outcome with certain intrinsic value and attractiveness, but above all useful (instrumental) to attain physical and psychological recovery from stress. This framework includes important variables to understand motivation: needs, values, and beliefs. The equation is also able to tell us that a tourist to natural setting does not go only to have an encounter with nature, but also to achieve a further self-indulgent goal.

Vroom's Expectancy Theory has proven its value, but there is another interesting concept to consider such as intention influencing behaviour, that according to Ajzen and Fishbein (1980) is influenced by attitudes and subjective norms. This model was called the 'Theory of Reasoned Action'. Ten years later they updated their model including 'perceived behavioural control' as another element influencing intention, calling this new model 'Theory of Planned Behaviour'. According to this theory changing beliefs will produce a change in behaviour, but this might not be enough if attitudes and/or subjective norms do not change. Attitudes "can be viewed as enduring general evaluations of people".

Subjective norms are what we expect other people will think of us if we carried out a certain action, in other words social pressure. The model states that beliefs influence attitudes and the perception of subjective norms, at the same time these attitudes and subjective norms influence intention, and intention determines behaviour. How does this model become useful to understand nature tourism motivation? It becomes relevant and useful if we relate it to the New Environmental

Paradigm and also to the general motives presented at the beginning of essay of why nature tourism has become so popular. The New Environmental Paradigm presents a new set of beliefs and values, including the desirability of restricting growth, of protecting the integrity of ecosystems, and of securing more harmonious relationships between man and nature.

Relating the Theory of Reasoned Action with the New Environmental Paradigm can be a clue to understand how this change of beliefs in society are affecting the motivation of people in their travel habits resulting in a desire to visit natural areas. The general motives presented by Lindberg, Wood and Engeldrum (1998): widespread changing environmental attitude, development of environmental education, and development of environmental mass media, seem more like reasons rather than motives, but are good reasons to understand this shift to a New Environmental Paradigm. If we include this new paradigm as a new set of beliefs rising in our post-modern world, which are influencing, according to Theory of Reasoned Action, the attitudes and subjective norms then we can understand why the intention of practising nature tourism has become such an important trend worldwide.

Through the combination of the New Environmental Paradigm and the Theory of Reasoned Action we have found a framework that includes several components of how behaviour is constructed together with actual contemporary trends in environmental beliefs. It also succeeds in covering all the requirements set beforehand to consider a theory a good travel motivation theory. For these reasons we can conclude that these combinations of perspectives are useful to understand nature tourism motivation.

Another conclusion to this approach of combining the theory and the paradigm can be that motivation, while it is an intrinsic process, when influenced by beliefs and these beliefs are a product of a social shared Environmental Paradigm then motivation becomes a socio-psychological process, influenced by external factors.

The revision of different theories under a scheme of requirements to find a proper one, we have come across a needs-oriented theory (Travel Career Ladder), we have disregarded any push and pull factors-based models, interpreted an all-inclusive framework of motivation (Expectancy Theory), and ended with a simple but comprehensive interpretation of the motivation of nature tourism through the complementation of the New Environmental Paradigm and the Theory of Reasoned Action. In conclusion we can say that a proper revision of travel motivation theories can help us understand what motivation is, and what elements must be considered to understand it, and then interpret the different findings to understand the motivation of a certain type of tourist. One important consideration is that when investigating what motivates a person to travel in a certain type of way we must concentrate on finding the intrinsic motivation while not distracting our attention to the "pull factors" of a specific destination. On the other hand we must say, as found while combining the Theory of Reasoned Action and the New Environmental Paradigm, that the trend of nature tourism becoming more popular can be better understood through a socio-psychological perspective, taking into account the influence of external factors, such as a new set of beliefs constructed by our post-modern western society. It is then proved that the behavioural perspective might not be enough and a psycho-sociological perspective gives us a better understanding.

5

Economic Perspectives on Nature Tourism

Introduction

Tourism has expanded to such an extent that it is Unfortunately there is no widely-agreed definition now claimed to be the world's largest industry of nature tourism, ecotourism or other related and provider of jobs, although measurement is forms of tourism, although notoriously difficult and accurate statistics are ecotourism is recognized as a subset of nature scarce. The World Travel and Tourism Council tourism. A largely prescriptive (WTTC) has estimated that international tourism literature describes what nature tourism, generated about 10% of global GDP in 1994, ecotourism, and so on should consist of, often in accounted for over 10% of all consumer terns of visitor motivation, philosophy and spending, created more than 12 million new jobs behaviour. Another body of literature describes

and provided more than $650 billion in tax the negative results when such alternative forms revenues to governments (WTTC 1995). Even if of tourism fails to follow these ideals. The tourism industry tourism is, or should be, a priority concern of itself has opportunistically used very broad governments worldwide interpretations of nature tourism and ecotourism to exploit these terms' suggestion of responsible This paper is specifically concerned with consumerism, economic perspectives on one sector of this vast industry-nature tourism in developing countries.

Nature tourism is defined here as those forms of All forms of tourism can make substantial tourism where natural attractions of ecological contributions to national income, foreign significance are the destination, leading to a exchange earnings, employment and government principal focus on tourism in state-run protected revenues. But nature tourism is particularly areas and land which is privately owned or under important in the context of sustainable communal tenure.

Although there are development because it offers the potential of considerable overlaps between nature tourism mobilizing resources through the private sector destinations and protected areas, it is important which can contribute to local and national to recognize that the terms are far from economic development while providing an synonymous.

Protected areas are only rarely incentive for conservation land uses and helping established because of their tourism potential and to finance biodiversity conservation. This is a by no means all-or even most-protected areas very appealing prospect, particularly in are viable nature tourism destinations developing countries where economic Conversely, nature tourism often takes place development alternatives in remote rural areas outside protected areas are very limited, where biodiversity investments are invariably inadequate, and where public A focus on tourist destinations of ecological funds to support either are usually scarce significance is not particularly restrictive, since this embraces activities as diverse as wildlife Economic Perspectives on Nature Tourism, Conservation and Development viewing, mountain trekking, exploring trends of higher personal disposable incomes, rainforests, diving on coral reefs and watching more leisure time, greater interest in nature and whales.

It includes small groups of independent outdoor activities as well as falling transportation and environmentally-sensitive travellers to remote costs all tend to support such positive growth and little-known areas as well as the thousands of forecasts, perhaps less environmentally-concerned visitors to such acclaimed destinations as Kenya's Given the credible and optimistic projections for Maasai Mara National Reserve, South Africa's nature tourism's future growth, it is not Kruger National Park, Egypt's Red Sea coast, surprisingly that high levels of interest have been Ecuador's Galapagos National Park, Caribbean aroused among government finance and economic marine reserves or Nepal's Royal Chitwan planning ministries and conservation agencies, National Park commercial tourism operators, private landowners, local governments,

NGOs and local Reliable data on nature tourism are very elusive, communities. But nature tourism's continued partly because of the lack of concensus on expansion will inevitably expose more defining the term. However, the few reliable ecologically-important areas to the opportunities estimates of the scale of the economic impact of and risks associated with greater numbers of nature tourism are impressive. Five World visitors. The opportunities are to generate Heritage Areas in Australia are estimated to increased income and employment, both generate an annual gross economic impact of nationally and in remote rural areas,. and to more than $1,000 million, excluding travel costs provide increased incentives for biodiversity. Annual expenditures of park conservation in state protected areas and on visitors in British Columbia, Canada have been private lands. The risks are continued estimated at $310 million. In developing countries, Kenya's wildlife on protected areas, most of which lack the tourism industry generates about $400 million in resources for effective management and are gross revenues annually. In Ecuador, $54 million of numbers annual tourist expenditures have been attributed to Galapagos National Park. Nature tourism in gap between nature tourism's actual and Costa Rica generated over $600 million in potential contribution to sustainable development foreign exchange in 1994, while the Monteverde.

While estimated to generate $10 million in gross tourist nature tourism in developing countries does receipts each year seems to be generating substantial opportunities Caution does need to be exercised in interpreting for the private sector, there is considerable doubt these figures due to some important limitations as to whether it is stimulating genuine social and variations in the methodologies used to economic development among rural communities estimate them or providing stronger incentives for biodiversity conservation. It is also not clear whether, or While nature tourism only accounts for only a under what circumstances, nature tourism in less-small fraction of the overall global tourist visited areas has more or less environmental industry, it is reported to be one of the fastest-impact than conventional or "mass" tourism growing tourism markets. A study for the which is concentrated in areas where Economist Intelligence Unit has forecast a environmental damage from uncontrolled doubling of expenditure on environmentally-development has already taken place sensitive tourism and ecotourism between 1995 and 2000.

Introduction

The objectives of this review are to explore the tourism? (2) How can nature tourism contribute use of economic analysis to help develop policies more to local economic development? (3) How which can enhance nature tourism's contribution can economic policies and instruments contribute to sustainable development, and to inquire into to mitigating nature tourism's environmental the conditions under which nature tourism is impact? The final section highlights gaps in the financially and economically viable as well as literature and identifies priority areas for further environmentally sustainable.

After a general research discussion of the economic analysis of nature tourism in the next section, the paper proceeds by Readers are referred to Hoagland et al. (1995) addressing two methodological and measurement for a methodological review of the net economic questions: (1) What has nature tourism's benefits associated specifically with the creation economic impact or contribution been? (2) What and operation of marine reserves, to Brandon are the net economic benefits of nature tourism? (1996) for a more general review of the next three sections explore three principal ecotourism literature, and to Goudberg et al. policy issues: (1) What are the options for (1991) for a review of site-specific ecotourism capturing more of the net benefits of nature planning issues.

Economic Analysis of Nature Tourism

Tourism's contribution to the economy can be measured. Such studies are the diverse types of businesses selling goods services to tourists do not constitute an easily separable economic sector and, as a result, very Key studies of nature tourism's economic few countries treat tourism as a separate category impacts as well as its economic value are in the national income accounts. Whether an economic difficult to isolate the economic impact of nature impact and/or a economic valuation study is tourism from other types of tourism. As a result appropriate or feasible depends on the priority of these complications, many economic studies of issues under consideration, the availability of nature tourism are based on uncertain data and adequate data and the cost-effectiveness of use a variety of methodologies to produce results generating new data.

Economic impact which are not easily comparable assessments of tourism have been much more influential with government policymakers due to Many so-called "economic" studies examine the their emphasis on money flows in the economy as contribution of nature tourism to the economy well as job creation and foreign exchange based on the amount of money which tourists earnings-all politically sensitive considerations spend on various aspects of their recreational Welfare analyses, although analytically more experience (travel, accommodation, food, comprehensive, have received much less attention souvenirs, and so on). This is equivalent to from decision makers who tend to be less measuring the proportion of transactions in the interested in economic benefits which they are economy which are dependent on nature tourism unable to capture or use in practical terms.

Such studies of the financial values of specific nature tourism destinations are an important but The critical distinction between nature tourism's incomplete step towards more complete economic impact and its economic value is analysis. Appropriately described as "economic illustrate. AD is the tourism impact assessments" (CNPPA 1996), such demand function showing how many visits will studies be made at each price and reflecting declining marginal benefits from additional visits to a In contrast, an economic welfare analysis destination. Tourists' direct expenditures at measures the value which society places on price B are equivalent to the area OBCE nature tourism destinations, i.e., the economic Consumer surplus, the amount which tourists benefits less costs over time. Welfare analysis would have been prepared to pay over and above requires not only market benefits (such as the prevailing price B, is equivalent to ABC tourism) but also non-market benefits (such as This is foregone income to the owners of the watershed protection and existence values) to be destination. The gross economic value of Environmental Economics Series tourism is then OACE. If the proportion of that it does not describe the broader economic tourist receipts from tourism that leak out of the benefits of conservation which can be associated economy is OF/OB, the retained gross impact of tourists is only one of the economic values which direct tourist expenditures on the economy is flow from nature tourism destinations. The other FBCG and leakages are OFGE (multipliers are values, although often substantial, are very excluded) difficult to quantify. The model illustrates the economic value of tourism.

What Has Nature Tourism's Economic *Impact or Contribution Been?*

The economic impact of tourism is usually. These indicative figures suggest measured in terms of tourists' overall spending that Nepal's parks may represent an attractive on accommodation, food, travel, souvenirs and public sector investment opportunity (higher user other expenditures. Assembling thic data usually fees were subsequently collected, although park requires estimates of the total number of visitor-management budgets have remained modest) days as well as average tourist spending per day. Although surveys may be needed to generate this Estimating the proportion of tourist expenditures data, many countries gather such information attributable to nature tourism or to a particular routinely for at least some categories of visitors nature tourism destination can be problematic, While economic impact data is not strictly especially in countries which offer a range of comparable with the costs of protected area conventional tourist attractions as well as nature management, the contrast between the two can tourist destinations.

Wells (1996) found a range sometimes be used to argue for higher of credible estimates that attributed between 10% management budgets. For example, the budgets and 90% of all international arrivals in South for managing five Australian World Heritage Africa to wildlife tourism. Other attractions in a Areas studied by Driml (1994) totalled less than complex set of visitor motivations included 4% of the estimated tourist expenditures in 1991, climate, scenery, post-apartheid curiosity, visits while revenues raised through user fees were less to relatives and add-ons to business trips than one third of one per cent of estimated tourist Similar complications can be found in many of expenditures the major nature tourism destination countries.

In Nepal, protected area tourism has expanded Theoretically, the key question in estimating the dramatically while the parks are becoming economic impacts of tourism attributable to a degraded and the financial resources provided for destination such as a protected area is: How their management have been inadequate. The much would tourism spending (and its related government collected less than $1 million in user impacts) decline if the protected area in question fees from protected area visitors in 1988, while was no longer available as a tourist destination?

reluctantly spending about $5 million in The answer depends partly on the extent to which managing these areas.

This suggests a $4 million other destinations provide acceptable substitutes, net expense, a significant amount in one of the and partly on the scale of the analysis. Creemers world's poorest countries. But tourism is (1996) has pointed out that the economic impact Nepal's largest foreign exchange earner and it of a nature tourism destination depends on the has been conservatively estimated that $27 geographic scale to which tourism spending million of 1988 tourist expenditures can be would be redirected if that destination was no attributed to the country's protected area network longer available. A thorough analysis would Economic Perspectives on Nature Tourism, Conservation and Development require information on where and how visitors that benefit from direct or indirect effects. The would spend the money which they would no direct, indirect and induced effects are used to longer be able to spend if a certain destination calculate economic multipliers which can then be became inaccessible, information which could be used to estimate the impacts of tourism elicited through surveys.

By definition, there can only be multiplier effects The economic impact studies described above if there are unemployed or underemployed have measured tourist spending at existing resources in an area. If destinations. In contrast, a recent South African there is full employment the resources purchased study considered the potential loss of tourism for the tourism sector must either have come revenues if the Greater St. Lucia Wetland Park from another sector or been attracted from was to allow mining instead of being developed elsewhere in the same economy. This is rarely an for conservation and tourism. Earlier estimates of the amounts of levels are so high as to place a considerable money which tourists were likely to spend in the premium on job creation.

Park were, unsurprisingly, orders of magnitude less than mining revenues projected for the Positive multiplier effects are limited by private sector. But a broader analysis using leakages, which reduce the positive economic reasonably conservative assumptions suggested impacts of tourism. At a national level, tourism that at least 20,000 fewer international tourists leakages are the proportion of the receipts would visit South Africa each year if mining derived from incoming foreigners which leave the went ahead at St. Lucia, a unique and highly country. Indicative values are shown in Table marketable attraction. At $3,750 per visit, the Leakage is often higher during start-up or foregone annual revenue to the national tourist rapid growth phases of tourism, when the local industry would be about $75 million, an amount economy is generally unable to provide many of comparable to the expected revenues from the goods and services demanded by visitors mining. Had the study had focused on High leakage rates for nature tourism are likely local/provincial as well as national impacts, the to persist in relatively undeveloped locations and potential deflection of domestic and international at those sites providing more luxurious and tourists to other destinations within South Africa expensive facilities would also have needed to be taken into account. Brown et al. (1995) analyzed the expenditures of international visitors to Hwange and Mana Pools National Parks in Zimbabwe.

As expected, the Estimating the aggregate or gross value of all largest component of visitor expenditures was transactions attributable to nature tourism at a international air fares, whose external component specific site does not take multiplier effects or (excluding Air Zimbabwe) averaged 40% of total leakages into account. Economic multipliers spending. Commissions paid to agents and to result from the process by which tourist spending ground operators in foreign currencies accounted stimulates further spending and increased for a further 7.4% and 5.8%, respectively. This economic activity.

There are three categories of meant that $53 out of every $100 spent by multiplier effects: (1) Direct effects are economic visitors did not enter Zimbabwe and primarily impacts directly related to nature tourism; (2) benefited the visitors' home countries (this might Indirect effects are expenditures incurred by a be referred to as pre-leakage). Of the $47 out of business or other entity when it re-spends its every $100 which was spent in Zimbabwe, gross income on wages, operating expenses or further foreign exchange leakages from agents' capital items; and (3) Induced effects arise from commissions and ground operator costs averaged the re-spending of wages earned in businesses $12. This left $35 in Zimbabwe out of every Multiplier models vary greatly in their $100 spent by visitors on their entire trip, sophistication and rigor, inadequate data are equivalent to 65% leakage.

Indirect and induced often a major drawback, and multiplier analysis multiplier effects were estimated to expand the in general appears to have fairly low credibility impact of this $35 by 56% to about $55. Even when adjusted for multipliers and leakages, estimates of total The items commonly included in analyses of tourist expenditures do not take into account the leakages are the import of materials and capital costs of the inputs to the tourism industry, and goods for the tourism industry, the import of thereby overstate tourism benefits. Gross consumables, the tourism expenditures are not comparable to gross employment of foreigners and the repatriation of domestic product (GDP), which is calculated on profits by foreign companies involved in the a value-added basis. Relatively few studies have industry. But Smith & Jenner (1992) have attempted to directly estimate value-added for the argued that leakages should also include interest nature tourism sector, although Norton-Griffith charges on foreign debt incurred for tourism & Southey (1995) estimated the value-added of development, overseas promotion by the national Kenya's wildlife tourism sector, an essential step tourism organization and by individual tourism in comparing nature tourism to alternative land companies, the depreciation of infrastructure use options (roads, airports and sewerage systems) due to international tourism, as well as damage to the In the mainstream tourism literature, the most built and natural environment, popular method of estimating indirect and Value Added induced effects has been input-output analysis.

Input-output tables usually require Estimating multiplier effects and leakages with a an extensive amount of work, which may not reasonable degree of accuracy is difficult be justified by the practical applicability of latest year for which needed data were available the Canadian economy, equivalent to 3% of Inputs included tourism expenditure surveys, a GDP, and supported 467,000 full-time jobs, national family expenditure survey, surveys of equivalent to 5% of all business sector travel agencies, tour operators and tour employment. These results indicated a much wholesalers, as well as the consumer price index greater tourism impact than earlier estimates and national input-output tables. The TSA Filion et al. (1994) report estimates that as much indicated that total 1988 tourist expenditures in as one quarter of tourist expenditures in Canada were $24.2 billion, 22% of which was can be attributed to wildlife tourism, suggesting spent by foreign tourists. These expenditures generated an economy.

Introduction

As the new millennium unfolds, we are becoming increasingly aware of the finite, interconnected and precious nature of our planet home. Likewise, tourism is becoming an increasingly popular expression of this awareness. Tourism not only provides an escape from the everyday working life of many, but it also represents the everyday working life of many more. With advances in transportation and information technology, ever more remote areas of the earth are coming within reach of the traveller. In fact, tourism is now the world's largest industry, with nature tourism the fastest growing segment. In response to this increasing appreciation of nature experiences, a new travel ethic has arisen which is now called ecotourism. This term has become increasingly popular in both conservation and travel circles. Most tourism in natural areas today is not ecotourism and is not therefore, sustainable. Ecotourism can be distinguished from nature tourism by its emphasis on conservation, education, traveller responsibility and active community participation. Specifically, ecotourism is not only the act of a foreigner visiting a foreign land, but also the participation of and effects on the local populations of touristed areas. These facilities and programs become part of the local culture, and it is up to the planning of tourism to make sure that they stay within the original framework of the culture.

With the definition of traditional tourism in mind, ecotourism can be discussed as a different entity based on the involvement of local populations in all aspects of tourism. Indigenous populations are the most knowledgeable about the area, and they "possess the practical and ancestral knowledge of the natural features of the area".

Maintaining the important bond between its education and its environment is important to the survival of an ecotourism program. This is especially important now, in a time when ecotourism is part of the development strategy of nearly every developing country.

Literature Review

The Definition of Ecotourism

There are various definitions of ecotourism, most of which have to do with combining the travel industry with an ideal that emphasizes conservation and preservation of the wilderness in which people spend their vacations. The Ecotourism Society defines ecotourism as "responsible travel which conserves environments and sustains the wellbeing of local people,".

Ecotourism is a relatively new concept, and it is still often misunderstood or misused. Some people have abused the term to attract conservation conscious travellers to what, in reality, are simply nature tourism programs which may cause negative environmental and social impacts. While the term was first heard in the 1980s, the first broadly accepted definition, and one which continues to be a valid "nutshell" definition was established by The International Ecotourism Society in 1990: *Responsible travel to natural areas that conserves the environment and improves the wellbeing of local people.*

As awareness and experience of the activity has grown, so has our need for a more comprehensive and detailed definition. Martha Honey (1999) has proposed an excellent, more detailed version: Ecotourism is travel to fragile, pristine and usually protected areas that strives to be low impact and usually small scale. It helps educate the traveller; provides funds for conservation; directly benefits the economic development and political empowerment of local communities; and fosters respect for different cultures and for human rights.

However, consensus exists among organizations involved with ecotourism including The Nature Conservancy around the definition adopted in 1996 by the World Conservation Union (IUCN) which describes ecotourism as:

Environmentally responsible travel and visitation to natural areas, in order to enjoy and appreciate nature and any accompanying cultural features, both past and present that promote conservation, have a low visitor impact and provide for beneficially active socioeconomic involvement of local peoples.

The Nature Conservancy has adopted the concept of ecotourism as the type of tourism that it recommends its partners use in most protected area management, especially for national parks and other areas with fairly strict conservation objectives. For The Nature Conservancy, ecotourism represents an excellent means for benefiting both local people and the protected area in question. It is an ideal component of a sustainable development strategy where natural resources can be utilized as tourism attractions without causing harm to the natural area. An important tool for protected area management and development, ecotourism must be implemented in a flexible manner. However, the following elements are crucial to the ultimate success of an ecotourism initiative. Ecotourism must:

- Have a low impact upon a protected area's natural resources;
- Involve stakeholders (individuals, communities, ecotourists, tour operators and government institutions) in the planning, development, implementation and monitoring phases;
- Respect local cultures and traditions;
- Generate sustainable and equitable income for local communities and for as many other stakeholders as possible, including private tour operators;
- Generate income for protected area conservation;
- Educate all stakeholders about their role in conservation.

Evolution of Ecotourism

Ecotourism is a concept that evolved over the last 20 years as the conservation community, people living in and around protected areas, and the travel industry witnessed a boom in nature tourism and realized their mutual interests in directing its growth. Ecotourism has brought the promise of achieving conservation goals, improving the wellbeing of local communities and generating new business promising a rare win-win situation. Relations among conservationists, communities and tourism practitioners have not always been smooth and collaborative.

However, the concept and practice of ecotourism brings these different actors together. Ecotourism has emerged as a platform to establish partnerships and to jointly guide the path of tourists seeking to experience and learn about natural areas and diverse cultures.

Conservationists and Ecotourism

Specific circumstances on all sides motivated this new interest in ecotourism. On the conservation side, protected area managers were in the midst of redefining conservation strategies. For practical reasons, they were learning to combine conservation activities with economic development as it became obvious that traditional conservation approaches of strict protectionism were no longer adequate and new ways of accomplishing goals were needed.

For years, conservationists established and managed protected areas through minimal collaboration with the people living in or near these areas. Circumstances in many countries, particularly in developing regions, have changed dramatically in recent years and have affected approaches to conservation.

Local Stakeholders and Ecotourism

Over the past two decades, many developing countries have experienced large populatión increases with declining or stagnant economic conditions. These countries have frequently been pressured into exploiting their natural resource base in an unsustainable fashion in order to meet immediate economic needs and to pay interest on foreign debt. This combination leads more people to compete for fewer natural resources.

Outside protected areas, the natural resources that many people have depended upon for sustenance and many businesses have relied upon for profit making have disappeared. For most countries, protected areas have become the last significant pieces of land that still retain important reserves of plant and animal diversity, water, clean air and other ecological services.

Meanwhile, protected areas have become increasingly attractive to farmers, miners, loggers and others trying to make a living. The economic development pressures on these areas have intensified on local, national and global scales. Thus, ecotourism has become very important for potentially reconciling conservation and economic considerations.

Because of this competition for resources, conservationists realized that local people and economic circumstances must be incorporated into conservation strategies. In most cases, local people need financial incentives to use and manage natural resources sustainably. Existing economic and political conditions often limit their options and increase their reliance on natural areas.

Conservation work often means creating alternatives to current economic practices so that multiple-use zones around protected areas can be maintained and threats to protected areas minimized. In looking for alternative economic activities, conservationists have become more creative and are exploring many options. Ecotourism is one such alternative. The rationale behind ecotourism is that local tourism businesses would not destroy natural resources but would instead support their protection. Ecotourism would offer a viable strategy to simultaneously make money and conserve resources. Ecotourism could be considered a "sustainable" activity, one that does not diminish natural resources being used while at the same time generating income.

Related Terms

As a popular word, ecotourism has been used loosely. But if implemented fully, it is a critically important conservation strategy for achieving sustainable development.

There are a variety of related terms that are frequently linked, and sometimes confused with ecotourism, including the following:

- Nature tourism is simply tourism based on visitation to natural areas. Nature tourism is closely related to ecotourism but does not necessarily involve conservation or sustainability. This is the type of tourism that currently exists in most natural areas before a plan is established and conservation measures are in place. As different elements of ecotourism are integrated into a nature tourism program, its effect on the environment may change.
- Sustainable nature tourism is very close to ecotourism but does not meet all the criteria of true ecotourism. For example, a cable car carrying visitors through the rainforest canopy may generate benefits for conservation and educate visitors, but because it represents a high degree of mechanization and consequently creates a barrier between the visitor and the natural environment, it would be inappropriate to describe as an ecotourism initiative. In altered and heavily-visited areas, sustainable nature tourism may be an appropriate activity. For example, larger "eco" resort development would not be considered low impact if it required significant clearing of native vegetation but may contribute to conservation financially and provide conservation education.

  The line between sustainable nature tourism and ecotourism is subtle but very important. A project must meet all of the necessary criteria listed above before it can accurately be defined as ecotourism. Projects that fall short on any of the criteria do not truly benefit conservation or the people involved over the long term.
- Cultural, ethno or cultural heritage tourism concentrates on local traditions and people as the main attractions. This kind

of tourism can be divided into two types: The first and conventional type is where tourists experience culture through museums and formalized presentations of music and dance in theatres, hotels or occasionally in communities themselves. In many instances, this has lead to the "commodification" of culture as it becomes adapted for tourist consumption, often resulting in degradation of the hosts" cultural traditions. The second type is more anthropological and contains a strong visitor motivation for learning from indigenous culture rather than simply viewing an isolated manifestation of it. For example, there is growing interest in learning how indigenous people use natural resources. It is important that cultural tourism be managed on terms defined by host communities and that indicators of the cultural impact of tourism be monitored to ensure visitation does not erode the cultural resource.

- Green/Sustainable tourism refers to travel operations that use natural resources judiciously. Green or sustainable tourism can be considered the "greening" of the tourism industry. Examples include the airline industry becoming more energy efficient, the cruise line industry recycling its waste or large hotel chains adopting environmental regulations. Large hotels have discovered that by advising guests to reduce water consumption or recommending that they not expect their towels to be washed every day, the hotels not only gain a "greener" image which is increasingly important to consumers, but they also reduce operating costs. Thus, green tourism is clearly an attractive proposition to the conventional tourism industry. In reality, reducing the hotel's water consumption by 15%, although desirable and relatively easy to achieve at most large hotels, is not enough to convert the hotel into a sustainable operation. Sweeting et al. (1999) review this issue comprehensively and make recommendations for reducing conventional tourism's impact on the environment.

While greening the existing conventional mass tourism industry will produce some benefits, new developments in natural areas, including beaches, need to address energy consumption, waste management and environmental interpretation in the design phase and not as an afterthought if they are to be truly sustainable.

Large hotels washing towels only every other day may not be enough to protect the water table in an arid area. Not building the hotel in the first place in an area where water resources are scarce may be the best option.

Developing a sustainable or green tourism industry in all its dimensions is as worthy a cause as working to maintain protected areas through tourism. In fact, some would argue that promoting sustainability of the broader tourism would be a better conservation mission than focusing on protected areas alone. However, for the present purposes the focus will be on ecotourism development. It may be easiest to think of ecotourism which works to protect natural areas through tourism and sustainable tourism which works to make the whole tourism industry more environmentally friendly as two valuable, but distinct, missions.

Key Considerations for Successful Ecotourism

These days, most conservationists recognize that working with communities is fundamental to achieving protected area goals and conservation strategies, including ecotourism. There are a number of basic principles that should be considered in planning for community involvement in ecotourism activities. Ecotourism organized at the local community level can rarely be successful without assistance or cooperation from tourism operators.

Links to the market, language skills and poor communications are three major aspects which limit communities ability to "go it alone" in ecotourism. Protected area managers must play a role in guiding ecotourism implementation outside of the protected area, but in many cases that role may have to be a "secondhand" one. NGOs are generally perceived as neutral parties and thus more acceptable as providers of technical assistance to local communities.

In some cases, the NGOs may be the protected area managers. Training, for example in basic accounting and guiding, is a key need for communities to effectively participate in ecotourism. This is a role that NGOs are best placed to provide. For ecotourism to promote conservation, local people must clearly benefit and understand that the benefits they receive are linked to the continued existence of the protected area. There must be a close working relationship between the protected area administration and the surrounding communities. Unfortunately, the limited benefits provided by many tourism projects frequently are not recognized by local residents as connected to the protected area. A huge range of players with varying interests and goals participates in ecotourism. Some play more prominent roles than others, but almost all are represented in the development and management of ecotourism sites.

A key to the success of ecotourism is the formation of strong partnerships so that the multiple goals of conservation and equitable development can be met. Partnerships may be difficult because of the number of players involved and their different needs, but forging relationships is essential. The key players can be classified as community organizations and individuals, private sector tourism industry members and a variety of government officials and nongovernmental organizations. Their effective interaction creates effective ecotourism.

Core Decision Makers

Local Government. Officials

Many government departments should participate in ecotourism planning, development and management. These departments include tourism, natural resources, wildlife and protected areas, education, community development, finances and transportation. Ecotourism involves officials primarily from the national level, although regional and local levels also contribute to the process.

Government officials have several significant functions in ecotourism. They provide leadership. They coordinate and articulate national goals for ecotourism.

As part of their overall tourism plans, they provide vision for this industry. They may even propose a national ecotourism plan; in Australia, the government created a National Ecotourism Strategy and then committed AUS$10 million for its development and implementation.

Government officials at the national level may also establish specific policies for protected areas. For example, government officials decide about visitor use fee systems at protected areas, and their policies outline what systems are established and how revenues will be distributed.

They may also delineate private sector practices, e.g., tour operators may be required to use local tour guides in certain areas or developers" property ownership rights may be regulated. Government policies direct ecotourism activities and may easily advance or hinder their growth.

Additionally, government officials are responsible for most basic infrastructure outside protected areas ranging from airline facilities in big cities to secondary roads leading to remote sites. The government generally takes the lead in all major transportation systems and issues. It may also provide other services important to ecotourism such as health clinics in rural areas.

Finally, government officials promote ecotourism. Sometimes the promotion is part of a national tourism campaign. At other times, advertisements for specific nature sites are created or perhaps a flagship species is identified and promoted. National government participation gives prominence to ecotourism destinations.

Local Communities.

People who live in or near protected areas are not a homogeneous group. Indeed, even within one small community there will be a diversity of people with a range of views and experiences.

But we can make a few generalizations about local residents and their relationship to ecotourism. First, some rural communities that once featured quiet living are finding themselves in the middle of an international trend. Nature tourists are invading their homelands, but they are generally just passing through the neighbourhood, not coming to meet residents. Residents have mixed reactions to this intrusion. Some want nothing to do with tourists; they want privacy and do not welcome the changes that tourism brings. Others are intrigued by tourism and are taking steps to develop it. Tourism may be particularly alluring if other employment options are limited or if residents feel tourism may help protect their precious resources.

Many communities in developing countries are hosting visitors and creating ecotourism programs. Sometimes their motivation is to protect their surrounding natural resources. For others, they may see ecotourism in a more economic perspective, as a means to gain income. Many communities have organized their own ecotourism programs.

Whatever their initial reaction to tourism, local residents are often unprepared for its demands. Those who do not want tourism have no means to stop it. They often cannot compete with the powerful tourism industry or the fiercely independent travellers who want to discover new areas. Those who are interested in pursuing tourism may not be familiar with its costs and benefits. Many have little experience in tourism business enterprises and are not connected to international tourism markets. The interests and concerns of local residents regarding tourism development need special attention.

Tourism touches all the other groups involved professionally, in a mostly economic sense. For members of communities, it also touches their personal lives by affecting their lifestyles, traditions and cultures, as well as their livelihood and their long standing ways of organizing themselves socially and politically. In addition, most of the other players enter into tourism voluntarily, whereas in many cases communities must deal with tourism impacts whether or not they choose to. Local residents play an important role in ecotourism for two main reasons.

First, it is their homelands and work places that are attracting nature travellers. Equity and practicality require that they be active decision-makers in ecotourism planning and management.

Second, local residents are key players in conserving natural resources both within and outside of neighbouring protected areas. Their relationship to and uses of natural resources will determine the success of conservation strategies for protected areas. In addition, local or traditional knowledge is often a key component of visitors' experience and education.

Tourism Industry

The tourism industry is massive. It involves a huge variety of people including: tour operators and travel agents who assemble trips; airline and cruise ship employees; minivan drivers; staff of big hotels and small family lodges; handicraft makers; restaurant owners; tour guides; and all the other people who independently offer goods and services to tourists. The complexity of this sector indicates how challenging it can be for protected area staff and local communities to learn about and form partnerships with the tourism industry.

Consumers are in contact with many members of the tourism industry throughout their journeys. For an international trip, the traveller often first contacts a travel agent, tour operator or airline. The agent will generally contact an outbound tour operator based in the tourist's country of origin, who in turn will contact an in bound tour operator based in the destination country. The in bound tour operator is best placed to make local travel arrangements such as transportation, accommodations, and guide services.

Once the traveller is at the destination, many local entrepreneurs will also become part of this scenario. One element that binds all businesses within the tourism industry is the pursuit of financial profit. There may be additional motivations for some businesses, particularly those involved in ecotourism, but tourism companies exist only when they are profitable.

Members of the tourism industry are valuable to ecotourism for many reasons. First, they understand travel trends. They know how consumers act and what they want. Second, the tourism industry can influence travellers by encouraging good behaviour and limiting negative impacts in protected areas. Third, the tourism industry plays a key role in promoting ecotourism. Its members know how to reach travellers through publications, the Internet, the media and other means of promotion, thus providing a link between ecotourism destinations and consumers.

Nongovernmental Organizations

Nongovernmental organizations are valuable players because they provide a forum for discussion and influence regarding ecotourism. They offer a means of communication with great numbers of interested individuals. These organizations can serve as vehicles for bringing together all the elements of ecotourism. NGOs can play many different roles in ecotourism implementation: directly, as program managers or site administrators; and indirectly, as trainers, advisors, business partners with ecotourism companies or communities and, in exceptional circumstances, as providers of ecotourism services. There are several different types of nongovernmental organizations. Among them are for-profit tourism associations consisting of private tour operators, airlines and hoteliers; ecotourism associations such as those in Belize, Costa Rica, Ecuador, etc., that bring together groups from all the sectors involved; and other trade organizations that handle travel issues. These NGOs often have members who meet regularly and communicate industry concerns through publications such as newsletters.

Members are often asked to subscribe to certain principles or "codes of ethics." These associations and organizations are effective at keeping the industry informed about current trends and events.

Another set of nongovernmental organizations involved with ecotourism includes the private, non-profit groups that focus on conservation and development or may be dedicated specifically to ecotourism. Their focus may be local, national or international. Frequently, these organizations serve as facilitators between protected areas, communities and all the other players in ecotourism, sometimes providing financial and technical assistance or directly managing ecotourism sites. Some of these NGOs have constituencies that enjoy nature and would be interested in ecotourism education and promotion.

NGOs play an important role in advancing ecotourism implementation through their positive interaction with local communities, the private sector tourism industry, government-dministered protected areas and others. The particular role adopted by an NGO depends upon the set of circumstances within which it operates, e.g., its mission and purpose, the degree of openness to NGO collaboration and the interest of the tourism industry. Opportunistic situations also arise which affect an NGO"s role, such as donation of a tract of land for ecotourism purposes or development of a friendly relationship with a community leader.

Supporting Players

Funders

Many different groups can fund the development of ecotourism through loans or grants: financial institutions, including investment corporations; bilateral and multilateral donor agencies; private investors; venture capital funds such as the Ecoenterprise Investment Fund; NGOs; and private banks.

These contributions are often critical for protected areas that pursue ecotourism. Typically there are studies to carry out, facilities to build, infrastructure to create and people to train. With protected area budgets so limited, outside funding is necessary.

Financial institutions do not generally participate in planning for ecotourism or in decisions about what is appropriate for a particular protected area. In this regard, they may be considered a second-tier player in ecotourism, but they are important nonetheless. For anyone that wants to develop ecotourism, access to funds is often the biggest obstacle confronted.

Academics

Academics at universities is another group that plays a secondary, though valuable, role in the planning and daily functions of ecotourism. It is a group that helps to frame the issues of ecotourism and raise questions to ensure that ecotourism meets its stated goals. Researchers and academics facilitate learning by asking such questions as: Who exactly is benefiting from ecotourism? How do we measure benefits? How does ecotourism contribute to our existing knowledge about conservation? What are the links between ecotourism and tourism? Academics can focus on the big picture and help us understand how ecotourism interacts with other concepts and global trends.

In addition to helping shape the hypotheses, academics conduct research. In coordination with NGOs, governments and local communities, they may:

- Educate and create naturalist guides;
- produce data about tourism patterns;
- inventory flora and fauna;
- document tourism impacts and share results to develop a good base of information;
- provide material to guide us in our discussions and conclusions about ecotourism;
- facilitate the sharing of this information and conceptual thinking through conferences, publications, the Internet, etc.

Travellers have a unique position as players in ecotourism. They are the most vital participants in the industry and provide motivation for everyone else's activities, but few participate in formal meetings about ecotourism. Nevertheless, the choices they make when they select a tourism destination, choose a tour operator or travel agent and, ultimately, the kind of tour in which they wish to participate, have a tremendous impact upon the eventual success or failure of ecotourism projects.

Ecotourism, then, is a multifaceted, multi-disciplinary, multi-actor activity requiring communication and collaboration among a diverse range of actors with different needs and interests. Consequently, achieving ecotourism is a challenging process though ultimately enormously rewarding for all involved.

Creating Naturalist Guides

Naturalist guides play a central role in the implementation of the ecotourism concept. They are the principal providers of the educational element to the ecotourism activity, and their capacity and commitment ensures that the negative impacts of tourism are minimized. At the same time, guiding is an obvious economic opportunity for people from local communities. These and other important benefits underline the importance of a protected area establishing and implementing a naturalist guide training and licensing program.

The use of tour guides in protected areas is not a new phenomenon. Guides have been a part of nature tourism in many places for many years. These tour guides usually were employed by private tour operators and had little or no relationship to the protected area they worked in even though they didn't have any background knowledge about the importance of environment. Over the years, this situation began to change as protected area managers realized the potential for using guides to increase contact with visitors and for accomplishing other ecotourism objectives as well.

The Roles of Naturalist Guides

Naturalist guides truly play a multifaceted role. They have responsibilities to their tour operator employers, to their clients the visitors, and to the protected areas and communities where they work. Tour operators count on guides to provide experience enriching interpretation of natural and cultural attractions to add value to the tourists' itinerary.

They also require guides to manage logistical aspects of trips in the field, such as coordinating with accommodation, food and transport service providers. Guides are responsible for the tourists" safety and in general represent their tour operator employer in the field.

Tourists look to the naturalist guide for information, interpretation and insight about the places they are visiting; for help preparing for a visit through formal briefings and informal talks; and generally to be a friendly, knowledgeable intermediary with unfamiliar places and people. Protected area authorities look to the guides as extensions of the park ranger staff, to educate the visitors, to protect the natural and cultural resources of the area visited, to participate in monitoring programs and generally to support the conservation objectives of an area. In addition to these roles, a naturalist guide should seek to inspire visitors to become supporters of conservation.

Nature Interpreters

Environmental interpretation is a subset of communication that focuses on how best to explain environmental and ecological concepts to the general public. One of the central tenets of ecotourism is to educate the visitor. Naturalist guides, who spend a considerable amount of time with visitors, are in a perfect position to educate through skilled interpretation. Many local residents have a detailed knowledge of the plant and animal life as well as of other natural and cultural attractions. They can also relate first-hand experiences with wildlife, medicinal plants and other local phenomena.

Conservationists

As the main contacts that visitors may have with an ecotourism site, guides serve as important role models both to visitors and their own communities. Their attitude and behaviour send an important message to others about the ecotourism concept. Does the guide pick up pieces of trash along the hiking trail? Does the guide actively support and cooperate with site managers by reporting illegal activities? Does the guide adapt ecotourism to his/her own home and community situation? Some tour guides make a point of discussing the importance of conserving the incredible diversity found at a site, what the major threats to it are and what visitors might do to help conserve it.

Park Rangers

Unfortunately, not all visitors to ecotourism sites know how to behave appropriately in sensitive natural and cultural settings. It is the guides' responsibility to ensure that visitors are aware of all applicable rules and regulations as well as other relevant ethical considerations. In a polite but firm manner, they must make sure that visitors comply with whatever restrictions there may be. This is perhaps the most difficult role that guides have because their major responsibility is to help provide visitors with an enjoyable experience.

As members of the private sector, it can, in rare situations, create a conflict of interest between the guides' conservation obligations and their obligation to the visitor and, in some cases, their employer. For example, a tour operator might promise clients a close encounter with a whale, but a guide may judge that at a given moment the whales seen in the distance are nursing young and should not be approached. The guide's obligations to an employer and to a park authority might be divergent at this point. Guides need special training in how best to deal with these situations. They also must be vested with the authority to report and deal with infractions of rules and regulations.

Monitors of Tourism Impact

Since guides visit the ecotourism site/protected area on a frequent basis, they are in a unique position to notice certain kinds of impact, such as trail erosion, increasing rareness of a particular bird species, etc. They are also in an excellent position to carry out formal monitoring observations for the site's managers. In many places, guides take the time to carry out observations of the number of nesting birds or of the regeneration of a plant species in a designated quadrant. This can be of valuable assistance to a site's managers when they are short-handed or simply do not have trained personnel to carry out these tasks.

Liaison with Local Communities

When guides are from local communities, they can serve an important role in improving communication between the site's administration and local people. This is particularly important when there may be some misunderstanding between the two different "communities," which there frequently is. Naturalist guides should establish government financed organizations to further conservation objectives.

Conditions for a Successful Naturalist Guide System

In order for a naturalist guide system to work well in an ecotourism site situation, several conditions must be met.

Control and licensing

The site must have effective control over the use of guides and the conditions under which guides will operate within the site. This implies that managers either own the site or that there is legislation or some other legal mandate for exercising this control. Most effective guide systems have a licensing mechanism. The site's administration, or some higher authority acting at the administration's request, will issue a license to guide visitors within the site if the guide complies with relevant rules and regulations. The site's administration reserves the right to suspend or revoke the license if a guide's behaviour is inappropriate. Licenses are usually extended to those individuals who pass a training course or a test. The site's administration reserves the right to set other criteria for attending a training course, such as: being a member of a local community, being of a minimum age, the absence of a police record and having a minimum level of education.

It is important to avoid flooding the market with too many licensed guides as this would force down wage levels as many compete for an insufficient number of jobs. However, it is necessary to have a sufficient number of guides to satisfy demand; a rough guide would be to license about 25% more guides than will be working each season.

In spite of the control that the site's administration must exercise over the guides' activities, the relationship between them should be more than one of employer and employee. Both the site administration and the guide have much to offer each other, and they should actively carry out their respective roles in order to benefit from each other's work. Unfortunately, it is not uncommon for one side or the other to lose sight of their mutually supportive roles and for the relationship to become nonproductive. Constant and positive feedback is the best way to avoid this situation. Involving tour operators and guides in the ecotourism program planning process from the beginning is also crucial.

Training

Naturalist guides need training in order to fulfil the many roles they are charged with. The primary themes for a training course curriculum are listed below.

- ***Natural history of the site and surrounding areas*:** What are the major species, plant and animal communities and ecosystems? How do they interact with one another? What is their conservation status?
- ***Cultural attractions:*** What are the historical, archaeological and traditional cultural activities that can be found in the site and surrounding areas? What is the relationship between natural and cultural attractions?
- ***Site conservation priorities and activities:*** Guides should be able to explain to visitors what the site's management is

doing to further the conservation of the natural and cultural resources found in the site as well as how the site relates to other protected areas and the surrounding communities.

- ***Rules and regulations:*** Guides need to be aware of all the rules and regulations governing public use of the site and its facilities. In particular, they need to be aware of what ecotourism is and how it is applied at this site.
- ***Group management:*** All guides need to learn how to best manage a group of visitors that can have widely varying attention spans and reasons for being there. Maintaining everyone's attention and keeping the group together can sometimes be a major chore. Experienced guides are sometimes the best people to teach this part of the course.
- ***Interpretive/communication techniques:*** There are very special techniques for communicating ideas to a group of disparate people. Learning the techniques comes easily for some guides; for others, a significant amount of time will need to be spent. Training should not be a one-time event for guides. Good guides should be continually refreshing and updating their knowledge, and the site's administration should consider carrying out periodic courses for this purpose. Courses should be developed with, and at least partly financed by, the tourism industry. In addition to specialists in each of the themes outlined, tour operators should be instructors in courses, as should older, respected members of the local community.

Young men often dominate the competition for places in guide training courses, but it is important to ensure that women participate too. They make good guides, and at least 50% of tourists are women! Rare (formerly the RARE Centre for Tropical Conservation), with the support of The Nature Conservancy, has developed a comprehensive guide training manual that is highly recommended (RARE, 2001).

Guide Availability

Ecotourism encourages the inclusion of local people in as many circumstances as possible. While it may be useful to utilize local people as naturalist guides, managers should realize that residents may not be "natural" naturalist guides. Their interests or educational levels may be obstacles to reaching the level of expertise required of guides at a site. Significant training may be needed before they can function effectively.

Work Availability

Work availability is a very sensitive issue in many situations. Naturalist guides have the potential to earn significantly more money than other members of their community. For this reason, when a site initiates a naturalist guide system, there are sometimes many more candidates than available work. Managers must be careful not to create high expectations among guide candidates, especially if visitor numbers are not sufficient to guarantee work for everyone. If some candidates for a training course are selected over others who appear to have similar qualifications, conflicts may arise. Site managers may do several things to minimize these problems:

- Ensure that specific criteria are used to select guide candidates and that the criteria are strictly followed.

  Limit training course size to a specific number of people and accept candidates on a first come, first serve basis.
- Initiate policies that encourage or mandate the use of local guides in the ecotourism site or in specific locations or zones within the site. This may cause conflicts with other, non-local guides.
- Encourage the creation of a naturalist guides association that will help to organize guides and their response to a limited number of guiding opportunities, e.g., a system of rotation. This is also an excellent way to minimize cutthroat competition and to standardize prices. The site could mandate that guides charge only a certain amount for a given service, but the mandate would be better received and complied with if the guides were allowed to determine their own price structure.

Language Skills

Local guides can face a language barrier since most ecotourists are from another country, usually one where a different language is spoken. Local guides can be very ingenious at communicating with visitors whose language they do not speak. However, they cannot express themselves at the level that a high quality naturalist guide would need to communicate effectively, expressing complex ideas and concepts.

It is not uncommon for organized tours to arrive at an ecotourism site with a guide who works with the tour company and comes from the capital city, or even another country. Sometimes these guides are very knowledgeable about the site, but many are not. However, local community members should be given priority for positions as naturalist guides. In the case of areas that are ancestral lands of local communities, hiring a trained local naturalist guide should be obligatory. If tour operators require higher level scientific interpretation, they may choose to hire a university educated non-local guide to also accompany their clients. Training courses for local guides will likely emphasize different themes than courses for university-educated naturalists. If the situation is developed appropriately, guides from both categories can learn a lot from each other. Regardless, all guides should take and pass the training course and be licensed. It should be mandatory to train and provide licenses to local guides.

Conclusion

The environment is one of the primary concerns of ecotourism, which often involves travel to relatively undisturbed areas. As the tourism product is often dependent upon nature, negative impacts upon that resource should be minimized. As Cater [1994] notes, even the most conscientious tourist will have some degree of impact on the environment and so ecotourism should therefore attempt to minimize that impact. Many studies of tourism attempt to identify an environmental carrying capacity but a major difficulty of this technique is that it "implies the existence of fixed and determinable limits to development and that if one stays below those threshold levels no changes or deterioration will occur".

Great importance is attached to the need for local participation in ecotourism. According to Wallace and Pierce [1996], ecotourism is a type of tourism that "maximizes the early and long-term participation of local people in the decision making process that determines the kind and amount of tourism that should occur". There are important reasons for local involvement other than a moral obligation to incorporate the people tourism will affect. The degree of control the local population has over tourism in their locality is generally perceived as being a significant element of sustainability. As was noted earlier, ecotourism is required to provide direct economic benefits to the local community and minimize negative environmental and sociocultural impacts. The most likely way these objectives can be achieved is if the local community are actively participating in and empowered through ecotourism.

The final principle to which ecotourism should adhere is that of education. Ecotourism should involve education among all parties – local communities, government, non-governmental organizations, industry and tourists before, during and after the trip. Guides should therefore have been taught conservation issues and the tourists should be told about local conservation efforts and why they are deemed important. Tourists should be made aware of the damaging potential of their stay and should be properly informed on "ecotourism etiquette" and how to behave to reduce any negative impacts they might have.

A pool of trained and licensed naturalist guides can be a tremendous asset to protected area conservation. Creating a naturalist guide program should be a high priority for all sites with an ecotourism program.

Proposal

The annual "yellow dust" spring storms, which originate in China's Gobi Desert before sweeping south to envelop the Korean peninsula and parts of Japan, are blamed for scores of deaths and billions of dollars in damage every year in South Korea. The dust picks up heavy metals and carcinogens such as dioxin as it passes over Chinese industrial regions, before hitting North and South Korea and Japan.

The state-sponsored Korea Environment Institute said the dust kills up to 165 South Koreans a year, mostly the elderly or those with respiratory ailments, and makes as many as 1.8 million ill so that volunteer tourism could be an another form of alternative eco-tourism for the theoretical development of EATOF members countries. Accepting that a person is rarely forced to go on vacation, we can then infer that tourism as an activity is voluntary. An exploration of volunteer tourism consists of the principles it adheres to, its goals, and the characteristics that define eco tourism.

The motivations of volunteer tourism can broadly be stated as volunteer-minded and vacation-minded. Push and pull factors also look at the motivations of participants. One of the example of volunteer tourism is to dispatch a voluntary team consisting of some EATOF youngsters and citizen to plant trees in desert areas in China and Mongolia to reduce damages from decertification and yellow dust.

It can provide people of EATOF countries with opportunities to realize the importance of voluntarism and environmental movement. The tourism strengthen partnership of cooperation on combating decertification and yellow dust. In cooperation with the all EATOF member, the Green forest is going to be established a long greenbelt, namely the Great Green Wall in Kubuqi desert in Inner Mongolia, China to fight decertification and yellow dust storm.

Through various programs such as tree planting, environmental education and cultural exchange, the Green Forest will provide young people and citizen with opportunities to realize the importance of voluntarism and environmental movement.

Goals

The volunteer tourism aims to arouse public awareness on the issues of decertification and yellow dust storms, to promote participation of the young generation in environmental activities, and to contribute to the establishment of ingenuous friendship among youths all over the world.

Vision

1. To combat decertification and yellow dust storms by constructing.
2. Organize Green Corps in cooperation with the all EATOF members.
3. Make a brighter future for the next generation.

I would like to close by proposing that consistent with ecotourism tourism ideals, the goals of volunteer tourism are to participate in community development activities, scientific research or ecological restoration. In other words, volunteer tourists provide a service to the destination. Capturing what can be considered the essence of volunteer tourism, a volunteer tourism product has an interaction element with both volunteer and community-a desired consonance of expectations and motivations among these participants. Inter cultural exchange between volunteer and community is a key aspect of volunteer tourism.

Net Economic Benefits of Nature Tourism

Ecotourism

1 Ecotourism, Definitions, Concepts and Visitor Types.

2 Actors in the Ecotourism "System".

3 Overview of Tourism and Ecotourism in the Asia-Pacific Region.

4 The Dimensions of Ecotourism.

Visitors have long been travelling to natural areas under the guise of recreation and tourism. This has led some observers to question whether ecotourism is simply a new name for an old activity. However, several changes apparently have occurred in the last decade. First, for reasons, there has been growth in visits to many natural areas, particularly in developing countries. Second, many economic development professionals increasingly have viewed natural-area visitation as a tool for providing employment in regions that have experienced decline, or lack of development, in other industries.

Third, many conservation and resource management professionals increasingly have viewed natural area visitation as an avenue for enhancing natural area finance and providing conservation-related benefits, particularly to residents living near natural areas. Fourth, there has been increasing attention paid to improving the sustainability of all tourism activities, including those occurring in natural areas. Thus, although ecotourism may not represent an abrupt departure from historic recreation and tourism, it does represent a change in the level of visitation for many areas and a change in the goals that various stakeholders attach to this visitation.

The Australia case exemplifies the development of the ecotourism phenomenon. In the late 1980s, ecotourism was an unknown entity that was just beginning to emerge in the popular lexicon. Its growth was spurred by the ongoing debate over tourism and the environment and as a direct result of the enthusiasm for ecologically sustainable development (ESDWG 1991). At first, its potential market base was seen to be small although, as a new product, its growth potential was seen to be large.

However, this niche concept changed in the early 1990s. The term ecotourism struck a chord with the tourism industry, the travelling public, and with private and public sector agencies charged with the promotion of tourism products. Ecotourism became a buzzword. The explosion of interest in ecotourism led to the emergence of a lively debate among academics and industry leaders about the merits of the activity. Ecotourism conferences resulted in the formation of a national ecotourism association, the Ecotourism Association of Australia. In the space of four years, the Commonwealth government, state governments (DCE 1992), and even regional associations (NPWS 1996) produced a variety of ecotourism policies designed to encourage the industry's development. This same period saw rapid expansion in the number of ecotourism operators and the emergence of specialist tour wholesalers and retail travel agents to market ecotourism products.

By the mid 1990s, ecotourism, as a concept, began to enter a period of maturity. Many of the claims made in earlier years began to be disputed, and the legitimacy of many players to call themselves ecotourism products was challenged. The travelling public either has become more aware of what ecotourism encompasses or more critical about the idea to accept blindly the claims that mass tourism destinations are ecotourism destinations. Assumptions regarding the benefits of ecotourism have been challenged through empirical research. As a result, a more realistic understanding of what the product entails and the benefits it can provide is emerging.

Ecotourism, Definitions, Concepts and Visitor Types

Much attention has been paid to the question of what constitutes ecotourism, and numerous concepts and definitions exist. The Ecotourism Society, based in the US and the most international of the ecotourism organizations, defines ecotourism as responsible travel to natural areas that conserves the environment and improves the welfare of local people. The Australian National Ecotourism Strategy defines ecotourism as A nature-based tourism that involves education and interpretation of the natural environment and is managed to be ecologically sustainable. Numerous other definitions exist around the world.

The variability in conceptual definitions like these is further complicated by the difficulty of moving from a conceptual definition to an operational definition. For example, a conceptual definition may involve sustainability, but when one tries to measure whether someone is an ecotourist or some tourism activity is ecotourism, a more precise definition of sustainability is needed. What are the criteria one uses to determine whether the activity is sustainable and thus qualifies as ecotourism?

Most conceptual definitions of ecotourism can be reduced to the following: "ecotourism is tourism and recreation that is both nature-based and sustainable," and it is this definition that is used here. Three features of this definition merit further discussion. First, the definition clarifies the descriptive and the prescriptive components of the ecotourism concept. The nature component is descriptive or positive in the sense that it simply *describes* the activity location and associated consumer motivations. The sustainable component is prescriptive or normative in the sense that it reflects what people *want* the activity to be. An important point is that, as used here, sustainability incorporates environmental, experiential, sociocultural, and economic dimensions.

The rest of this section shows that there is significant diversity in definitions of ecotourism and in the characteristics of ecotourism experiences. Typically, and as used here, most tourism activities that occur in natural areas are loosely considered ecotourism. In practice, ecotourism is concerned with making all nature tourism activities more sustainable-with achieving the conceptual definition presented above.

Second, this basic conceptual definition incorporates more complex definitions. For example, some definitions focus on minimizing negative environmental and cultural impacts while maximizing positive economic impacts. Such a focus is a means to the end of achieving sustainability. Likewise, the definitional focus on environmental education tends to reflect a desire to satisfy tourists or to use education to reduce negative environmental impacts. In the former case, it is a means to the end of achieving a sustainable experience. In the latter, it is also a means to the end of sustainability. Because most components of ecotourism definitions either focus on the goal of sustainability or on means to achieve that goal, it is practical to use the simple conceptual definition of ecotourism being sustainable nature-based tourism and recreation.

Third, and related to the second feature, by focusing on ends (the desired condition of sustainability), this definition forces critical evaluation of what constitutes ecotourism. For example, is sport hunting ecotourism? Many observers feel that hunting is not ecotourism, but under this definition it would be if it met the sustainability criterion. Though hunting will be inconsistent with concepts of sustainability in some natural areas (or may be rejected on other grounds), it may be appropriate in others. Similarly, a large commercial group of tourists paying an entry fee to visit a hardened visitor centre and associated rainforest board walk may qualify as ecotourists to the same degree as a small group of visitors following low-impact principles in a pristine wilderness.

Given the importance of sustainability within the ecotourism definition, a fundamental question is "What is sustainability?" In simplified terms, tourism sustainability is postulated to result from a positive overall balance in environmental, experiential, sociocultural, and economic impacts ("experiential impact" is used to describe the effect of visitors on each other and "sociocultural impact" is used to describe the effect of visitors on local residents). Thus, tourism activities that generate more positive net benefits would be more sustainable, in general, than tourism activities that generate fewer positive net benefits.

The focus on benefits also clarifies ecotourism-related objectives. Historically, many sites have sought to increase the number of tourists, but this objective slowly is giving way to increasing tourist expenditure (a positive benefit), which does not always require increasing the number of tourists. Hopefully, this objective will progress to one of increasing income generated in the region of question (again, which need not involve an increase in expenditure). Ultimately, the objective should be to increase net benefits, a measure of benefits less costs. This refinement of objectives to focus on net benefits enhances the likelihood that ecotourism will be sustainable.

With respect to visitor types and activities, a key consideration is the diversity within the ecotourism market. Ecotourists may differ greatly in several aspects, including:

- distance travelled;
- length of stay;
- desired level of physical effort and comfort;
- importance of nature in trip motivation;
- level of learning desired;
- amount of spending;

- desired activities; and
- personal demographics.

For example, ecotourism experiences can range from: 1) a foreigner spending thousands of dollars coming to Australia on a commercial tour to visit the Great Barrier Reef and the Wet Tropics rainforests to, 2) a local resident camping over the weekend at an adjacent national park. Ecotourists might engage in a wide range of activities, including trekking (hiking, bush walking), climbing, camping, hunting, photography, sightseeing, fishing, bird watching, whale viewing, and general exploration of remote natural areas.

Of particular interest, visitor surveys and anecdotal reports indicate that many ecotourists feel it important for their visit to contribute to conservation and local development. Though this is not important for all ecotourists, it does present additional motivation for businesses and government agencies to support conservation and development efforts.

Lindberg (1991) provides a typology of nature/ecotourism types, though many other typologies are possible:

- ***Hard-core:*** scientific researchers or members of tours specifically designed for education, environmental restoration, or similar purposes.
- ***Dedicated:*** people who take trips specifically to see protected areas and who want to understand local natural and cultural history.
- ***Mainstream:*** people who visit the Amazon, the Rwandan gorilla park, or other such destinations primarily to take an unusual trip.
- ***Casual:*** people who partake of nature incidentally, such as through a day trip during a broader vacation.

Actors in the Ecotourism "System"

Ecotourism often involves numerous actors, including:

- Visitors;
- Natural areas and their managers, including both public and private areas;
- Communities;
- Businesses, including various combinations of local businesses,

in-bound operators, outbound operators, hotel and other accommodation providers, restaurants and other food providers, and so on;

- Government, in addition to its role as a natural area manager; and
- Non-governmental organizations, such as environmental and rural development NGOs.

The relevant actors will vary across sites. For example, local communities may be present at some sites, but not others. Likewise, businesses may play a large role at some sites, but little or no role at others.

A common phenomenon is that ecotourism can generate both symbiosis and conflict between the actors. The potential for ecotourism to result in symbiosis between conservation and development has been widely touted, but the potential for conflict should not be ignored. For example, natural area managers and ecotourism businesses have a shared interest in conserving the natural environment. However, there often is conflict regarding the point at which tourism activity jeopardizes this conservation.

Overview of Tourism and Ecotourism in the Asia-Pacific Region

* Tourism in the Region

* Future Growth in Tourism in the Region.

* Ecotourism in the Region.

* Past and Future Ecotourism Growth in the Region.

This section provides quantitative and qualitative information regarding tourism and ecotourism in the Asia-Pacific region. The statistical data are based on World Tourism Organization (WTO) and World Travel and Tourism Council (WTTC) estimates. In addition, the WTO figures in particular generally are for international tourism and do not include domestic tourism, which often is quite substantial.

More importantly, readers should remember the inherent limitations of tourism and ecotourism statistics. There are a several problems associated with measuring tourist flows and resulting economic impacts (WTO 1997). One of these problems is the lack of a universal definition of tourism. *Thus, the data presented here should be treated with caution.* Caution is even more important when one turns to ecotourism, as definitions of this activity are even less universal. There have been relatively few attempts to develop an operational definition of ecotourism, one that allows the number of ecotourists or their economic impacts to be measured. Therefore, there have been very few estimates of the importance of ecotourism, either in absolute terms or as a proportion of tourism generally. Moreover, for practical reasons, the estimates that have been made typically are based on definitions focused on the nature component, with little or no consideration of the sustainability component. Thus, estimates typically reflect nature tourism rather than ecotourism. *In short, currently it is all but impossible to estimate with any accuracy the importance of ecotourism in the Asia-Pacific region.*

Given these important caveats, the following information provides an indication of tourism and ecotourism in the region.

Tourism in the Region

As noted by the WTO (1996), the Asia-Pacific region has experienced rapid tourism growth during the past decade. The absolute and relative growth in arrivals and receipts. As illustrated by the figures, tourism in the East Asia and Pacific region has grown much faster than in the South Asia region, and somewhat faster than global tourism. WTO (1997) estimates that the East Asia and Pacific region had 87 million international arrivals in 1996, with South Asia having 4.5 million international arrivals in that period. These arrivals generated US$80.8 billion and US$4.0 billion in receipts, respectively. The importance of tourism relative to other economic sectors is illustrated by the share of tourism receipts in services and merchandise exports (WTO 1997:18):

The Asia-Pacific region thus accounted for about a sixth of world international arrivals and nearly a quarter of receipts in 1996 (editor).

Region	*Share of tourism receipts in services*	*Ratio of tourism receipts to merchandise exports*
Northeast Asia	30.3%	3.6%
Southeast Asia	42.3%	8.8%
Australasia (AU + NZ)	46.7%	13.9%
Other Oceania	260.4%	63.5%

Though tourism plays a particularly important role in Oceania, these figures indicate its importance throughout the East Asia and

Pacific region. WTTC (1997) estimates of travel and tourism's impact on regional output are (includes domestic tourism, amounts in US$ billions):

Northeast Asia	751
Southeast Asia	105
South Asia	46
Oceania	67

Within the East Asia and Pacific region, the top ten countries in terms of international tourism receipts, excluding transport, for 1996 are (WTO 1997:51, amounts in US$ billions):

Hong Kong	10.8
China	10.2
Australia	8.7
Thailand	8.5
Singapore	7.9
Indonesia	6.1
Korea (Rep.)	5.4
Japan	4.1
Malaysia	3.9
Macau	3.5

The top ten East Asia and Pacific countries in terms of average annual growth rate for receipts, 1986-1996, are (WTO 1997:40, 43, 46):

Indonesia	26.3%
Australia	20.9%
China	20.9%
Vanuatu	20.9%
Macau	20.8%
Malaysia	19.9%
Thailand	19.6%
N. Mariana Is.	17.0%
Hong Kong	16.8%
Singapore	16.2%

Importantly, the region is not solely a recipient of visitors from outside the region. Indeed, the following figures for market share (percent of total arrivals in East Asia and the Pacific coming from each source region, 1996) indicate that countries within the region generate most of the region's tourism arrivals (WTO 1997:54):

East Asia/Pacific	79.3%
Europe	11.4%
Americas	6.9%
South Asia	1.6%
Africa	0.5%
Middle East	0.4%

Using a different country grouping, the Pacific Asia Travel Association (1996) reports that 61% of the international arrivals in the Pacific Asia region originated from Asia, up from only 45% a decade ago.

The current importance of intraregional travel is illustrated by the case of Malaysia. As of 1994, the ten largest markets for Malaysia were, in decreasing order (MCAT 1995):

The future importance of intraregional travel is illustrated by efforts by national tourism organizations and the private sector to increase such travel. For example, Tourism Malaysia's bimonthly publication *Malaysia Tourism* summarizes efforts to attract the Japanese, Chinese, Indonesian, and Indian markets.

Future Growth in Tourism in the Region

As noted by the WTO (1997: 10, 34), the reasons for regional tourism growth include:

- rapidly growing income;
- freer intraregional travel;
- increased leisure time;
- dynamic trade and investment;
- government promotion measures, such as launching "visit years"; and
- political stability in many of the region's countries.

Many of these factors are expected to continue, with the result being continued tourism growth into the future. Indeed, the East Asia and Pacific region is expected to surpass the Americas to become the world's number two tourism region by 2010, with 229 million international arrivals (WTO 1996). Of all the WTO regions, East Asia and Pacific is forecast to have the highest average annual growth rate (7.6%) between 1990 and 2010, with South Asia having the second highest rate, at 6.7% (the world rate is forecast at 4.1%).

The growth in arrivals is expected to result from roughly equal growth in the various source markets, including East Asia and the Pacific countries. Intraregional source market growth is particularly expected from the emerging economies of China, Korea, Malaysia, the Philippines, and Singapore (WTO 1997).

The WTTC (1997) estimates that regional tourism output will increase by the following percentages in the ten years from 1997 to 2007:

Northeast Asia	52%
Southeast Asia	103%
South Asia	119%
Oceania	44%

Ecotourism in the Region

There has been much discussion and debate regarding the size and growth of the ecotourism market. Although supporters of ecotourism, or any other phenomenon, like to provide large estimates, others question this growth in some contexts. Estimates of market size depend on the definition used to describe the market. As noted above, the lack of a widely-accepted operational definition of ecotourism hinders estimates of the ecotourism market and prevents effective comparisons across sites. Moreover, because the sustainability component of ecotourism definitions is particularly difficult to measure, most existing estimates are based solely on the nature-based component. Therefore, most estimates of ecotourism really are estimates of nature tourism.

Keeping in mind that estimates should be treated with caution, Ceballos-Lascurin (1993) reports a WTO estimate that nature tourism generates 7% of all international travel expenditure. Campbell (1994) reports that approximately 20% of all foreign tourists to Thailand (in 1990) visited nature tourism sites. In some countries, such as Australia, the percentage is even higher. *Assuming that the Asia-Pacific region follows the global pattern, 7% might be used as an extremely rough estimate of the region's international tourism that can be viewed as ecotourism, with several countries exhibiting higher proportions.*

Lew (1997) divides ecotourism in the region into three zones: 1) South and Southeast Asia, which together comprise the major international destination region, 2) Australia and New Zealand, which have substantial domestic ecotourism industries, as well as a secondary international market, and 3) the peripheral ecotourism areas, including China and Japan to the north, and the Pacific islands to the east.

A thorough evaluation of ecotourism offerings and experiences across the region's countries was not possible given limited project resources. However, one ecotourism operator with many years of experience in Southeast Asia ranks countries in the following decreasing order in terms of ecotourism experiences: Papua New Guinea, Malaysia, Indonesia, Thailand, and the Philippines. Several other countries are not ranked and do not play major ecotourism roles, including: Laos, Burma (Myanmar), Cambodia, and Vietnam.

Currently, most nature tourists at some sites and for some activities are foreigners, typically from North America, Europe, and Australia/ New Zealand. For example, Chudintra (1993) reports that 90% of Thailand's jungle tour clients are foreigners. However, domestic visitation predominates at many sites. For example, Campbell (1994) reports that about 90% of visitors to Indonesia's national parks are domestic tourists, while Chudintra reports that the percentage of such visitors in Thailand increased from 58% in 1986 to 85% in 1990. Further information on adventure and ecotourism source markets is provided in Aderhold (1996) and Weight.

The characteristics of ecotourists and ecotourism vary widely across sites in the region. Nonetheless, Taman Negara in Malaysia illustrates some of these characteristics (DWNP 1996a, 1996b; Stecker 1996). From 1984 to 1993, visitor numbers increased 360%, from 8,200 to 30,000, respectively. Numbers have continued to increase, reaching 36,924 in 1994 and 43,491 in 1995 (an 18% growth rate from 1994 to 1995). Of the 1995 visitors, 48% were Malaysian, 8% Singaporean, 7% British, and 7% German.

The majority of the visitors were male (58%), young (89% under 40 years old), university educated (71%) and of high income. Motivations for visiting the park include:

* To see and experience rain forests (45% of respondents).
* For a holiday (16%).
* To get new experience (10%).
* For relaxation and sightseeing (8%).
* To see wildlife (8%).
* For recreation and adventure (6%) and
* To enjoy the camping life (3%).

Activities undertaken by visitors include (in decreasing order of frequency) jungle trekking, bird watching, swimming, caving, visiting indigenous forest dwellers, botany, mountain climbing, and fishing. Somewhat more than a third of the visitors were on prearranged package tours from Kuala Lumpur, while somewhat less than two-thirds made their own travel arrangements.

Past and Future Ecotourism Growth in the Region

Though estimates of ecotourism's growth are rare, due to the definitional problem, most observers feel that ecotourism has grown faster than tourism generally during the past several years. Based on a survey of ecotourism operators in the region, Lew (1997) found that average annual growth rates have been steady at 10% to 25% over the past few years, and many are projecting higher growth in coming years.

There are various explanations for ecotourism's growth, including:

- increasing environmental awareness and interest, including the desire to be perceived by others as environmentally sensitive;
- increased media exposure to natural areas around the world;
- related to the above two, a desire to see natural areas before they disappear;
- increasing dissatisfaction with traditional tourism destinations and products, and a desire for more educative and challenging vacations;
- desire to go to novel destinations, sometimes as a way to "outdo" others; and
- easier access to remote ecotourism destinations through development of air routes, roads, and other infrastructure.

Insofar as the increased motivations to experience and preserve natural environments stem in part from more fundamental changes in societal values, the continuation of these fundamental changes, particularly in developing countries, should lead to continued growth in demand for ecotourism. Many observers believe that the growth rate for ecotourism will be higher than for tourism generally. Thus, assuming an increase in the proportion of tourism represented by ecotourism from 7% to 10% and assuming that the WTO forecast of 229 million international arrivals by 2010 is accurate, *an extremely rough estimate of the region's international ecotourism arrivals for 2010 would be 22.9 million.* To this, one must add the substantial number of domestic visitors to natural areas.

The ecotourism market is expected to evolve over time. Much of the ecotourism growth probably will stem from intraregional travel. As noted above, growth in intraregional travel is expected for tourism generally as incomes rise and infrastructure improves. Moreover, intraregional ecotourism in particular is expected to grow as regional population centres become increasingly crowded and polluted, and as increased wealth and education lead to greater knowledge of, and interest in, the natural environment.

The growth in Asian ecotourism source markets will affect the type of experience sought by visitors. In general, it is expected that Asian ecotourists will travel in larger groups and will demand a higher degree of comfort than is the case for western ecotourists. They also may be more interested in ecotourism day trips while lodging and dining in comfortable resorts. An example of this is the Juldis Khao Yai resort and golf course on the border of Khao Yai National Park in Thailand. Asian visitors (mostly Japanese) flock to see the park, play golf, and stay in luxury in the middle of jungle surroundings.

Evolution probably also will result from demographic changes occurring in society. For example, in source countries the "babyboomer" population is ageing, which will increase leisure time amongst this group. However, the group may require ecotourism experiences that are less physically demanding, more easily accessible, and with more comfortable facilities.

In addition, various factors affect the types of ecotourism experiences sought. For example, substantial media attention has been focused on the loss of tropical rainforests, and many tourists wish to visit them partly out of a concern that they may be lost entirely. Future interest in forest visitation may depend on continued media coverage and public concern about forest issues.

Other trends, such as the increased popularity of SCUBA diving, may affect forest-related ecotourism to varying degrees, depending on individual site characteristics. For example, forest areas near dive sites may benefit from add-on trips to the forest by divers. On the other hand, some forest areas may lose visitation as potential visitors choose diving-oriented trips rather than terrestrial-oriented trips. Unfortunately, it is extremely difficult to identify future trends of this sort.

Several other factors, many of them external, may affect demand at individual sites and countries. For example, political or economic instability may cause strong decreases in visitation, an event that has at times affected tourism demand for many countries in the Asia-Pacific region. In summary, historic data, trends, and expectations indicate that:

- tourism makes a substantial contribution to the region's economy;
- tourism has experienced rapid growth in the region (though less so in South Asia), and this growth is expected to continue;
- ecotourism in the region and globally has grown faster than tourism generally, and this probably will continue over the next several years;
- domestic and intraregional visitors are an important component of the region's ecotourism, and this importance is expected to increase in the future; and
- ecotourism demand will evolve over time, and the region's ecotourism sites will need to adapt to these changes.

The Dimensions of Ecotourism

* Environmental Dimension.
* Experiential Dimension.
* Sociocultural Dimension.
* Economic Dimension.

Environmental Dimension

By definition, the descriptive component of ecotourism involves the natural environment as an attraction. Conversely, the prescriptive component involves the impacts of visitation on the natural environment.

Although most discussions of this dimension focus on negative impacts, ecotourism also can generate positive environmental impacts. For example, some tours involve cleaning trails or undertaking rehabilitation work. Also, ecotourism indirectly can generate positive impacts by increasing political and economic support for natural area conservation and management.

Some argue that ecotourists are motivated to preserve the environment, so one would expect them to generate little or no negative environmental impact. However, as Wall (1994) pointed out:

- ecotourists often go to environmentally fragile areas, such as alpine and arid areas;
- visitation may occur during sensitive periods, such as during breeding or hatching periods;
- visitation by ecotourists eventually may lead to mass tourism at the site, such that the ultimate impact is much greater than the initial impact; and
- visitation may cause off-site impacts, such as the consumption of aeroplane fuel.

Despite the centrality of the environment to ecotourism, there is relatively little accumulated knowledge regarding ecotourism's impacts on the environment and the effect of these impacts on the ecotourist experience. In part, this is due to the complexity of these impacts, the difficulty of evaluating them rigorously, and the comparative lack of research in this area. Most of the analysis that has been undertaken has focused on North America or Europe and has appeared within the recreation or natural science literatures. Although several recent publications deal with tourism's environmental impacts, there also is relevant literature from the recreation field.

Ecotourism's impacts often are categorized using groups like "direct" (effect or the visitors themselves) and "indirect" (effect of the infrastructure or activities necessary to provide the visitor experience) or "on-site" and "off-site". Using the latter groups, some on-site impacts include:

- soil erosion and compaction;
- disturbance of wildlife;
- trampling of vegetation;

- removal of vegetation (e.g., collection of plants or firewood);
- accidental introduction of exotic species;
- increased frequency of fire; and
- litter and vandalism.

Some off-site impacts include:

- reclamation of land for infrastructure;
- generation of solid waste;
- water and air pollution; and
- purchase of souvenirs utilizing threatened or endangered species.

Given that ecotourism can generate some negative environmental impacts, the critical questions become:

- What are the acceptable levels of these impacts?
- What is the relationship between use and level of impact?
- How is this relationship affected by management activities?

The question of acceptable levels is particularly thorny and has frustrated resource managers and other stakeholders for years. The answer is political rather than technical, and different stakeholders provide different answers.

The relationship between use and level of environmental change is difficult to evaluate, in part because few environmental parameters are amenable to the requirements of experimental design needed to establish causal relationships. As a result, many studies are correlative rather than causal. The reliance on monitoring as a replacement for experimental analysis is an example of this problem. Monitoring can provide useful information, but one should be careful when inferring causality from monitoring studies due to the potential presence of confounding factors.

The research that has been conducted indicates that use-impact relationships generally are non-linear and vary across parameters. For example, the relationship between use and soil compaction may be different than the relationship between use and wildlife disturbance. Commonly, the relationship is asymptotic curvilinear, with marginal impacts at high use levels being small or nonexistent. That is, a medium number of visitors may cause significant change, but additional visitors may not cause significant additional change. Studies of recovery from impacts indicate that recovery occurs more slowly than the initial impact. Given such relationships, the common strategy of dispersion may be misguided, and concentration may cause less overall impact.

To further complicate matters, several factors may affect use-impact relationships, including:

- level of site hardening;
- types of visitors and their activities;
- characteristics of the organism impacted; and
- timing and location of interaction.

Experiential Dimension

Most of the attention within ecotourism, and within sustainable tourism generally, has been on environmental sustainability. However, tourism should be sustainable in other dimensions, including the experiential dimension. If the visitor experience is sufficiently degraded there will be a reduction in visitation that jeopardizes sustainability. Despite the relative inattention paid to experiential impacts within the ecotourism literature, they have been a focus within the recreation literature. For some sites, experiential impacts may be a greater limiting factor than environmental impacts.

At the most basic level, managers should monitor the quality of the visitor experience to determine what can be done to address concerns and to improve experience quality. Often, experiential improvements focus on the addition (or removal) of specific infrastructure or programmes. However, the experience often depends on how visitors affect each other. Such experiential impacts can be grouped into three categories:

- ***Crowding***, in which the quality of the experience is reduced by visitor perceptions that they saw too many other people during their visit.
- ***Conflict***, in which the quality of the experience is reduced by visitor perceptions of incompatibility or animosity with other visitors.
- ***Environmental degradation***, in which the quality of the experience is reduced by visitor perceptions of environmental deterioration caused by other visitors.

These impacts, and the associated concept of satisfaction, often are complex, affected by a variety of factors, and can be difficult to measure accurately. Satisfaction is particularly problematic because simplistic measurement of this concept is popular amongst natural area managers yet can provide misleading information. For example, high levels of reported satisfaction may lead managers to become complacent. However, current visitors may report satisfaction while nonetheless desiring improvement in facilities, activities, or conditions. In addition, previous visitors who were unsatisfied during their visit likely would not be represented in the sample of current visitors, as they would have stopped coming to the site, a process known as displacement in the recreation literature. Similarly, potential visitors may never have come to the site due to word-of-mouth or otherwise-obtained knowledge regarding the experience offered.

The concern over environmental degradation, resulting from tourism or other causes, and its effect on the visitor experience is widespread. It has been argued that environmental integrity must be preserved if the visitor experience is to be maintained, thereby providing an additional rationale for conservation. However, the extent to which visitor experiences are affected by environmental degradation has not been well researched, and the research that has been conducted suggests that visitors often do not notice tourism-related environmental degradation. This is an area that would particularly benefit from additional research.

Sociocultural Dimension

As with the natural environment, the sociocultural environment serves as both an ecotourism attraction and a recipient of ecotourism's impacts. If these impacts become, on the whole, too negative, the local sustainability of ecotourism can be jeopardized. In some areas local residents have been sufficiently unhappy with ecotourism development that they sabotaged the natural resource on which this development was based. Many ecotourism activities involve relatively intense interaction between greatly differing cultures, and these differences may exacerbate the negative sociocultural impacts of ecotourism.

The impacts of tourism on host communities, and resulting resident attitudes toward tourism, have been popular research topics in the past several years. In addition, many policy makers are now becoming aware of the need 1) to incorporate local communities into the tourism development and natural area management process and 2) to understand and address the negative impacts on communities.

Though the difference between cultural and social impacts is blurry, one grouping might include the following as cultural impacts:

- Commodification of culture, in which cultural symbols are treated as commodities to be bought and sold;
- Changes in group social structure, the way in which lives are ordered and patterned;
- Changes in cultural knowledge, the body of information possessed; and
- Changes in the way in which cultural property is used and viewed.

The following grouping is of common social and sociophysical impacts. Depending on how tourism is developed, these impacts might on balance be positive or negative, and this balance may affect resident attitudes toward tourism:

- Economic—tourism can generate a wide variety of economic benefits (such as jobs) and economic costs (such as inflation).
- Disruption—tourism can generate an increase in traffic congestion, crowding in stores and other areas, and crime.
- Recreation facilities—tourism can increase both the number of recreation facilities and the demand for such facilities (recreation is used broadly here to include outdoor recreation, urban entertainment, and related activities).
- Aesthetic—tourism can contribute to an aesthetically pleasing environment, for example, by catalyzing waterfront revitalization; however, it can also detract from an aesthetically pleasing environment by, for example, leading to construction that is deemed inappropriate or by increasing the amount of litter or vandalism.
- Interaction with nonresidents—tourism can lead to satisfying relationships with nonresidents, even if those relationships are brief.
- Interaction with residents—tourism can affect local social relationships among residents, such as by reducing the friendliness of local residents.

- Community/culture—because tourists often are motivated by the desire to experience the host community and its culture, tourism can affirm that culture and lead to community pride; it also can disrupt local cultures, particularly when international tourists visit remote areas with little historic foreign contact.
- Influence over community decisions—studies have shown that residents are more supportive of tourism when they have been able to influence the tourism development process.

These impacts, and resulting attitudes, can strongly affect the viability of ecotourism.

For example, commercial tourism activity in natural areas in Australia is undergoing a period of rapid expansion. In Victoria's Alpine National Park, the number of licenses granted to tourist operators has increased fourfold in the past five years to more than 110. This level of growth, and the perception that park policy now favours tourism interests over use by local residents, has resulted in antipathy toward tourism. This may lead to ecotourism becoming the next target for the national park movement, thereby jeopardizing access privileges to natural areas.

Economic Dimension

The final dimension is economic. There are various stakeholders in ecotourism, from operators to natural area managers to local communities. One thing they have in common is that they often seek economic benefits from ecotourism, whether it be sales and profits for operators, user fee revenues for natural area management, or jobs and income for local communities.

With respect to natural area finance, many public natural area systems around the world have encountered severe financial difficulties as the number of national parks and other areas has grown while funding has remained stable or declined. As a result, many area managers and environmentalists have turned to ecotourism as a source of revenue, as a means to at least cover the ecotourism-related park costs that historically have been financed by governments.

There have been numerous studies of user fees in the ecotourism context. Though a full discussion of this issue is beyond the scope of this paper, several points are worth noting. First, the appropriate fee system will depend on the objectives for the area. If the objective is to generate revenue, fees should be relatively high. If the objective is to maximize the number of visitors to provide job opportunities for local businesses, than the fees should be low or nonexistent.

Second, there are strong economic reasons for charging user fees, including that ecotourism generates costs that would otherwise need to be financed by non-users. In the case of developed country visitors to developing country public natural areas, it is particularly inappropriate for relatively poor local non-users to subsidize the visits of relatively wealthy users.

Third, most analyses conclude that current fee levels at most sites could be increased with little or no impact on the number of visitors. In cases where fee increases would reduce the number of visitors, such increases may remain appropriate as a means to maximize total revenue and/or reduce negative environmental, experiential, or social impacts. Fourth, often, there are opportunities for increasing non-fee revenues, such as through donation programmes or through souvenir sales.

With respect to job creation, natural areas provide many benefits to society, but few are tangible. Ecotourism-related jobs are one of the most tangible benefits provided by these areas.

In some cases, these jobs can provide direct alternatives to practices, such as poaching of forest products, that threaten natural area conservation. In other cases, the jobs will simply, but importantly, diversify local economies. As ecotourism jobs increase, it is likely that support for the natural areas providing the jobs will increase. Conversely, if ecotourism is perceived to generate more costs than benefits, it may reduce local support for natural areas.

The economic impacts of tourism, or any economic activity, can be grouped into three categories: direct, indirect, and induced. *Direct impacts* are those arising from the initial tourism spending, such as money spent at a restaurant.

The restaurant buys goods and services (inputs) from other businesses, thereby generating *indirect impacts*. In addition, the restaurant employees spend part of their wages to buy various goods and services, thereby generating *induced impacts*. Of course, if the restaurant purchases the goods and services from outside the region, then the money provides no indirect impact to the region, it *leaks* away.

Figure 3: Tourism's Economic Impact

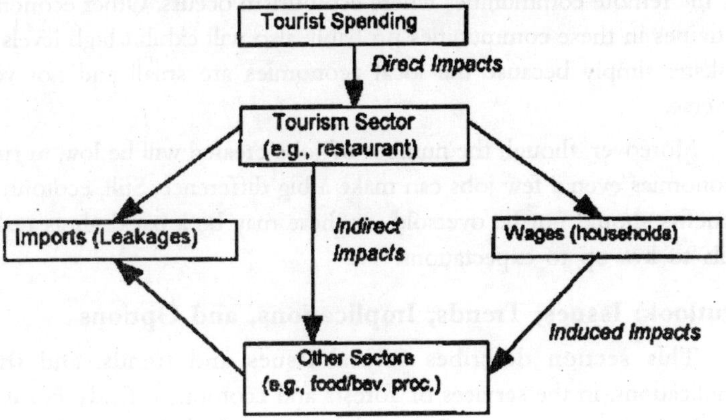

Several studies have assessed the local employment benefits of ecotourism. Not surprisingly, the level of benefits varies widely. In part, this is due to variations in the level of direct impact (tourist expenditure), which may depend on the quality of the attraction, access, and so on. In part, this is due to variations in the level of linkage (or, conversely, the level of leakage), which may depend on the size of the economy and other factors. The following estimates provide indications of the percentage of tourism spending leaking away from host country economies:

- 70% in Nepal.
- 60% in Thailand.
- 55 % for the typical developing country.

There is often wide variation in leakage estimates across sites. This is partly a result of the type of tourism development and the size of the economy being evaluated. Small-scale nature tourism tends to use more local goods than does large-scale traditional tourism. However, smaller economies may have more leakages because a lower diversity of goods is produced in small economies than in large economies. Variation in leakage estimates may also be due to definitions and methods used. More than 90% of tourism spending is thought to leak away from communities near most nature tourism sites.

Though the high level of leakage should be considered and should be reduced where possible, one should remember that this leakage not only results from the nature of the tourism industry, which requires substantial expenditure before arrival on-site, but also from the nature of the remote communities where ecotourism occurs. Other economic activities in these communities probably also will exhibit high levels of leakage simply because the local economies are small and not very diverse.

Moreover, though the number of jobs created will be low, in rural economies even a few jobs can make a big difference. Still, ecotourism benefits should not be oversold, or there may be a backlash as reality fails to live up to expectations.

Outlook: Issues, Trends, Implications, and Options

This section describes several issues and trends, and their implications, in the services of forests and ecotourism fields. For each of these, one or more options are presented for achieving objectives given the trends, with ecotourism objectives focusing on sustainability in the dimensions.

Issues and options relevant to tourism generally, such as infrastructure development and promotion, are not addressed in detail. Rather, this section focuses on issues and options that are particularly relevant to ecotourism and may be overlooked by traditional tourism planning and development. The issues tend to be interrelated, such that the grouping is somewhat arbitrary and is used as an organizational tool.

Many of the options will be familiar to readers. They are commonly-noted means for achieving the potential benefits of ecotourism. It is recognized that political and economic realities may hinder implementation of these options and thus achievement of ecotourism objectives.

In short, ecotourism rhetoric does not always translate into ecotourism reality. Nonetheless, the options are presented here to offer a vision of future possibilities and to guide those actions that are feasible. Many of the issues relate to achieving a balance between private and public objectives, between providing economic and other benefits from natural areas and conserving those areas.

Preserving Services Derived from the Forest: Protected Area and Social Forestry Approaches

Issue/trend: Though forest production provides important economic benefits in many of the region's countries, it (and other activities) also negatively impacts services of forests and ecotourism potential. Therefore, there is a need to implement programmes that maintain or enhance services of forests and ecotourism potential.

Options: Two options for maintaining and enhancing services derived from forests and ecotourism are implementation and management of *protected areas* and *social forestry* programmes.

Elsewhere in the world, notably in southern Africa, sometimes successful efforts have been made to bring wildlife into agricultural areas and basing tourism on this (Editor).

Protected areas and Their Management

Protected area systems can be seen as conservation mechanisms that incorporate social and cultural factors alongside legal, economic and political mechanisms and ecological insights. The movement towards a more inclusive policy context that integrates local people and their rights within protected area management frameworks is indicative of this.

In a report outlining the role of protected areas in the Asia-Pacific region, Braatz (1992) prioritized the need for integrated national strategies and investment focusing on programme development rather than species preservation. Braatz has identified three major objectives that will be crucial to the protection of biodiversity in the Asia-Pacific region:

- modifying policies that adversely affect biodiversity;
- reconciling local people's needs with protected area management; and
- ensuring the sustainability of investments.

In relation to participation, Braatz suggests there are three countries well suited to demonstrate the importance of participation:

- Indonesia because of its importance for biodiversity and its foreign assisted development programme;
- India because of its active NGOs and strong participatory process; and
- Papua New Guinea because some 97% of land there is under customary tenure.

Finally, in relation to sustainability of investments, Braatz suggests ecotourism and forest development as priority components.

Movements Towards a Community/Social Forestry Approach

Many government agencies and non-governmental organizations in the region are assessing the usefulness of community and social forestry approaches. In the specific context of policies and policy directions, these represent, at least potentially, an acknowledgement of the rights of local populations and the movement towards a policy context that incorporates a more inclusive range of interests and values.

Social forestry is seen as an important option for forest protection and the maintenance of services of forests. At least potentially, it exemplifies the characteristics of community involvement, participation, and development of some degree of self-reliance. In addition, it provides opportunities for reforestation and the maintenance or even enhancement of biodiversity with benefits accruing at the local level. It can also enhance the possibility for tourism and ecotourism. Social forestry programmes are those which are designed as to:

- motivate large numbers of people to plant trees;
- promote the kind of tree growing that best supplies firewood, small timber, grasses and income; and
- provide increased benefits to the poorer strata in society.

These programmes are especially aimed at involving farmers and the landless. Social forestry can incorporate a wide variety of activities, including farmers growing wood to sell or use for firewood, and individuals earning income from the gathering, processing and sale of minor forest products such as fruits nuts, mushrooms, herbs, basketry materials, honey, and vines. It can also include government and other groups planting trees on public lands to meet local village needs.

Unlike in conventional production forestry, where the focus is on the wood that trees produce, a social forestry approach focuses on people, on community involvement and on the trees that provide direct and indirect benefits locally. The approach therefore is used to create immediate economic and social benefits to local people or communities from their immediate locality. According to Gregersen, Draper and Elz (1989), social forestry is important for the following reasons:

- *Environmental protection connection:* Deforestation causes decline in agricultural land quality, soil degradation, flooding downstream results in loss of crops, and so on.

- *Agricultural productivity:* Social forestry can contribute to the livelihood of the poor by improving soil, providing food supplements, and providing wood for construction, fencing, fibre, shade, and fodder. Social forestry also can provide income for farmers and rural communities and can help raise people from mere subsistence. In many parts of the world, agroforestry, or the integration of tree growing into farming systems, is a main tool in social forestry programmes involving farmers. Agroforestry is a collective name for all land use systems and practices in which woody perennials are deliberately grown on the same land management unit as crops and/or animals.
- *Fuelwood:* Fuelwood is the primary source of energy for poorer urban households and for the vast majority of rural households in developing countries.
- *Employment:* Whilst social forestry cannot solve the problem, it can contribute to increasing locally available jobs and income.

However, social forestry is not a panacea. The assumption that local knowledge and management is preferable to western scientific knowledge and centralized management does not always hold true. Likewise, the role of women within social forestry does not always take into account the reality of family and class power relationships.

In summary, social forestry is an important option for resource management approaches incorporating a local development framework. At least potentially, it exemplifies important characteristics such as community involvement, participation, and building some degree of self-reliance. In addition, it provides opportunities for reforestation and the maintenance or even enhancement of biodiversity with benefits accruing at the local level. In this context, it also can enhance the possibility for tourism and ecotourism. It is probable that protected area establishment and social forestry programmes will expand in the future. However, a critical issue will be the level of financial and political support for both approaches, and thus the wealthier countries of the region probably will achieve the most progress in this regard. Protected area and social forestry programmes are not the sole options for preserving services of forests, but they can make important contributions toward this goal. If they are not effectively implemented, alternate approaches must be sought if this goal is to be achieved.

Need for Increased Research and Utilization of Results

Issue/trend: Ecotourism occurs within a competitive and complex environment, and this competition and complexity probably will increase in the future. As a result, the collection and utilization of information increasingly will be critical if effective policies and programmes are to be developed and implemented.

Options: Enhanced implementation of ecotourism-related research and utilization of research results. The research focus will depend on local information needs. However, a general recommendation is that topic areas be expanded beyond the common focus on identification and management of environmental impacts to include identification and management of social, economic, and experiential aspects, with the latter two categories including market research.

Insofar as research provides valuable information in decision-making processes, the conduct of research and use of results will enhance a site's ability to benefit from ecotourism while reducing its negative impacts.

Importance of Social Issues in Management

Issue/trend: There is a global tendency for protected area staff to be trained in the natural sciences, particularly biology or ecology. However, it has become clear that the challenges natural area managers face often are more social and political than ecological and technical, and it is likely that future challenges also will be significantly social/political in nature. As noted by Fazio and Gilbert (1986), natural resource management is 90% managing the public and 10% managing the resource. In particular, ecotourism has a technical ecological component, but it also has a significant social and political component.

Due to their training, and associated world view, it is natural for ecologically-oriented staff to seek technical solutions to problems that are at least partly sociopolitical. The focus on carrying capacity is an example of this. Likewise, planning and management tends to focus on the natural environment rather than on the human environment, and on visitation in particular.

In addition, often it is difficult for natural area staff to work effectively with tourism professionals, who typically have very different training, priorities, and personalities. As a result, it is difficult to develop the trust and personal relationships that contribute to effective cooperation. Lastly, often it is difficult for staff to work effectively with local communities.

Options: As part of the skill enhancement noted, there may be a focus on developing and/or recruiting social science skills amongst natural area staff. An increased focus on social issues and corresponding staff skills will enhance the ability of natural area managers to respond effectively to ecotourism and broader conservation challenges.

Continued Funding Difficulties in Natural Areas

Issue/trend: There has been a trend in many countries of stable or decreasing government funding for natural area management, despite increased pressure on these areas, including increased visitation. This imbalance between available resources and management needs may lead to deterioration at many natural areas.

To varying degrees, developing countries in the region have benefited from bilateral or multilateral (e.g., GEF) funding for natural area management. Moreover, economic growth in many countries may lead to increased financial and political support for natural areas in the future. Of course, this will vary across countries, in part based on varying levels of economic development. For example, funding for natural area protection and management is more likely to increase in Malaysia than in Burma or Laos.

However, any increase in funding may be offset as expenses increase. In particular, ecotourism generates financial and non-financial costs for natural areas. The historic and projected increases in ecotourism mean that these costs are likely to increase. However, ecotourism also provides a potential source of revenue. Though fees have been instituted or increased at various sites in the region, in general Asia-Pacific remains behind Latin America and Africa in terms of generating ecotourism-related funding for natural areas.

Options: Where the need for revenue outweighs other ecotourism objectives (such as the desire to provide open access to all visitors), visitor fees can be implemented/increased.

Collection and retention of fees not only increases available funding, but may also increase support for ecotourism amongst natural area managers. Many agencies responsible for natural areas have had strong conservation ethics of "resource protection" at all costs. Managers often are ambivalent and even hostile to the idea of tourism. This is made worse by tourist revenue being transferred to the central treasury. It is also reinforced by low budgets, few staff, and "all the tourist problems". Thus, retention of fees at the local level probably would increase managerial support for ecotourism.

At the most basic level, ecotourism can help address natural area funding difficulties only when fees are charged and when they benefit the area financially, usually through retention of fee revenue directly by the area. A recent survey of protected areas around the world indicates that only about half of the areas responding to the survey collected fees at that time.

Though there has been a trend toward implementation of fees over the past several years, many areas still charge little or no fee. Moreover, it is common for revenues from fees that are charged to be directed back to the general government treasury, thereby providing no direct benefit to the natural area.

An example of a site that charges fees but receives little direct benefit is the Dinghushan Biosphere Reserve (DBR) in China. DBR received an estimated 13.5 million yuan (approx. US$1.7 million) in entrance and related fees in 1995. However, this revenue has made little contribution to reserve management, as only 5% is allocated to the management agency (most of the money goes to the local government tourism bureau). Thus, substantial revenue is generated, but the revenue primarily has contributed to infrastructure development by local government rather than to environmental interpretation, visitor management, or general reserve management.

It is worth noting that results of a visitor survey at DBR indicate visitor support for a greater portion of entrance fee revenues to be dedicated toward reserve management, as opposed to local government. When asked how revenues from entrance fees should be distributed, 18% selected the "100% to conservation, research, and education" option while 43% selected the "75% to conservation and 25% to construction for tourism" option. Both options would represent a substantial change to the current distribution.

A similar distribution situation was found in study of tourism at Tangkoko Duasudara Nature Reserve in Indonesia. Kinnaird and O'Brien found that the Department of Forestry, which manages the reserve, receives only 2% of ecotourism revenues, and the reserve itself receives only a fraction of that. Mt. Everest in Nepal, where the climbing fee is US$50,000, provides an excellent example of capturing potential fee revenue. Though few sites are able to charge such high fees, the distribution of revenue from this fee to conservation programmes serves as an example for other sites. In addition, a portion of the US$700 per person fee for ten days of trekking in the Mustang region of Nepal goes to conservation and development programmes, while the 1993 amendment to Nepal's Wildlife Conservation Act provides for the distribution of 30% to 50% of protected area revenue to surrounding communities.

If it is determined that fees should be charged, there are various ways they might be applied, including:

- ***Entrance fee:*** collected when tourists enter the site.
- ***Admissions fee:*** charged for admission to a specific facility, such as a visitor centre.
- ***Use fee:*** charged for use of a specific object, such as rented equipment, or opportunity, such as a camping place.
- ***License or permit:*** like a use fee, this includes fees such as hunting or fishing permits.
- ***Sales and concessions:*** includes 1) profits from natural area sales of souvenirs, lodging and others goods or services, 2) license fees from concessions to sell these goods and services on site, and 3) revenues from licensing area logos and trademarks.

Experience in various countries suggests that:

- Fee systems will be most efficient if, within overall objectives, flexibility is provided for each site to implement the fee structure most appropriate to local conditions (that is, a single fee structure for the whole system may not be efficient).
- Earmarking at least a portion of fee revenues directly to the area collecting them (as opposed to the general government treasury) encourages efficient collection and enhancement of visitor experience quality.
- When fees are earmarked, this portion of the site's income becomes dependent on cyclical variations in visitation, such

that an endowment should be considered as a means to even out income over such variations.

- Multi-tier fee systems, in which some groups pay more than others, can be used to reduce concerns about equity; for example, foreigners might pay more than nationals, or pensioners might pay reduced fees.
- In areas with low visitation and/or multiple entry points, it simply may not be practical to collect entrance fees, though alternative systems (e.g., annual passes) can be used.
- The responsiveness of demand to fees may be reduced by "hiding" fees in larger expenditure items (such as by incorporating fees as part of the price of a whole tour) or by explaining the importance of fee revenue for maintaining the natural attraction.
- Often, there are opportunities for increasing non-fee revenues, such as through donation programmes or through souvenir sales.

Depending on how they are implemented (as well as on site characteristics and other factors), fees have the potential to significantly supplement traditional natural area funding

sources. If they are not implemented, ecotourism may make natural areas worse off because of the costs imposed by this activity.

Ecotourism Management: Low Level of Funding and Reliance on Simplistic Strategies Like Carrying Capacity

Issue/trend: The previous section notes the problem of insufficient natural area funding. With respect to ecotourism in particular, many countries and sites have devoted insufficient funding, political support, and research/analysis to managing ecotourism given the complexity of this activity with respect to both the natural and social environments. One of the results of the lack of support in the face of increased pressure is the reliance on simplistic management strategies such as carrying capacity.

Options: At the basic level, an important option is to provide to natural area managers the funds needed to implement the types of management strategies described. These funds will need to be supplemented by the development of staff skills, through training of existing staff and/or through hiring of new staff.

Next, a commitment to planning at various geographic levels may be made. In particular, effective planning requires explicit statements of ecotourism-related objectives and ongoing monitoring to determine whether those objectives are being achieved. UN FAO (1988), Inskeep (1991), MacKinnon et al. (1986), and WTO and UNEP (1992) are examples of resources available to guide and facilitate planning efforts.

Of particular concern is the popularity of the carrying capacity concept. Though this concept is appealing in its simplicity and helps draw attention to the possibility of "overdeveloping" ecotourism, it simply is not adequate to deal with the complexity found within the ecotourism context.

Therefore, it is proposed that this concept be avoided in favour of alternate frameworks that focus on identifying and maintaining desired conditions (these conditions might be environmental, experiential, social, and/or economic; for further discussion, see Harroun and Boo 1996; Lindberg, Mc Cool and Stankey 1996). Alternative frameworks not only are more appropriate, but also may be more accepted by the tourism industry, as the focus on conditions rather than numbers encourages management actions that reduce negative impacts per visitor rather than the number of visitors. Moreover, planning processes, such as the Limits of Acceptable Change system (LAC), that involve standards can be used to avoid the tendency, through multiple small developments, for tourism to undergo an undesirable amount of succession. For example, a wilderness site may slowly become more developed as the site is hardened, more and different types of people come, and hardening and infrastructure development continues. By setting standards reflecting wilderness qualities at an early stage, management has a guide and rationale for implementing actions consistent with the standard or rejecting actions that are inconsistent with the standard. Succession, and thus the value of good planning, is also relevant at the community scale. Pattaya (Thailand) has been used as an example of tourism that gradually developed well beyond its small village origin.

The recognition of ecotourism's complexity and the devotion of sufficient funding and support to its management will greatly enhance the likelihood of achieving ecotourism objectives in the long term.

Growth in International and Domestic Visitation

Issue/trend: As noted, the expected trend to 2010 is for continued ecotourism growth within the region. This growth can lead to increased impacts, both positive and negative, on natural areas.

Options: Strengthen visitor management in natural areas in order to achieve ecotourism objectives. Several strategies for doing so are provided below.

Much has been written about the management of tourists, particularly in natural areas. On-site management options include:

- ***Site hardening,*** such as building boardwalks.
- ***Selective marketing and restrictions on activities,*** such as marketing non-motorized uses and restricting motorized use.
- ***Managing behaviour,*** such as through education and persuasive communication (including use of visitor guidelines)-everything from keeping appropriate distances from animals to carrying out rubbish.
- ***Overall limitations on use,*** such as a maximum number of visitors per period for the site.
- ***Selective limitations on use,*** including:
- Refuge zoning, such as permanently prohibiting visitation in certain geographic areas.
- Buffer zones, such as prohibiting visitation within X meters of active bird nests or within Y meters of whales while whale watching.
- Temporal limitation, such as limiting visitation by season or time of day.

Of course, a combination of these strategies might be used. For example, visitors might be allowed within 50 m of bird groups during non-nesting periods, but only within 150 m during nesting periods. In addition, management of behaviour and spatial limitations can be achieved passively through trail/track and infrastructure design and layout rather than solely through more intrusive visitor guidelines. Though user fees typically are promoted as a way to generate revenue, they are also a potential management tool insofar as they can be used to limit use overall or distribute use spatially or temporally. Much attention recently has been directed at low impact design, construction, and management of visitor-related infrastructure in natural areas (CDOT 1995; Hawkins, Wood and Bittman 1995; US NPS 1993). Significant potential exists for the indirect environmental impacts of tourism to be reduced through utilization of alternate energy sources, the implementation of recycling programmes, and so on. The substitution of kerosene for firewood in Nepal is a widely-cited example of reducing such indirect impacts.

For both experiential and social reasons, it is recommended that buildings be designed in harmony with the local architecture and use traditional construction materials. Unfortunately, in many ecotourism areas, such as in Namche Bazaar in the Everest region of Nepal, lodges have been constructed of cement, which is unattractive to many western visitors.

Governments can play important roles in managing the environmental impacts of tourism infrastructure and operations through regulation and incentives. For example, in Malaysia the government has granted various incentives, such as pioneer status and income tax exemptions, to promote tourism investment. These incentives could be used to encourage environmentally sensitive practices, such as energy and waste minimization.

Strategies for managing environmental impacts also can be used to manage experiential impacts. For example, conflict often is caused by visitor behaviour, in which case there may be opportunities to manage conflict by managing behaviour through visitor education and guidelines. At the most general level, crowding can be managed by limiting the number of visitors.

A site might disperse and spatially limit certain activities to reduce crowding or conflict. For example, motorized activities might be allowed in some areas, but only non-motorized activities in other areas. If the area is of limited size, managers may need to determine the most appropriate or desirable activity, and then market and manage for that activity. The strategy of dispersal illustrates the potential for conflict between strategies to manage environmental versus experiential impacts. It may be sensible to *concentrate* use to minimize the real extent of environmental impacts, but it may be sensible to *disperse* use to minimize experiential impacts. With respect to increasing positive economic impacts, the issue of user fees and natural area finance is discussed.

With respect to increasing jobs and other economic benefits, the traditional approach is to increase the number of visitors. Given that negative impacts (environmental, experiential, sociocultural, and economic) correspond, to varying degrees, to visitor numbers, generally it will be preferable to increase local benefits by:

- increasing spending per visitor;
- increasing backward linkages (reducing leakages); or
- increasing local participation in the industry.

Spending per visitor can be increased through, for example, provision of handicrafts where such provision does not currently exist. Backward linkages can be increased through greater use of local agricultural and other products.

Though visitor management traditionally focuses on environmental and experiential impacts and, to a lesser degree, economic impacts, social impacts on local communities may have at least as great an effect on sustainability as do these other impacts. As one ecotourism operator put it, "ecotourism cannot be achieved if development is opposed by the community".

Probably the best way to minimize negative social impacts and enhance local economic benefits is to ensure local involvement in, and control over, tourism development. There are obstacles to local involvement, including local factionalism and a tendency toward centralized government planning. Moreover, this involvement may make tourism development slower and more expensive. However, it also probably makes it more sustainable. As noted by Brandon (1996), local residents can (and should) decide what level of tourism they want, what cultural practices they wish to share, and where tourists will be allowed to go. Several different levels of community involvement are possible, from full local development of facilities to partnerships or joint ventures with industry, to delegation of rights in exchange for fees. The Annapurna Conservation Area Project (ACAP) in Nepal is a commonly-cited example of effective local development of ecotourism.

The local involvement process should include education about probable tourism impacts so that residents can make an informed decision regarding the desirability of tourism. Lastly, development should keep in mind the impacts listed Sociocultural Dimension and should pursue opportunities for minimizing costs and maximizing benefits. For example, reduced access to resident recreational areas (e.g., beaches) is a commonly-cited cost of tourism, so continued resident access to these areas should be preserved.

Future increases in visitation can bring important economic and other benefits. However, it also can generate increased negative impacts. If effective visitor management is implemented, the benefits can be enhanced while the negative impacts are minimized. Indeed, in some cases it may be possible, through effective management, to reduce negative impacts from current levels despite an increase in visitation. On the other hand, if visitor management is not strengthened, increased visitation may severely jeopardize resource management and other objectives.

Change in the Visitor Market

Issue/trend: As noted in the previous section, the number of visitors is expected to increase at many of the region's natural areas. In addition, it is expected that the types of visitors (the visitor market) will change.

One of the primary changes will be in the balance of western and Asian visitors (with Asian visitors being both domestic and intraregional). Though growth is expected for western ecotourists, faster growth is expected for Asian ecotourists, such that the latter will comprise a larger proportion of all visitors. In general, Asian visitors are more likely to prefer larger group sizes, relative comfort, and easy site accessibility. They may seek forest-oriented experiences, but are more likely to do so in the context of trips taken for other purposes, such as golfing or diving.

Moreover, there often is divergence between the on-site experiences sought by Asians and westerners, and this will compound the need for effective management. The issue of divergent experiences is illustrated by the case of Dinghushan Biosphere Reserve (DBR) in China. Visitor survey results suggest that many DBR visitors (almost all of whom are domestic) are motivated by the opportunity to view scenery in the reserve, as well as to learn about nature. These motivations lead to support for restricting activities, including infrastructure development, that might threaten natural features. Nonetheless, observation of visitor behaviour in DBR suggests that these responses should be interpreted cautiously and with due regard to the cultural context. For example, there is a much higher tolerance for littering in the reserve than would be the case in many western reserves.

Moreover, cross-cultural evaluations of human relationships with the natural environment suggest that, relative to western cultures, eastern cultures tend to favour human manipulation of nature in order to enhance its appeal, in contrast to preservation of nature in a pristine state. Thus, DBR visitors may be more tolerant of human changes to the nature reserve than would be true of visitors in many western reserves (this tolerance extends to the acceptance of, and possibly preference for, buildings with modern material like concrete rather than more natural materials like wood).

Though little empirical research has been conducted on cross-cultural motivations and desired experiences in ecotourism settings, observation and discussion with researchers and reserve managers in many countries suggest that substantial cross-cultural differences exist. The example of litter suggests that perceptions of depreciation and environmental degradation caused by other visitors varies across cultures. Similarly, perceptions of crowding may vary across cultures. Of the 242 respondents (in the DBR visitor survey) who reported that they saw at least 200 other people during their visit, fewer than 25 % selected the number 5 or higher on a scale of 1 to 9, with 1 being "not at all crowded" to 9 being "extremely crowded." The reserve is located within two hours of a city of six million people, and it is unlikely that visitors expect a wilderness experience. Nonetheless, the level of crowding in the reserve probably is much more tolerable to Chinese visitors than to western visitors.

Of course, there is variability within cultures, with certain individuals and groups in Chinese society being more sensitive than others to environmental degradation and crowding. For example, Xing (1993) notes the high levels of visitation at Wuyishan, Changbaishan, and Huangshan reserves (with the latter having more than 10,000 visitors per day during peak periods) and observes that such visitation levels, and associated infrastructure, may devalue the natural beauty of the reserves.

Other trends also will cause changes in the visitor market. For example, the population in many source countries is ageing. Though older visitors may still seek ecotourism experiences, they are more likely to desire more comfort and greater site accessibility than their younger counterparts.

Options: Ecotourism is a business and, therefore, the ecotourism product needs to adapt to changes in the marketplace (or choose to accept static or declining visitation if adaptation will lead to changes that are unacceptable with respect to other management objectives). Thus, if natural areas are to take full advantage of ecotourism, they will need to evaluate the market most suited to the ecotourism product offered, as well as tailor the product to the desired market as far as practical and desirable. It may be difficult to simultaneously satisfy markets with disparate desires and tolerances, such that a variety of spatially or temporally separated ecotourism experiences may need to be offered within or across natural areas.

Continued or Increased Competition, Particularly for International Visitors

Issue/trend: Though regional ecotourism visitation levels are expected to increase, competition for these visitors also is expected to increase as new destinations are developed and as visitors become more sophisticated and discriminating in their choice of destinations. On the supply side, various countries in the region, such as Mongolia, have begun developing their ecotourism potential. On the demand side, many visitors are seeking more than a generic visit to a rainforest. They may search for specialized itineraries, trips involving significant contact with local communities, and high-quality interpretive programmes. Increased sophistication and expectations have been noted for westerners, but also will be increasingly true for Asian visitors in the future.

Thus, sites not only have to attract visitors in the face of increased supply, but they also have to provide a high quality experience once the visitors arrive, thereby helping to attract future visitors through word-of-mouth referrals.

Options: One innovative option for reaching potential visitors in a competitive marketplace is the Worldwide Web (WWW). Though the Web offers small ecotourism companies the opportunity to reach visitors around the world, Web marketing must be done well to be effective and should not be viewed as a panacea for attracting visitors. Numerous ecotourism operators and government agencies already are on the Web. Marketing efforts generally, and Web marketing in particular, provide excellent opportunities for public-private partnerships. In addition, destinations can maintain and enhance the quality of the visitor experience and offer the visitor something different than other sites and/or what the same site offered previously. Some sites have a natural advantage with respect to offering unique experiences.

For example, only China can offer giant pandas in their native habitat. However, other sites can develop competitive advantages through, for example, enhancing access or predictability, enhancing trip quality through improved interpretation, developing or linking with complementary attractions, and so on.

Increased competition, increased expectations on the part of visitors, and the apparent trend for ecotourists to be less likely than sun and sand tourists to make repeat visits presents substantial challenges to natural areas. A flexible, business-oriented approach to marketing and trip quality can help ensure continued visitation and visitor satisfaction. If sufficient action is not taken, traditional ecotourism destinations in the region may lose their market share to new destinations as they are developed. For example, Choegyal (1996) states that Nepal has lost market share to regional competitors.

Importance of Interpretation

Issue/trend: There is a need to more actively manage visitors and to enhance the quality of the visitor experience.

Options: Implement interpretive programmes as a means for achieving both of these objectives.

Development of interpretive centres and other interpretive material has occurred at many sites within the region. For example, the Malaysia Department of Wildlife and National Parks recently constructed interpretive centres at Bota Kanan and Sungkai (DWNP 1996a). However, interpretation has been largely neglected at many sites in the region. For this reason, and due to its importance in ecotourism, it is discussed in some detail here (further discussions are available in Ham (1992) and other interpretation resources). Though the focus here is on using interpretation to manage visitors and enhance the visitor experience, it also serves to develop a keener awareness of an area or issue and to promote public understanding of the natural area management agency and its policies.

Put simply, interpretation seeks to help people understand and appreciate the environment through various communication processes. Interpretation is more than just providing information or explaining the environment. Tilden (1977) defines interpretation as "an educational activity which aims to reveal meaning and relationships through the use of original objects, by first-hand experience and by illustrative media, rather than communicate factual information." The concept of interpretation is illustrated by the saying, "through interpretation understanding, through understanding appreciation, through appreciation protection".

The following are some of the considerations for effective interpretation:

- the level and type of education will depend on the interests and expectations of the tourist and will include a broad range of educational opportunities through interpretation, interactive and participative approaches, and the use of various media;
- the interpretive component may acknowledge the natural and cultural values of a destination and also can address issues such as resource management and the role and attitude of the host community;
- content can include information and orientation, rules and regulations, activities, local flora and fauna, ecological processes, management issues and the cultural history and prehistory of the area (in short, topics can be broad and varied, and are only limited by the imagination of the interpreters); and
- interpretive material should be easily accessible, accurate and stimulating to encourage responsible behaviour and an ongoing interest in the environment and conservation after the visit.

The "art" of interpretation has been well-developed in many countries, but planning has been slower to progress. It has frequently been omitted, ad hoc or in many cases reinvented. However, planning for interpretation can help managers:

- decide what they want to achieve, by identifying what opportunities are offered to raise public awareness, and what management issues can be addressed through interpretation; and
- work out the most effective and efficient way to achieve goals.

Proper planning is required for effective evaluation, and thus effective strategic planning. Upitis (1991) summarizes the questions that should be asked when planning interpretation:

- why communicate?
- what is the objective?
- what is the message?
- who is the audience
- how/when/where is the best way to communicate with the audience?
- what have we achieved?

Interpretation can be included as part of the management planning process of the site, rather than being considered as an afterthought. Interpretive considerations can have a major influence on the placement of facilities, such as trails/tracks and campsites.

The range and type of interpretation will vary considerably from country to country as well as site to site. In Asia and the Pacific, interpretive services have traditionally been fairly basic, and often have been designed for a limited domestic market. Interpretation is one area in which consideration must be given to the differences between domestic and international visitors. This is not just a challenge in terms of language, but also in terms of the type of media, style of presentation, and the content. Often, there will need to be provision for multilingual interpretation, whether in the written media or guides.

Interpretation also can be a valuable tool to increase the awareness and understanding of local people who may live adjacent to the natural area. Interpretation can illustrate how they can contribute to the protection and sustainability of the area's natural resources upon which they may depend for subsistence or income. Indeed Ceballos-Lascur in (1996) suggests that there is increasing evidence to indicate that on-site interpretive programmes in developing countries have an important strategic environmental education function.

Ceballos-Lascur in (1996) goes on to describe the case study of the Kanah National Park interpretive centre in India. The interpretive centre was created entirely by local staff and utilized local resources. The development of this highly successful interpretive centre has resulted in a number of spin-offs. It has demonstrated the abilities of the Indian staff and has encouraged other park managers to develop their own interpretive services. It has given interpretation a higher profile within the Indian parks system and has allowed the continued development of expertise in planning, design and development of other interpretive facilities. It is also significant that this project was developed as a partnership between the managers and the local people who had been relocated from the park when it was designated.

The effective implementation of interpretive programmes can greatly enhance the visitor experience, thereby making the site more competitive. In addition, interpretation can be used to manage visitors in a non-intrusive manner, thereby reducing negative impacts and increasing positive impacts. Moreover, it can be used to raise the general awareness and level of support for resource management policies and agencies.

Importance of Partnerships Among Ecotourism Actors

Issue/trend: Almost every ecotourism observer notes the importance of forming partnerships among ecotourism actors. Such partnerships not only promote the setting of balanced objectives, but also promote achievement of these objectives through utilization of the varied skills and contributions each actor can make. For example, government clearly has an important role in ecotourism, but the private sector and NGOs offer skills, flexibility, and political independence that government agencies and local communities may lack. Moreover, the private sector and NGOs may be more efficient in achieving objectives, even in such traditional public sector activities as conveying the importance of conservation to surrounding communities.

Despite significant barriers to forming and maintaining such partnerships, the fact that they can provide substantial benefits but currently are relatively rare leads many observers to expect a future increase in partnerships.

Options: Though the roles of actors within a partnership will vary across sites, Eagles (1995) provides some broad categories of roles that each sector might take on. *The public* sector role in ecotourism typically is to:

- provide environmental protection (the natural area itself);
- provide infrastructure, such as roads and airports;

- provide security and enforcement;
- monitor and control impacts;
- allocate access;
- provide information, such as through interpretive programmes; and
- resolve conflicts.

The *private* sector role in ecotourism typically is to:

- provide accommodation and food;
- provide transportation, such as busses and airlines;
- provide information, such as guides and brochures;
- promote sites to potential visitors; and
- provide consumer products, such as souvenirs.

Various types of partnerships might be pursued, with national or regional ecotourism councils as one option. A specific example of public-private partnership is the formation of the Nepal Tourism Board, with representation from both the private and public sectors.

An example of inter-agency cooperation is the Joint Committee on Nature Attraction Utilization in Indonesia, with representation by the Directorate General of Tourism and the Directorate General of Forest Protection and Nature Conservation. Joint marketing between natural areas, regional/national tourism agencies, and ecotourism businesses is another example of opportunities for partnerships to achieve mutual objectives in a cost-effective manner.

More extensive partnership opportunities also exist and likely will expand in the future. These include co-management of natural areas (e.g., government-NGO and government-local communities) and joint ventures between the private sector and local communities.

Depending on the type and effectiveness of the partnership, it can be an important means for achieving ecotourism and natural area management objectives more efficiently or in ways that individual actors alone simply cannot do.

Greater Private Sector Roles in Management of Natural Areas

Issue/trend: For a variety of reasons, including private sector pressure to access natural areas and lack of public sector funding for natural area management, there is a trend toward greater private sector roles in the management of natural areas. These roles vary across countries, but often involve private sector management of infrastructure and activities within parks.

The greater private sector role can increase funding for infrastructure development. Moreover, it can bring skills, including hospitality and tourism management skills, that may be lacking in natural area management staff. However, this trend also may jeopardize natural area conservation objectives. When private concessionaires lead infrastructure development, there may be a loss of economic benefit and management control. Important revenue-generating opportunities may be lost by natural area management agencies by offering "crown jewels" of tourism in concessions that do not reflect true financial value.

Options: The value of private sector participation should be recognized, but this participation must be balanced with conservation objectives if the latter are to be achieved. New public-private relationships need to be explored. Rather than react to lack of funding by inviting private sector leadership, other options may be pursued. One of these options is for the public sector to charge user fees and to take on a greater role in infrastructure. For example, it may be possible to follow the common hotel owner-management relationship, with public agencies investing the capital needed for infrastructure development and ownership, but with private companies hired as managers.

In simplified terms, natural area managers face three options with respect to pressure for increased private sector roles. First, the natural area can resist this pressure and retain the status quo, which limits negative impacts and loss of control, but also limits ecotourism-related benefits. Second, the natural area can follow a traditional concessionaire model, which may generate some additional revenue and may obviate the need for the natural area management agency to be involved in tourism itself. However, the revenue benefits may be less than their potential, and control may be lost.

Third, more creative relationships may be explored, such as the hotel model noted above. Though such an option would require some natural area agency involvement in tourism, this commitment likely would be repaid in terms of retention of control and greater financial benefits.

Pressure to Use Natural Areas for Activities that are Not Nature-Dependent

Issue/trend: Related to the previous issue/trend, there is pressure to use natural areas for activities that are not nature-dependent. For example, golf courses have been proposed, and in some cases developed, in several national parks and other protected areas in the region. At the same time, the supply of natural areas with little or no environmental degradation continues to decline. Therefore, it should be questioned whether it is either environmentally desirable or economically efficient to locate non nature-dependent activities in natural areas preserved for conservation or nature tourism purposes.

Options: In simplified terms, two options are to allow or to not allow non nature-dependent infrastructure and activities in national parks and similarly-designated natural areas. If they are allowed, the natural areas may gain concession fees and/or political support, but negative environmental and experiential impacts may outweigh these benefits.

Insofar as the infrastructure and associated activities are less dependent on intact ecosystems than is the case for ecotourism activities like bird watching, it may be better to locate them outside protected areas for both economic efficiency and conservation reasons.

Professionalization of Operators and Desire to Exclude Those Not Meeting Professional Criteria

Issue/trend: There is a trend toward enhancing the skills of ecotourism operators as part of the need to ensure high quality visitor experiences and to sustain the economic viability of these operators. Simultaneously, many *"bona fide"* ecotourism operators (those that adhere to ecotourism principles) are trying to differentiate themselves from operators who use the label solely as a marketing tool.

Options: Recognize the inherent difficulties for ecotourism operators, arising from the nature of small scale businesses operating in remote regions, and provide appropriate assistance through government agencies, industry associations, and vocational and/or university training programmes.

The following section describes some ecotourism operator difficulties and needs, using the Australian context as an example. Though there is variability across countries, similar difficulties exist elsewhere, and several observers stress the importance of enhancing professionalism amongst ecotourism operators.

Best estimates suggest that about 600 businesses are involved in the Australian ecotourism sector. Dozens of new operators are entering the industry monthly and a similar number likely are deciding the leave the sector. Cotterill's profile of the industry suggests that (in Australia):

- the industry is comprised of small operators with most having four or fewer staff;
- the average life of enterprises is 10 years; and
- each operator primarily provides either day tours or extended tours to one to three natural areas.

The industry faces many operational issues that will affect the long term viability of many businesses. Given a goal of sustainability, the industry as a whole, if not individual operators, must remain viable. A major issue for the sector is the lack of business expertise on the part of new entrants.

Most new entrants have little practical business or business planning background, and many also are woefully undercapitalized. Business planning emerged as one of the three most critical issues identified by Australian tour operators in a survey of new eco and adventure businesses conducted by the Victorian Tourism Operators Association (VTOA 1995).

Information needs include basic business planning, business development, marketing issues, accounting and book keeping, accessing finance, pricing, booking and reservations procedures, taxation issues, cost control and new business development. Indeed, the issues identified by the ecotourism sector are similar to those identified by the small business in general.

The lack of business expertise affects all aspects of the ecotourism operation including such fundamental issues as product development. Cotterill's (1996) research identified the need to package products better, coordinate itineraries, and improve product quality and presentation. The ecotourism sector is unique in that it serves small numbers of clients, often has a limited number of trips, and often is constrained by seasonality issues. As a result, gross revenues often are low and the industry as a whole faces seasonal cash flow crises.

Marketing often emerges as a key issue for ecotourism businesses. Traditionally, ecotourism products have not been marketed effectively through the travel trade. Many operators do not understand how the travel trade works. Moreover, many have not developed their pricing structure to accommodate the up-to-30% commissions demanded by wholesalers and in bound operators. On the other hand, the travel trade largely has been uninterested in selling ecotourism products. The in bound, wholesale, and retail travel system is geared to selling mass tourism experiences in which large numbers of people purchase carefully packaged and standardized products. Until recently, few travel agencies have been interested in selling specialist tourism products.

Practical operational problems that affect the profitability of some ecotourism operations also were identified. Cotterill (1996) cited the need to ensure product consistency. He notes that in some locations the accommodation is substandard for the quality and price of the experience offered. The end result is deficient product quality, which threatens to reduce consumer satisfaction.

Although many ecotourists are prepared to trough it, the facilities and services must be at suitable standards. A more strategic approach to planning the tour and a better understanding of satisfying client needs would address this weakness. In a similar manner, the effective hiring, management, training, and rewarding of staff emerged as a significant issue in the Cotterill (1996) study. The first imperative is to determine the appropriate staffing level. Some larger businesses have a client to staff ratio as high as 20:1. For specialist products, the client-staff ratio can be as little as 2:1.

The second imperative is to find enough suitably skilled staff to perform the necessary duties. Sourcing suitable staff in rural areas can be a problem, and training staff is costly. The third imperative is efficient employment in the face of seasonality. Like most tourism businesses, ecotourism operators experience peak periods in which large numbers of staff may be needed. During the rest of the operating season, a few key staff people may be suitable for operating the business. In the off season, an organization may have no need for any salaried staff.

Finally, Cotterill's (1996) research identified a number of personal issues as important factors that limit the commercial profitability and, in some cases, viability of ecotourism operations. The greatest personal challenge facing all small business operators is the risk of burnout. This risk is especially strong with ecotourism operators who may face the gruelling combination of a heavy work load, a lack of support systems, and a lack of financial resources to hire additional staff. Many ecotourism businesses offer their trips on weekends, yet they also must work a full Monday to Friday schedule to operate the office, prepare for trips, and be available to answer customer inquiries. As a result, operators may find themselves working seven day weeks for the entire operating season.

To some degree, these weaknesses and difficulties can be overcome by appropriate assistance through government agencies, industry associations, and vocational and/or university training programmes.

Accreditation has been pursued in part as a means to exclude businesses that do not follow ecotourism principles. The term "ecotourism" has become a positioning statement and a politically correct form of mass tourism. As such, virtually any type of tourism activity has claimed to offer an ecotourism experience. In Australia, bus tours that once were sold as day sightseeing trips from Sydney or Melbourne now are being marketed as ecotourism experiences because the tours stopped at wildlife parks. Yet there was no change in the tour itinerary nor the qualifications of interpretive staff.

Locations outside Australia have followed similar paths. Golf resorts in Hawaii became ecotourism resorts. Singapore, possibly the most urban of all nations, promoted itself as an ecotourism destination because of its renowned zoo (STPB 1993). The Desaru resort being developed in Johor, Malaysia will have 12 hotels with 5,000 rooms and three golf courses, yet will "promote ecotourism" by setting aside 242 of the 1,600 hectares as a natural reserve. South Pacific island nations like Fiji and Western Samoa began to promote themselves as ecotourism destinations, though three years earlier they had been positioned as mass tourism resort destinations.

The danger of abusing the ecotourism label comes not so much from large resorts using the term, because consumers presumably will be able to easily determine the type of experience they are purchasing. Rather, the confusion occurs when operators working in natural areas use the term while not complying with ecotourism principles. Such operators may be able to underprice those complying with the principles and may provide inferior experiences that, through negative word of mouth, can jeopardize demand for site and thus the viability of other businesses. Accreditation is an option that enables consumers to identify those operators that comply with ecotourism principles. Australia is in the process of implementing such an accreditation programme. The pluses and minuses of accreditation programmes, and the different types of such programmes, have been widely debated, and the experience of implementation in Australia and elsewhere can be used to guide future accreditation efforts.

Tendency for Dominance by Larger Operators and Those Located in Regional or National Centres

Issue/trend: There is a tendency, particularly for developing countries within the region, for ecotourism to be dominated by larger operators and/or those in regional or national centres. This results from economies of scale, differential access to capital, and the tendency for individuals with the necessary entrepreneurial and linguistic skills to be located in such centres.

Often, larger operators play important roles as intermediaries between consumers and small local operators. However, the dominance of larger operators can work against the goal of providing local economic benefits. Moreover, there is a common perception that large and out-of-region operators are less environmentally and socioculturally sensitive than smaller and/or local operators.

Options: Recognize the reasons for dominance by larger operators (and the important roles they can play), but implement programmes to facilitate local involvement where practical and desirable. Various options for achieving this include:

Local training: This training would cover a range of topics, including general overviews of the ecotourism industry, hospitality management (including hygiene), relevant language skills, interpretive material, cross-cultural considerations, and so on. Training can be based on existing tourism programmes, such as those conducted by the Malaysian Tourism Promotion Board, but should be supplemented with material specifically for ecotourism. This training also is relevant to guides and businesses from outside local areas.

Provision of Local Capital through Microcredit and Other Programmes: Facilitation of outreach to visitors and to other sectors of the ecotourism industry, such as in bound operators. One of the key needs for local businesses is to reach potential visitors directly or through in bound operators. For many ecotourism sites, it is important to identify appropriate marketing outlets. For example, getting information into "backpacker" guidebooks may be more important than putting glossy brochures in tourist centres.

Natural area requirements that local guides be used: Opportunities for greater local benefits from ecotourism exist not only within the ecotourism industry itself (such as guides or operators), but also within related industries. For example, training and capital might be targeted at developing the type, quality, and reliability of agricultural products used by local restaurants and lodges. Various resources relating to business development, community ecotourism development, and guide training are available, including Bushnell (1994), Pedersen (1995), and Pond (1993).

Finally, innovative strategies for small operator marketing can be pursued. One strategy, that of utilizing the Worldwide Web. This is an important potential strategy, but its usefulness should not be overstated, as it may become more and more difficult for small operators to become noticed on the Web as the number of sites proliferates. Indeed, it is possible that the Web ultimately will favour larger operators that are able to establish and maintain a higher Web profile. Again, partnerships may play a critical role here. Groups of operators, possibly in conjunction with natural area management agencies, can pool resources for combined sites that may be more attractive and useful to consumers than would be sites for individual operators.

Summary of Issues, Trends, Implications, and Options

Various demographic, tourism, and other trends will present challenges and opportunities for the region's natural area managers into the future. To some degree, these trends will put pressure on managers to maintain and improve their present activities. However, they also will put pressure on managers to take on new and different responsibilities and perspectives. For example, effective resource management will require increasingly greater social and political skills.

An overarching issue is the need for ecotourism to be dealt with in a business-like approach in terms of reacting to changes in the marketplace and satisfying ecotourists as customers. There are two general options for doing so: either natural area management agencies can take on this responsibility themselves or they can invite the private sector to do so in a partnership mode.

It should be stressed that this does not mean that important resource management objectives should be sacrificed to the desires of tourists or the tourism industry. Indeed, it may be critical for natural area managers to cultivate additional political support for such objectives in order to resist desires that are inconsistent with the objectives. Rather, it means that a more flexible, business-like approach can be taken within the constraint of achieving these objectives. Such an approach will enhance the probability that ecotourism objectives will be achieved into the future.

Nature Tourism Contribution to Local Economic Development

There are many different benefits that can be derived from Ecotourism if it is used as a tool by local communities rather than large outside interests. However, the results are a direct reflection of the motivation behind the project. Since these motivations are often mixed it follows that the results are often mixed too.

The following article was originally published by USAID, an organization that helps fund various ecotourism projects in many developing nations. Win Approaches to Development and the Environment, Ecotourism and Biodiversity Conservation.

Centre for Development Information and Evaluation

Whether called nature tourism or ecotourism, recreational and educational travel based on natural attractions is a promising means of advancing social, economic, and environmental objectives in developing countries. It offers countries new opportunities for small-enterprise investment and employment and increases the national stake in protecting their biological resources. However, making ecotourism a positive economic and environmental tool requires policies that foster responsible nature tourism development, broad-based and active local participation in its benefits, and conservation of developing countries' biological heritage.

The Problem

Forest and marine habitats are being destroyed and some of the wildlife they contain is being driven to extinction under the pressures of hunting, logging, agriculture, and fishing. Where areas have been officially reserved for nature conservation, many developing country governments lack sufficient funds to manage and protect them. These areas are being destroyed because they are not fully valued for their role as nature's genetic reservoirs of the world's biological resources.

The Win Solution

A recent USAID evaluation has identified ecotourism as an enterprise with potential positive contributions to the conservation of endangered biological resources. Contributions of ecotourism include raising local awareness about the value of biological resources, increasing local participation in the benefits of biodiversity conservation (through new sources of jobs and incomes), and generating revenues toward conservation of biologically rich areas.

Wildlife and its habitats in developing countries are becoming increasingly popular attractions for international tourism. Many of the richest areas, biologically, are in the developing world. Growing numbers of ecotourists are flocking to the mountains of Nepal and Madagascar, the tropical forests of Costa Rica and Thailand, and the beaches of Belize and Sri Lanka. Nature tourists bring with them money to spend, money that creates jobs and incomes for households and communities in and around national parks and other protected areas. Ecotourism enterprises tour agencies and guide services, lodges and private reserves as well as such satellite activities as crafts industries and transportation and food services, also generate revenues and foreign exchange. Governments can use this income in operating and protecting natural habitats.

By recognizing the importance of protecting biological diversity, ecotourism is raising appreciation for biological resources and leading to better conservation practices by developing country populations. It must of course be properly regulated and managed to protect against adverse environmental and cultural effects that can come with overbuilding of tourist facilities and influx of populations around fragile ecosystems. Assuming such oversight, nature tourism can benefit both the environment and economic development.

The Role of USAID

USAID supports nature-based tourism activities as part of its biodiversity conservation programs in more than a dozen countries worldwide. The Agency's ecotourism activities include support for developing national park systems, demarcating and equipping new national parks, recruiting and training park staff, and encouraging government reforms that promote regulated investments in private lodging, guide service, and other tourism ventures.

The Agency's involvement is recent, beginning in the mid-1980s, and the effect of these activities is only starting to emerge. USAID biodiversity conservation programs have demonstrated that potential local resistance to setting aside forest and fishing areas for conservation can often be softened by employment and income-producing opportunities ecotourism can generate.

In Costa Rica, Jamaica, and Sri Lanka, USAID support led to the creation of entirely new wildlife parks that have begun to spawn tourism facilities around them. Tourist demand for food, lodging, souvenirs, educational materials, and guide and transportation services stimulates local investment, employment, and incomes. Costa Rica has introduced revenue retention arrangements to keep earnings from entrance fees for park operations; it awards contracts to local communities to operate food and souvenir concessions as a means of building local involvement in and commitment to park conservation. Costa Rica has also included a variable park entrance fee structure (charging higher fees to international tourists than to local visitors) to increase revenues. In Nepal, Madagascar, and Thailand, USAID has supported integrated conservation and development activities to promote new livelihoods including nature tourism based employment as alternatives to encroaching into protected national parks for hunting, logging, and farming. Engagement of local people in planning and conducting ecotourism activities has generated a new group of stakeholders with a vested interest in protecting parks. The new nature jobs depend on it.

USAID's Central American Paseo Pantera ("Panther Walk") project has helped establish national nature tourism councils in Guatemala and Honduras to involve local communities and tourism enterprises. The councils also enlist international conservation organizations as advisers to promote green, self-sustaining tourism activities.

In 1989 the Agency began a Parks in Peril project to improve management of 20 parks in Latin America and the Caribbean. The project also seeks to enhance recreational and educational use of the parks. For example, in Bolivia, Parks in Peril is working through a U.S. environmental nongovernment organization (NGO) to assist a Bolivian NGO in providing nature tourism packages in two national parks. The project has helped create jobs for tour guides, park rangers, educators, and the like in several countries in the region.

These experiences suggest that ecotourism can be a constructive component of strategies to promote, at the same time, both environmental protection and development of private enterprise. USAID can help promote nature tourism in a way that maximizes its contribution to both the economies and the ecologies of developing countries. Specifically, USAID, other donors, NGOs, and developing country governments can work together to:

1. Identify and mobilize funding for potential private nature tourism investments. Ecotourism enterprises, like most business ventures, need operating capital. USAID and other donors can help identify promising funding sources.
2. Formulate fiscal policies to promote nature tourism and to maximize its economic and environmental benefits. USAID can encourage public policies (such as visitor fees, regulations for tourism operations, and investment incentives and land-use zones for tourist facilities) that promote environmentally sound tourism as well as community involvement in providing services and products such as guides, lodging, transport, and crafts.
3. Encourage international exchange of information and know-how about nature tourism opportunities and operations. USAID can foster participation by developing country public agencies and private service providers in international nature tourism associations that can help them, through technical and management training, to meet the needs and interests of international and domestic nature tourists.
4. Monitor and certify the performance of ecotourism activities. USAID can support emerging international movements aimed at promoting "green tourism." Green tourism takes ecotourism a step further, promoting environmentally responsible tourist

operations that conserve energy, recycle waste, and instruct staff and tourists on proper behaviour in parks and protected areas.

5. Fund research on ecotourism's developmental and environmental impact. Information is needed to demonstrate to decision-makers the economic contributions nature tourism can make. Better understanding of the impact of ecotourism (such as in resort development) is needed to regulate and enforce against environmentally damaging investments.

Outstanding Issues

***Risk*:** Unregulated, nature tourism can damage the environment and corrode local cultures. Pollution from runaway resort and hotel development around fragile park areas in Costa Rica, Nepal, and Thailand exemplifies poorly managed tourism activity.

***Distribution of benefits*:** Where international travel and resort chains or urban investors control the tourism industry, the local economic effect of ecotourism may be reduced. Early studies of ecotourism expenditures suggest that in such cases not much perhaps 20 to 30 cents of the tourist dollar stays in the national economy; even less reaches local communities.

***Perceptions*:** Developing countries fear that their parks and protected areas will become playgrounds for international tourists, with the land reserved for conservation and no longer available for farming to feed and employ their growing populations.

***Lack of information*:** More and better information is need about the actual and potential economic contributions of nature tourism ventures and practices. Inclusion of visits to natural attractions as part of regular recreational tourism needs to be explored along with "purer" forms of nature tourism and travel.

The tourism industry does not extract natural resources, while destroying the habitat. However its activities and infrastructure may or may not have negative impacts over the environment. Nevertheless, tourism and especially ecotourism provides and opportunity to develop an industry that does not destroy the environment but in fact supports nature conservation.

Nature tourism is the industry segment with the highest rate of growth. It can best be defined as "*tourism that consists in visiting natural areas with the aim to study, admire or enjoy the natural landscape, its wild species of flora and fauna as well as any cultural attraction that can be found in these areas.*"

Nature tourism has shown in recent years annual growth rates between 25% and 30% in comparrison to an annual growth of 4% in the tourism industry in general (WTO). Nature tourism generates 7% of the spending in tourism on an internacional level and contributes a total of $US 223 billion.

Examples for Nature Tourism

Bird watching: The number of bird watchers was estimated to be only in the US a total of 65 million people, of which 24 million travel at least once a year. In 2001 a study estimated that here are 6.5 million people in the US being interested to visit Peru. 700,400 of these (10.3%) are bird watchers.

Whale watching: There is an estimated 10 million bird watchers worldwide, spending every year more than 1.2 billion $US. Peru with 30 species of whales and dolphins being registered in our ocean and rainforest rivers could become a prime whale watching destination.

Scuba diving: According to the "1999 Travel Agent Planner" there are only in the US 3 million scuba divers, spending annually US$ 2.3 billion and do travel 2 to 4 times per year to diving destinations.

According to the Ecotourism Society 40%-60% of the international tourists are interested in nature tourism and 20%-40% of international tourist visit nature destinations.

Examples for other Countries with an Important Nature Tourism Industry

- Costa Ricas natural protected areas received in 1982 around 65,000 visitors, a number that increased to 273,000 in 1991 (320 %). Nepal had 175,000 foreigners visiting its protected areas in 1982, a number that increased to 334,000 in 1991 (91 %). Ecuador had an increase in number of visitors in protected areas of 17 % between 1986 and 1998.

However, the label "nature tourism" does not mean that the tourism activity itself would be sustainable or would be carried out taking a special care about the environment.

Contrary to this "ecotourism", being a sub segment of nature tourism, is the strictest form of sustainable tourism. Ecotourism has been defined by the International Ecotourism Society as *"responsible travel that aims to conserve the environment and improve the situation of the local population"*. A study undertaken in seven major cities in the US and Canada identified 1995 a market of 13 700 000 people. We do use the word "ecotourism" according to the definition of the International Ecotourism Society, while we call other forms of tourism, that do not comply with these standards, nature tourism.

Sadly the term ecotourism has lately become a fashion word and only very few tourism operations that call themselves "ecotourism" are actually complying with the above cited definitions.

In order to be an ecotourism it is not enough to merely offer a visit to a natural area. It requires real corporative responsibility that aims for sustainable use of tourism resources.

Ecotourism must Meet the Following Criteria

(A) The tourism operation must be designed and implemented in a way that creates minimum environmental impact.

(B) Tourism must contribute to the local economy and use where ever possible local services.

(C) Tourism must contribute financially to nature conservation.

(D) Tourism must be designed in order to educate visitors and local communities about the importance of nature conservation.

Agricultural Diversification Through Nature Tourism

The Texas Department of Agriculture (TDA) has a strong interest in rural economic development. As commodity prices decline, ranchers, farmers and the communities that depend on them continue looking for ways to diversify their income. The Rural Economic Development Division focuses on assisting landowners in their efforts to diversify and strengthen the economy in communities that surround them. As a result, many landowners have found nature tourism a good way to maintain their rural way of life.

TDA has compiled this guide to provide you with information about agricultural diversification through nature tourism. It is intended as a starting place for people interested in establishing or expanding an agricultural-based nature tourism business, and it includes many references and resources for additional information. Texas Yes! is a new initiative from the Texas Department of Agriculture designed to promote the growth and prosperity of every rural Texas town, city and county. Membership in Texas Yes! is free and open to communities, businesses, and associates.

Today's farmers and ranchers are increasingly on the lookout for ways to maintain their land and lifestyles in rural Texas. The Texas Department of Agriculture is working hard to assist producers, including partnering with the U.S. Department of Agriculture's Natural Resources Conservation Service and Texas Cooperative Extension to provide the information and connections necessary for agricultural diversification. One of the most challenging and rewarding means of agricultural diversification is through nature tourism.

In 2001, Texas Parks and Wildlife commissioned Southwick Associates to do a study on the impact of hunting, fishing and wildlife watching on nature tourism in Texas. The purpose of the project was to help resource managers and the public develop a better understanding of the economic contributions of these activities. The study concluded that 4.5 million residents and nonresidents participated in some form of fish and wildlife-related recreation in Texas.

These anglers, hunters and wildlife viewers spent $5.2 billion in retail sales ($4.8 billion by residents and $400 million by nonresidents), creating $2.6 billion in salaries and wages, and supporting more than 96,700 jobs. The total economic effect (multiplier effect) from fish and wildlife-related recreation was estimated at $10.9 billion.

Recreational and nature tourism is not a silver bullet to save farms and ranches, but its potential as an additional income source appears to be growing in Texas, where 97 percent of the land is privately owned and the urban population continues to rapidly increase, accounting for more than 87 percent of the total population.

Texas farmers and ranchers are known for their innovation and persistence when making a living off the land. With our state's growing urban population seeking nature activities, more producers are considering nature and recreational tourism as a new income source to help diversify and sustain their operations.

Message from the Commissioner

Nature Tourism

Farmers and ranchers have always been innovators and experts at diversifying their operations. In that tradition, some producers in Texas are now examining nature tourism, based upon natural, recreational, cultural or historical assets, as a way to supplement conventional agricultural incomes.

Nature tourism may not work for every farm or ranch, but it does have potential as an additional income source for some operations. Nature tourism on private land also has a great potential to grow in Texas where 97 percent of the land is privately owned and where more than 85 percent of the state's population is urban. Nature tourism is defined by the Texas Nature Tourism Task Force as "discretionary travel to natural areas that conserves the environmental, social and cultural values while generating an economic benefit to the local community." Nature tourists are travellers who spend their time and money enjoying and appreciating a broad range of outdoor activities.

Tourism as an industry is growing, and that growth includes great increases in spending on nature-based travel. In Texas, the overall economic effect of fish and wildlife-associated recreation (fishing, hunting and wildlife viewing) in 2001 is estimated to have been $10.9 billion. The urban population is increasingly interested in connecting with nature and chooses to do so in a number of ways. Biking, nature and hiking trails have been ranked by Texans as among the top 10 most-needed recreation facilities in our state. Bird and wildlife viewing are also popular.

For landowners interested in diversifying, nature tourism offers a large market. In addition to the more traditional nature activities of hunting and fishing, landowners can open their property to cyclists, hikers or horseback riders, providing travellers with additional destinations and landowners with additional income.

According to research done by the Economic Development and Tourism division of the Office of the Governor and others, people are looking for "experiences," and if you can provide a great experience, you're off to a good start. Remember, some of the experiences that you may take for granted-the view of the water tank in the morning or the "critters" that may be a pest to you-may be the very things that your target market seeks. Hosting tourists is hard work, requires good people skills and takes research and marketing. Landowners who think this sort of diversification will work for them should know up front that it is a lot of work. But that work can be very rewarding for the host as well as the tourists.

Cultural and Heritage Tourism

Rural Texas is also fertile ground for developing cultural and heritage tourism. This type of tourism is travel directed toward experiencing the culture and heritage of a city, region, state or country.

Today's travellers expect more out of their vacation experience. A growing segment of the travelling public is retired baby-boomers. This group, as a whole, is more educated and experienced. More and more are taking time to travel, and as a result, cultural and heritage tourism are the fastest growing segments of the travel economy. Additionally, they're good customers: heritage travellers spend more per day and stay longer on their visits.

Texas has a unique culture and heritage that many people would like to learn about. Spanish, French, Czech, German, Mexican and many other nationalities have influenced the culture and the history of our state. Since 97 percent of Texas land is privately owned, much of the culturally significant property is in private hands. Providing a rich experience for travellers depends on the collaboration of landowners and communities.

A cultural and heritage tourism plan can begin with an honest appraisal of your land and community assets. What can the landowner or business offer as a destination? Is there a dominant theme in the region? To attract tourists, it is important for landowners to work with businesses and other landowners in the local community to create a multilevel experience, ideally including several possible destinations with a similar theme and places to stay and eat.

Additionally, working with the local city or county economic development or chamber of commerce staff can provide benefits. Rural cities and counties with populations less than 20,000 are eligible for full membership in TDA's Texas Yes! program, which helps promote tourism in rural Texas. Businesses and individuals are also welcome to participate as business and associate members.

An excellent resource for information on cultural and heritage tourism is the Texas Historical Commission (THC). THC has worked with the Texas Commission on the Arts, the Texas Association of Museums and the Texas Travel Industry Association to create a Web site, *Uniquely Texas*, which serves as a resource for cultural and heritage tourism. THC also supports a number of Heritage Trails around the state that bring together businesses and communities to develop heritage tourism in a region. Information about these programs can be found on the Texas Tourism Resources page in this guide.

Business Considerations

As with any start-up business, one must carefully consider many factors before launching a nature tourism operation. Most small business owners will tell you that owning your own business is very gratifying, as well as very time consuming. Be sure to consider lifestyle changes that owning a nature tourism business may bring. If you will be managing the business, ask yourself if your personality is well suited for the service industry. Being a "people person" is an important attribute for the person in charge of the operation. Many businesses never reach their full potential because they do not develop and follow a good "roadmap." A well-written business plan is essential to develop and/ or expand any small business. There are many different types of business plans, but most incorporate the following core elements:

Business Description

Include a description of your proposed nature tourism business. How will this business fit in with any existing agricultural enterprises?

Product Description

Identify your product. A very important consideration is "What makes my product unique?" Include your pricing strategy. Service, amenities and location all impact the price that your target market will be willing to pay.

Market Description

Marketing is probably the area that most distinguishes nature tourism from traditional operations. Identify your customers, where they are located and how you intend to target and service them. Remember that research indicates that most tourists in rural areas come from within 250 miles. The Internet is increasingly important for getting the word out about your product and services. Having a Web site and promoting it properly can be crucial.

Collaboration Opportunities

Identify others in your region that you could work with to provide a more balanced and complete experience to the traveller. Working with a community and highlighting all local attractions could provide a stronger draw to tourists who are expecting more from their travel experience, which could mean longer visits.

Competition

Identify your competitors. Remember, in many cases, a nature tourism enterprise that provides a minimum level of service or amenities may be competing with public parklands for customers. Identify your competitive advantage. Other components the business plan should address are location, facilities, management/personnel, financial needs and liability.

Pricing your Nature Tourism Business

While pricing is only one element of a business plan, it is an issue that landowners are often curious about as they consider how nature tourism might enhance their existing operation. Our research indicates that pricing varies widely, but here are a few things to consider.

The most successful businesses are providing "value-added" services in addition to a primary activity such as camping, horseback riding or nature tours. For example, businesses may offer lodging, professional guides or some "unique experience" that attract customers.

A review of various nature tourism operations indicates a range of advertised rates for activities with limited service or amenities:

- $5-$65 per day for birding (tours on public land are generally on the lower end, while tours on privately owned land are typically on the upper end of the price scale).
- $18-$25 per hour for horseback riding and $50 per hour for private lessons on privately owned land.
- $2-$6 per day for mountain biking in state parks or on privately owned land. Revenues can increase dramatically when services are added. The following are examples of advertised rates of activities involving higher levels of service or amenities. These value-added services provide the customer with a unique

experience that is not available elsewhere and therefore justifies a higher price.

- Birders may pay $195 per person for a full weekend, which includes birding classes, field trips and lodging.
- Trailriders may pay $90 or more per person for two hours of horseback riding, lodging, meals and other ranch activities.
- Mountain bikers often pay an additional $5 per person per night for basic camping facilities or $10 per night for trailer hook-ups. Mountain bike races are very popular events and attract large numbers of entrants and spectators. Race fees are charged in addition to land access fees for each rider, and spectators may pay an entry fee as well.

Landowner Liability Facts

Beginning in 1985, the Texas Legislature offered landowners limited liability protection by adding the Texas Civil Practices and Remedies Code. In its current amended form, provides that the owner of agricultural land used for recreational purposes does not incur liability for injury or damage caused by an act of the user if:

- there is no entry charge, or
- annual charges for entry did not exceed 20 times the property taxes on the agricultural land during the preceding year, or
- the owner has liability insurance in the amount of at least $500,000 per person and $1,000,000 per occurrence for injury or death and $100,000 per occurrence for damage to property.

Agricultural landowners are not totally absolved of liability for recreational use. Landowners are liable for:

- gross negligence,
- deliberate, wilful, or malicious injury, and
- injury to children under the attractive nuisance doctrine.

The information presented in this Guide regarding landowner liability is intended for informational purposes only and is not intended as and should not be relied upon as legal advice to any person or entity. It is important that anyone interested in bringing recreational guests onto their property seek individual legal advice regarding their specific circumstances.

6

Option for Mitigating Nature Tourism's Environmental Impacts

Sustainability

- "Development that meets the needs of the present without compromising the ability of future generations to meet their own needs"
- Brundtland Report, World Commission on Environment and Development (1987)
- "The relevant metric of sustainability is the production of human wellbeing (not necessarily material goods) per unit of extraction from or imposition upon nature."

Sustainability's Components Economic Footprint

Sustaining the ability of future generations to eliminate poverty, generate wealth, and meet the economic requirements of basic human wellbeing.

Societal Footprint: Supporting social, economic and Political conditions that enhance People's ability to meet their Fundamental needs.

Environmental Footprint: Managing and minimizing human impact on biodiversity, the ecosystem, and the Planet's "natural capital" Managing and Reducing the demand for nonrenewable Resources.

Sustainability and Climate Change

- *Economic Impact of Climate Change:* unmitigated climate change would damage economic growth on a global scale, causing a reduction in consumption per capita of 20% by late in the 21st century. The Stern Report, Cambridge University (2006).

- ***Political Impact:*** Climate change is a national and international security risk, and a primary potential source of political instability, as a result of resource shortages and economic impacts. UN World Tourism Organization/UN Environment Program (2007).
- The integrated effects of climate change will have far-reaching consequences for tourism businesses and destinations.

Tourism, Sustainability and Climate Change: a Partial History

- International Institute for Environment and Development (IIED), *Tourism, Conservation and Sustainable Development: Case Studies from Asia and Africa.*
- 1st International Conference on Climate Change and Tourism, *Climate Change and Tourism ("Djerba Declaration),* Djerba, Tunisia.
- 2nd International Conference on Climate Change and Tourism, *Climate Change and Tourism: Responding to Global Challenges ("Davos Declaration"),* Davos, Switzerland (October 2007).
- UNEP, *Climate Change Adaptation and Mitigation in the Tourism Sector: Frameworks, Tools, Practices* (2008).
- 1st International Capacity Building Seminar on Climate Change Adaptation and Mitigation in the Tourism Sector, UNEP (2008).

Climate Change Impacts on Tourism

- ***Direct Climatic Impacts:*** heat waves, droughts, floods, tropical cyclones, changes in duration of seasons.
- Indirect Environmental Change Impacts: water availability, reduced landscape aesthetic, increased natural hazards, coastal erosion and inundation, damage to infrastructure, increased vector-borne diseases.
- Regional impacts vary. NE Asia will suffer less impact on balance.
- Impact of Mitigation Policies on Tourist Mobility: increased transport costs; tourist environmental attitudes; change in travel patterns.

- Particularly affects long-haul destinations.
- Indirect Social Impacts: reduced discretionary wealth available to consumers of tourism; greater political instability and social unrest.

Tourism's Contribution to Climate Change

- Tourism accounts for 5% of global CO2 emissions (2008).
- 75% of this is generated by transport.
- Up to 70% of tourism's contribution to CO2 emissions attributable to air transport.
- Trips by bus and rail account for 34% of all trips, but only 13% of tourism-related emissions.
- Long-haul travel is only 2.7% of all tourist trips, but contributes 17% to global tourist emissions.
- SOURCE: UNEP, *Climate Change Adaptation and Mitigation in the Tourism Sector* (2008)

Global Tourism's Projected Growth by 2035

- Global tourism will grow by 179%.
- Passenger kilometres travelled will rise 222%.
- Guest nights will increase by 156%.
- CO2 emissions from tourism will rise 152%.
- Tourism's contribution to radiative forcing that contributes to global warming through all greenhouse gases will increase 188%.

Source: UNEP, *Climate Change Adaptation and Mitigation in the Tourism Sector* (2008).

How Should the Tourism Industry Respond?

- "Climate change as well as poverty alleviation will remain central issues for the world community. Tourism is an important element in both. Governments and the private sector must place increased importance on these factors in tourism development strategies and in climate and poverty strategies. They are interdependent and must be dealt with in a holistic fashion."
- UNWTO Secretary General Francesco Frangialli (2007).

Adaptation and Mitigation in the Tourism Industry

- ***Adaptation:*** adjustment to environmental conditions; modification of behaviour to more easily fit the conditions of a particular environment.
- Reduces the costs of climate change impacts, thus reducing the need for mitigation.
- ***Mitigation:*** to directly address and change environmental conditions; to cause an environment to become less harsh or hostile.
- Adaptation and Mitigation are complementary. They must be considered together.

Adaptive Capacity of Tourism Subsectors

* Tourists Tour Operators Hotels/Resorts,

* Transport Providers Attraction, Operators,

* Travel Agents Communities.

Mitigation by Sector

Transportation

- "Transportation is by far the most important sector contributing to emissions of greenhouse gases by tourism, and within the transport sector, aviation is most relevant." — UNEP (2008)
- Airlines; cars; rail and coach travel,
- Accommodation,
- Hotels and restaurants.

Tour Operators

Transportation: Airline Industry

- "For trips involving air travel, the journey to the destination will account for 60-90% of the trip's overall contribution to climate change." UNEP
- The aviation industry is growing at a compounded rate of 5% per annum, though there has been recent retraction.
- In Asia, airline traffic is projected to grow from 1,100 billion Revenue Passenger Kilometres (RPKs) in 2006 to 3,700 billion RPKs in 2026, or 31% of the total global market (Europe: 27%; North America 24%).

- Air travel contributed only 1.6% of total global GHG emissions in 2006 (CO_2; CH_4; NO_x); this will grow to 2.7%-4% by 2030.
- Source: Association of Asia Pacific Airlines conference on "Aviation and the post-2012 climate change policy regime," Hong Kong, 25-26 February 2008.

Transportation: Airline Mitigation Strategies

- Technology: replacing old aircraft can reduce emissions per passenger kilometre by 20-30%.
- Increase load factor to 80% or more.
- High load factors = reduced energy use per traveller.
- Denser passenger seating.
- Higher prices for First and Business class seating.
- More efficient flight paths: direct flights coupled with integrated surface transportation.
- Adjusted bonus programs.
- More non-travel-related benefits.

Transportation: Other Modes

- Railways and Coaches: Trips by rail and coach account for 34% of all trips but only 13% of transportation-related CO_2 emissions in tourism.
- Long distance rail needs to be better integrated with air transportation.
- Rail offers the advantages of comfort, on-time arrival at city centres, and a potential for carbon-free operation.
- Cars: The tourism industry remains inordinately dependent on the automobile. Changes will accompany changes in the wider society, to electric and hybrid technologies, biofuels and other technological innovations.
- Seaborne tourist travel: A relatively modest contribution to tourism's total carbon footprint.

Accommodations Mitigation Strategies

- Globally, accommodation is responsible for 21% of tourism-related GHG emissions (when considering energy throughput).
- Mitigation strategies include:

- Lower electricity and gas consumption through adjusted room temperature settings, energy-efficient lighting, and more efficient water-heating systems.
- Passive energy conservation efforts in building design.
- Water conservation.
- Reduced use of materials, especially disposable packaging.
- Environmentally sensitive waste management.
- Restaurants: more local-source products, fewer carbon-intense meat offerings.
- "Green Certification" and environmental impact mapping.

Tour Operators: Mitigation Options

- Avoid promoting long-haul destinations that are dependent on air travel and contribute inordinately to carbon emissions.
- Rethink the choice of destinations, giving preference to closer destinations over those more distant.
- Market low-carbon tourism options that can use surface transportation, particularly rail.
- Offer carbon offsetting payments (shared with consumer) for journeys by air.

Consumer (Tourist) Options

Consumers have more flexibility than tour operators, transportation providers or hotel and resort operators.

- Consumer mitigation options:
- Minimize air travel.
- Agree to carbon offsetting for unavoidable flights.
- Travel less and stay longer.
- Reward pro-environmental transportation providers, tour operators, and hotels/resorts.
- Stay home.

Destination Mitigation Strategies

- "Destinations have the greatest potential to contribute to fast reductions in greenhouse gasses. This is because destinations, even though they can vary considerably in size, comprise various stakeholders that can work together to achieve emission reductions."

- Destination-wide transport management (such as free or inexpensive public transportation); energy from renewable sources; closer cooperation with marketers in taking energy efficiency and environmental sensitivity into account as a tourism promotion strategy.
- Seek "Green Certification;" engage in environmental impact and disaster mapping.

Long Term Implications

- There will be pressure to retard the growth of the airline industry. Air travel will be much more expensive.
- Carbon taxation will increase transport costs.
- More use will be made of ground transportation options, particularly rail.
- Less emphasis will be placed on long haul destinations, and more on local and regional travel.
- Destinations more reliant on the long-haul market will be more heavily impacted by changes.
- More emphasis on group tourism packages.
- Consumers will travel less and stay longer.
- Environmentally sensitive low carbon tourism options will receive greater emphasis.
- Tourism development strategies will be more consciously articulated with economic and social policy objectives.

Some Potential Risks Associated With Mitigation Strategies

- Investment Risks.
- Forced downsizing or abandonment of existing operations because of bad investment strategies/decisions.
- Market Risks.
- Changing market conditions: consumers have less disposable income.
- Reputational Risks.
- Local actions become global news almost immediately.
- Political and Social Risks.
- Civil unrest, political deadlock, local interest group issues.

- Environmental Risks.
- Long term environmental change risks; disaster.

Mitigating Investment Risk

- Realistically assess the implications of long-term market shifts and other factors.
- Pursue multi-stakeholder, open development processes that forthrightly address community issues.
- Seek public/private partnerships; leverage local government funding to share in infrastructure development.
- Many financial institutions now adhere to environmental and social impact standards in making financing decisions.
- Equator Principles (2003; updated 2006).

Mitigating Market Risk

- Assess the balance between a widening global market with new entrants and the risk of reduced disposable income.
- Put greater effort into the local and regional market, and less into long-haul tourism.
- Market low-carbon tourism options that use surface transportation.
- Compensate for greater costs.

Mitigating Reputational Risk

- Partner with local government entities.
- Melbourne Principles for Sustainable Cities (2002).
- Work openly with local and national stakeholders.
- Take account of "special interests," particularly indigenous groups and environmental groups.
- Partner with NGOs in developing "green" tourism options. Seek "Green Certification."
- Bolster and complement local economic development; hire locally.
- Take care to preserve "heritage sites."
- Have a sustainability plan.

Mitigating Political and Social Risk

- "Political risk" lies along a spectrum from (at one end) regulatory issues and relations with local and national governments and interest groups to (at the other end) serious political instability and civil unrest.

- Tourism is now too important and pervasive an activity for governments to ignore.
- Any evidence of domestic turmoil is likely to result in a decision not to visit that country.
- Examples abound: Egypt (late 1970s); Fiji (1987); China (1989); Former Yugoslavia (1991); Mexico (1994); North Korea (today); Zimbabwe (today); Middle East generally for extended periods.

Davos World Economic Forum Global Risks

Political And Social Risk Cont'd

- The tourism industry can do little to mitigate the impact of political instability and civil unrest. It must "ride out" such cataclysms.
- Even so, the tourism industry cannot ignore politics.
- Lower-order political risk can be mitigated through.
- Transparency in business operations.
- Public/private partnerships.
- Outreach to government entities and interest groups.
- Active presence at those places where political power is exercised and public choices are made.
- Greater awareness of the political and social consequences of business planning.

Adaptation to Environmental Risk

- Adhere to the Hannover Principles (1992) in designing buildings and other facilities, consuming energy and water, and providing for waste management.
- Use eco-engineering and "green architecture" measures.
- Incorporate ecological safety measures in facilities design.
- Engage in "hazard mapping" – particularly important in coastal and mountain areas.
- Example: Setback from beach areas.
- Make necessary seasonal adjustments to climate change.

- Adapting to more extreme temperatures, wetter seasons, or diminished natural snowfall
- Be mindful of tourism's ecological footprint and the need to preserve biodiversity.

Sustainability, Climate Change, and Risk

- Mitigation and adaptation processes that respond to sustainability and climate change issues will create their own risks.
- At the same time, "if any function can mitigate against the uncontrollable risks, sustainability can."
- Kariann Aarup, Rio Tinto Alcan (2008).

Where do we go from Here?

(1) Capacity Building: capacity for adaptation and mitigation in response to climate change and sustainability needs across government bodies, tourism institutions, and the tourism industry at the global, national, regional and destination level.

(2) Addressing Gaps in Knowledge: further research should include "assessment of uncertainties in climate change projections themselves, as well as socioeconomic uncertainties within the tourism sector." — UNEP, *Climate Change Adaptation and Mitigation in the Tourism Sector (2008)*

(3) Developing Innovation Strategies: innovation, both technical and programmatic, must be understandable in terms of standard tourism business practices.

(4) Reducing "Hotspot" Vulnerabilities: some regions and destinations are more vulnerable to the impacts of climate change or to the economic impact of changes in the tourism industry.

(5) Effective Policy Implementation by Diverse Stakeholders Working Together: national governments, regional and local administration, the tourism industry, international bodies, NGOs.

On The Positive Side: What can the Tourism Industry Gain From Adaptation and Mitigation?

- Improved financial performance.

- Reduced operating costs.
- Enhanced reputation and image.
- Increased sales and customer loyalty.
- Reduced regulatory oversight.
- Improved access to capital.
- A more supportive external environment.

"We tend to do the things we know how to do, instead of trying to do the things we ought to do."

The tourism industry's interaction with climate change and sustainability issues has set it on a new course. We have no choice but to learn to do new things.

- Climate Change.
- Inter-governmental Panel on Climate Change (IPCC).
- Declared the 'warming of the climate system is unequiyocla'
- 0.76! 1850-1899 & 2001-2005.
- 1.8! to 4.0! by the end of the 21st Century.
- Global Warming Impacts.
- More extreme weather patterns (too hot, cold, dry or wet for some);
- Less predictability.
- Melting of ice in polar regions and retreat of glaciers in alpine regions.
- Variable and unpredictable snowfall reductions in areas that have supported winter tourism activities.
- Decertification (the world's tropical forests are disappearing at the rate of 13 million hectares a year).
- Unusual flooding and increasing storms .
- Grow now, clean up later vs. Green Growth.
- Current Growth pattern must change.
- Leapfrogging is possible.
- Decoupling of economic growth and environmental pressure is doable.
- Green growth.
- Maintains or restores environmental quality and ecological integrity.

- Decouples negative environmental impact from economic growth pressures.
- Key elements of Green Growth.
- Improving eco-efficiency
- Satisfying unmet needs with less resource and waste
- Incorporating environmental costs in socioeconomic development planning
- Creating synergies between economic growth and environmental protection
- Promoting green business opportunities
- Environment as an opportunity for growth – not a cost or burden
- "Tourism is both a victim and a vector of climate change."
- Secretary-General United Nations World Tourism Organization
- Tourism's Contribution to Climate Change
- The tourism industry is a significant contributor to climate change, making up as much as 5% of all carbon emissions from human activities (2008).
- 75% of this is generated by transport.
- Up to 70% of tourism's contribution to CO2 emissions attributable to air transport.
- Trips by bus and rail account for 34% of all trips, but only 13% of tourism-related emissions.
- Long-haul travel is only 2.7% of all tourist trips, but contributes 17% to global tourist emissions.
- If trends continue, emissions are projected to more than double in the next 30 years.

Change and Tourism

- Climate Change Impacts on Tourism.
- Direct Climatic Impacts.
- Heat waves, droughts, floods, tropical cyclones, changes in duration of seasons.
- Indirect Environmental Change Impacts.
- Water availability, reduced landscape aesthetic, increased natural

hazards, coastal erosion and inundation, damage to infrastructure, increased vector-borne diseases.

- Impact of Mitigation Policies on Tourist Mobility
- Increased transport costs; tourist environmental attitudes; change in travel patterns.
- Particularly affects long-haul destinations.
- Indirect Social Impacts.
- Reduced discretionary wealth available to consumers of tourism; greater political instability and social unrest.

Climate Change and Tourism

- Global Tourism's Projected Growth by 2005.
- Global tourism will grow by 179%.
- Passenger kilometres travelled will rise 222%.
- Guest nights will increase by 156%.
- CO2 emissions from tourism will rise 152%.
- Tourism's contribution to radiative forcing that contributes to global warming through all greenhouse gases will increase 188%.

Source: UNEP, Climate Change Adaptation and Mitigation in the Tourism Sector (2008).

Climate Change and Tourism

- How should the tourism industry respond?
- Climate change as well as poverty alleviation will remain central issues for the world community.
- Tourism is an important element in both.
- Governments and the private sector must place increased importance on these factors in tourism development strategies and in climate and poverty strategies.
- They are interdependent and must be dealt with in a holistic fashion.

Sustainable Tourism

- Definition.
- ST meets the needs of present tourists and host region while protecting and enhancing opportunities for the future.

- Stakeholders and Principles.
- Tourism Industry, Environmental Supporters and Local Community.
- Economic, Sociocultural, and Environmental Sustainability.
- Principle of Sustainable Tourism.
- Conserve the Nature.
- Raise Tourists' Environmental Awareness.
- Insure Economic-, Social-, Environmental-Benefits.
- Sustainable vs. Conventional Tourism.

Sustainable Tourism

- Tourism, Sustainability and Climate Change: A Partial History.
- International Institute for Environment and Development (IIED), Tourism, Conservation and Sustainable Development: Case Studies from Asia and Africa (December 1998).
- 1st International Conference on Climate Change and Tourism, Climate Change and Tourism ("Djerba Declaration), Djerba, Tunisia (April 2003).
- 2nd International Conference on Climate Change and Tourism, Climate Change and Tourism: Responding to Global Challenges ("Davos Declaration"), Davos, Switzerland (October 2007).
- UNEP, Climate Change Adaptation and Mitigation in the Tourism Sector: Frameworks, Tools, Practices (2008).
- 1st International Capacity Building Seminar on Climate Change Adaptation and Mitigation in the Tourism Sector, UNEP (2008).

Adaptation and Mitigation in the Tourism Industry

- Adaptation: adjustment to environmental conditions; modification of behaviour to more easily fit the conditions of a particular environment.
- Reduces the costs of climate change impacts, thus reducing the need for mitigation.
- Mitigation: to directly address and change environmental conditions; to cause an environment to become less harsh or hostile.
- Adaptation and Mitigation are complementary.
- They must be considered together.

Adaptation and Mitigation in the Tourism Industry

Mitigation of Tourism's Impact: Four Steps :

(1) Eliminate greenhouse gas (GHG) emissions by avoiding certain activities that can be avoided without a substantial change to the tourism product or service quality.

(2) Reduce the emission of GHGs by focusing on energy efficiency.

(3) Substitute practices responsible for large GHG emissions with practices that have a lower carbon footprint.

(4) Offset remaining emissions to achieve full carbon neutrality.

Carbon offsetting means that an amount of GHG emissions equal to that caused by an activity (such as a flight) will be reduced elsewhere through investment in energy-efficiency measures, renewable energy, or carbon sequestration (such as forestry projects).

Adaptation and Mitigation in the Tourism Industry

- Mitigation By Sector.

Transportation

- "Transportation is by far the most important sector contributing to emissions of greenhouse gases by tourism, and within the transport sector, aviation is most relevant." — UNEP (2008).
- Airlines; cars; rail and coach travel.

Accommodation

- Hotels and restaurants.
- Tour Operators.
- Consumers (Tourists).
- Destinations.

Transportation

Airline Industry

- "For trips involving air travel, the journey to the destination will account for 60-90% of the trip's overall contribution to climate change." UNEP.
- The aviation industry is growing at a compounded rate of 5% per annum, though there has been recent retraction.
- Air travel contributed only 1.6% of total global GHG emissions in 2006 (CO2; CH4; NOx); this will grow to 2.7%-4% by 2030.

Airline Mitigation Strategies

- Technology: replacing old aircraft can reduce emissions per passenger kilometre by 20-30%.
- Increase load factor to 80% or more.
- High load factors = reduced energy use per traveller.
- Denser passenger seating.
- Higher prices for First and Business class seating.
- More efficient flight paths: direct flights coupled with integrated surface transportation.
- Adjusted bonus programs.
- More non-travel-related benefits.

Other Modes

- Railways and Coaches: Trips by rail and coach account for 34% of all trips but only 13% of transportation-related CO2 emissions in tourism.
- Long distance rail needs to be better integrated with air transportation.
- Rail offers the advantages of comfort, on-time arrival at city centres, and a potential for carbon-free operation.
- Cars: The tourism industry remains inordinately dependent on the automobile. Changes will accompany changes in the wider society, to electric and hybrid technologies, biofuels and other technological innovations.
- Seaborne tourist travel: A relatively modest contribution to tourism's total carbon footprint (not to be confused with shipping).

Accommodations

Mitigation Strategies

- Globally, accommodation is responsible for 21% of tourism-related GHG emissions (when considering energy throughput).
- Mitigation strategies include:
- Lower electricity and gas consumption through adjusted room temperature settings, energy-efficient lighting, and more efficient water-heating systems.

- Passive energy conservation efforts in building design.
- Water conservation.
- Reduced use of materials, especially disposable packaging.
- Environmentally sensitive waste management.
- Restaurants: more local-source products, fewer carbon-intense meat offerings.
- "Green Certification" and environmental impact mapping.

Tour Operators: Mitigation Options

- Avoid promoting long-haul destinations that are dependent on air travel and contribute inordinately to carbon emissions.
- Rethink the choice of destinations, giving preference to closer destinations over those more distant.
- Market low-carbon tourism options that can use surface transportation, particularly rail.
- Offer carbon offsetting payments (shared with consumer) for journeys by air.

Consumer (Tourist) Options

- Consumers have more flexibility than tour operators, transportation providers or hotel and resort operators.
- Consumer mitigation options.
- Minimize air travel.
- Agree to carbon offsetting for unavoidable flights.
- Travel less and stay longer.
- Reward pro-environmental transportation providers, tour operators, and hotels/resorts.
- Stay home.
- Sustainable Travellers.
- Social.
- Environmental.
- Economic.
- Respect Cultures.
- Call Ahead Rethink.
- Expectations and Learn about a Region.

- Choose Sustainable Transportation.
- Leave No Trace and Bring Travel Mug/Water Bottle.
- Support Local Businesses.
- Eat Local Foods.
- Buy Locally Made Souvenirs.

Destination Mitigation Strategies

- "Destinations have the greatest potential to contribute to fast reductions in greenhouse gasses. This is because destinations, even though they can vary considerably in size, comprise various stakeholders that can work together to achieve emission reductions."

Source: UNEP Climate Change Adaptation and Mitigation in the Tourism Sector (2008)

- Destination-wide transport management (such as free or inexpensive public transportation); energy from renewable sources; closer cooperation with marketers in taking energy efficiency and environmental sensitivity into account as a tourism promotion strategy.
- Seek "Green Certification;" engage in environmental impact and disaster mapping.
- Essential Elements of an Adaptation Strategy.
- Risk management plans.
- Link with other planning processes.
- Legislation and enforcement.
- Support networks.
- Financing adaptation.
- Information and good science.
- Education and communication.
- Responsibility for development.
- The eight elements of an adaptation strategy.
- Sequence of steps in the Process of Adaptation.
- Strategies to Achieve Low Carbon, Green Growth.
- Use 10 strategies to the tourism industry for the policy consistency.

- Use the frameworks, tools, and practices by UNEP, UNWTO, WMO to meet the international standards.

Korea's Tourism in the Era of Low Carbon, Green Growth

- Use the 10 strategies to the tourism industry.
- Use the frameworks.
- For Adaptation.
- Use the frameworks.
- For Mitigation.
- Eliminate greenhouse gas (GHG) emissions by avoiding certain activities that can be avoided without a substantial change to the tourism product or service quality.
- Reduce the emission of GHGs by focusing on energy efficiency.
- Substitute practices responsible for large GHG emissions with practices that have a lower carbon footprint.
- Offset remaining emissions to achieve full carbon neutrality.
- Sectors.
- Transportation.
- Accommodation.
- Tour operators.
- Tourists.
- Destinations.

The promoters of 'adventure-' or 'ecotourism' have popularized slogans such as: "Go visit the last paradises… before they'll be destroyed by tourist hordes." In a similar fashion, the British daily *The Observer* recently suggested that world travellers need to hurry up if they want to see the '10 wonders of a *vanishing* world'. According to the related article, the most wondrous natural tourist attractions we can no longer take for granted due to global warming include:

Africa's highest mountain-the spectacular Kilimanjaro in Tanzania will never look the same as snows are disappearing at an alarming rate.

The Caribbean coral reefs – particularly the Meso-American reef, the world's second biggest, stretching from the coast of southern Mexico down past Belize and into Honduras, is threatened by a threefold environmental disaster: Warmer water disrupts coral growth; acidic water affects coral's abilities to secrete new skeletons; and increasingly intense hurricanes break it up. As a result thousands of marine species are on the brink of extinction.

The Maldives in the Indian Ocean-many tropical islands forming the Indian Ocean archipelago are likely to become submerged in the next two decades as a result of rising sea levels and increasing numbers of heavy storms. Traditional ski resorts in the Alps such as Kitzbuhel in Austria for example will disappear from the tourist map within 20 years because of the lack of snow.

Furthermore, the future of many unique animal species that have attracted wildlife tourism is in jeopardy as habitats, breeding grounds and migration routes are changing. If global warming gets worse, entire populations of polar bears in the Arctic region, Wildebeests in East Africa, Mountain Gorillas in Uganda and Rwanda or Monarch Butterflies in Mexico may be destroyed.

Tourism World Wakes up to the Climate Crisis

Climate is an essential resource for tourism, and especially for beach, nature and winter sport tourism, and the phenomenon of global warming already gravely affects the industry and an increasing number of destinations. In 2003, the Madrid-based UN World Tourism Organization (UNWTO) convened the 1st International Conference on Climate Change and Tourism in Djerba, Tunisia, to help the travel and tourism industry to respond to these issues. The UNWTO, that only a few years ago became a special UN agency, is traditionally driven by a strong Business Council that aggressively advances the interests of the world's most powerful tourism-related corporations. That the UNWTO declared climate change a priority issue shows the growing awareness among industry leaders and policymakers that the impacts of global warming pose a serious threat to tourism-one of the world's largest and fastest growing industries, generating over 10.4 per cent of world GDP, according to the World Travel and Tourism Council (WTTC).

Notably, the Djerba conference recognized that the relationship between climate change and tourism is twofold: Not only is tourism affected by a changing climate, at the same time it contributes to climate change by the consumption of fossil fuels and resulting greenhouse gas emissions. It was concluded that there was an "urgent need for the tourism industry, national governments and international organizations to develop and implement strategies to face the changing climate conditions and to take preventive actions for future effects, as well as to mitigate tourism's environmental impacts contributing to climate change.".

Also the burgeoning international ecotourism industry feels challenged. At the recent Global Ecotourism Conference 2007 (GEC07) that was jointly organized by The Ecotourism Society (TIES), Ecotourism Norway and the UNEP in Oslo, Norway, it was agreed that "Climate change has increasingly become a major threat affecting the very resources on which ecotourism depends – natural areas and local and Indigenous communities around the world....Stronger leadership and strategies are needed in order to substantially decrease ecotourism's carbon footprint generated from multiple sources including facility operations and transport-related greenhouse gas emissions."

This article will offer some explanations as to why travel and tourism leaders are now feverishly working at the climate change front. Firstly, the economic costs of climate change for the industry will rise inexorably if it takes a business-as-usual attitude. Secondly, tourism relies more than other industries on a good image, but its reputation as a beneficial and environmentally acceptable activity has rapidly faded during recent debates on the causes of global warming.

Economic Factors

Critics have always pointed out the fickle nature of tourism, and indeed the industry's special vulnerability to bad news and events has been proven many times in recent years; just consider the slumps following terrorist attacks such as 9/11 and the Bali bombings, the threat of diseases such as SARS and avian flu or environmental crises. The Indian Ocean tsunami in 2004 and Hurricane Katrina that hit New Orleans in 2005, caused immeasurable costs for the travel and tourism industry. What needs to be calculated here are not only the costs of lost property and for the reconstruction of tourist infrastructure in case of disasters, but also the costs of tourists staying away from crisis-hit destinations for a long time as well as the high expenditures for promotional campaigns to get tourists visiting again.

To enable the tourism sector to respond promptly and effectively in cases of emergency, the UNWTO and international business associations such as the Pacific Asia Travel Association (PATA) have already made major investments to establish crisis centres and risk management task forces. Further efforts are underway to develop climate change policies for the tourism sector that offer adaptation and mitigation measures aimed to prevent or reduce high expenditures in tourist areas affected by climate-change-related problems.

How urgent it is to take action is shown by the case of Fiji. Like uncountable other small islands around the world, Fiji's islands are highly vulnerable to climate change, and the tourism industry is already suffering from the impacts in the form of cyclones, storm surge and flooding, sea level rise, erosion, transport and communication interruption, and reduced water availability. These are the findings of a research by Susanne Becken, published by the University of the South Pacific in August 2004. The "climate-change-related hazards have the potential to destroy existing tourism capital and severely undermine efforts to attract new investment from within Fiji and overseas. Increasing insurance premiums aggravate the risk.".

Aviation, Cruise Ship Industry Major Climate Change Culprits

The aviation industry in particular is now facing enormous pressure since the Intergovernmental Panel on Climate Change (IPCC) and environmental campaign groups have singled out the responsibility of air travel in accounting for a considerable portion of global greenhouse gas emissions. Globally, the world's 16,000 commercial jet planes generate more than 600 million tones of CO_2 per year, almost as much as from all human activities in Africa each year, according to Friends of the Earth. The huge increase in aircraft pollution is largely due to the rapid growth of tourism and related air traffic. A WWF briefing paper on 'Tourism & Climate Change' (2001) states that the actual tonnage of CO_2 emitted will increase by over 75 per cent by 2015; concomitantly, from almost 700 million international travellers in 2000, numbers are expected to jump over one billion by 2010 and 1.6 billion by 2020. "As a consequence, the role of air travel within the tourism industry is likely to expand, cause considerable environmental damage, and to have knock-on effects on the tourism industry itself," concludes WWF.

Given the recent negative publicity, tourists in Western countries are changing their behaviour and tend to fly less. There are now even voices in Europe that go so far to suggest that flying away on holiday is immoral and should be stopped altogether.

"Warming stops global roaming", wrote the Australian newspaper *Daily Telegraph* recently. A survey in Australia done by a holiday website found nearly 20 per cent of respondents considered giving up air travel as it causes irreparable harm to the environment, while only 16 per cent said they do not care about climate change and it would not affect their travel choices at all. Similarly, a study prepared for Greenpeace in the UK showed a clear shift in consumers' perception: 61 per cent of the respondents were of the opinion that "We should limit our air travel voluntarily", 33 per cent agreed that "Air travel is now too cheap", 52 per cent agreed that "There should be a tax on fuel for air travel", and 61 per cent of the respondents supported the idea that "There should be a pollution warning on air tickets".

Apart from aviation, the worldwide booming cruise ship industry has also come under fire. Cruise ships that can carry up to 5,000 tourists are not only notorious for creating tremendous amounts of waste and sewage but also belong to the biggest contributors to greenhouse gas emissions within the travel and tourism industry. The US-Blue water Network that campaigns against the pollution of the world's oceans by ships has found that in one port visit, a single cruise ship can generate the emissions of more than 12,400 cars. The ship smokestacks release toxic emissions that lead to acid rain, global climate change, and damaging health effects to communities situated near ports. Despite the fact that ocean cruise liners are more energy efficient than other forms of commercial transportation, marine engines operate on extremely dirty fuels, known as 'bunker oil'. To compound the problem, engines on these ocean-going ships are currently not required to meet the same strict air pollution controls as cars and trucks are required to do.

Global travel and tourism could only grow by leaps and bounds because the transport networks that enable the movement of people and goods around the world are heavily subsidized. Tourists can enjoy to travel the world at incredibly low prices. As the New Economic Foundation study 'Up in Smoke?' explains "...much international trade lives in a bubble. International aviation and marine fuels are immune from any kind of taxation that would indicate and internalize the real environmental cost of freight and shipping. Greenhouse gas emissions from international freight are also exempt from the emissions targets set for rich countries to meet under the Kyoto Protocol of the UN Climate Change Convention."

Growing consumer awareness on these issues and a burgeoning citizens movement calling for fuel taxes and stricter regulation of the transport industry can severely curb future tourism growth targets and, thus, cut deep into the profits of plane-makers, airlines, travel agencies, cruise ship-operators and other tourism-related businesses. No wonder then that companies are now scrambling to talk about hard-earned environmental advances and new initiatives to protect the environment.

At the Paris Air Show in June, for example, Airbus' top salesman John Leah, told a press conference that Airbus is "saving the planet, one A380 at a time". The company's promotional brochures featured a silhouette of the new two-deck super-jumbo-dubbed the "gentle green giant"-set against images of dolphins, rain forests and fishing boats on a misty pond. Boeing representatives were also keen to display ecological bona fides and claimed the industry has reduced fuel consumption by 70 per cent since the jet age began, reported *Dow Jones Newswires*.

Image is All

While the global travel and tourism lobby has adopted the rhetoric of corporate social and environmental responsibility, reality checks on the ground show that tourism's environmental performance has remained very poor. Neither the UN-initiated International Year of Ecotourism 2002 or multilateral environment agreements such as the Tourism Guidelines under the Convention of Biological Diversity (CBD), have achieved anything to stop tourism from pervading pristine coastal areas, islands, forests and mountainous areas. On the contrary, more fragile ecosystems and biodiversity are destroyed, local communities displaced and traditional livelihoods destroyed-all for the establishment of huge exclusive resorts, golf courses and marinas. These massive tourism complexes are also notorious for high per capita consumption of energy and water. But however damaging and wasteful these projects may be, with the right PR efforts, they can still pass as 'ecotourism' developments and even raise their profile thanks to eco-accreditation schemes, or environmental Best Practices awards. As long as no proper legally binding frameworks are in place to check and redress excessive and damaging tourism activities, 'green-washing' continues and climate change culprits are likely to get away scot-free.

Ecotourism promoters' intention to help minimize tourism's carbon footprint is laudable. The GEC07 Oslo Statement, for example, outlines an action plan that aims at "encouraging adapted travel patterns; promoting more energy-efficient, alternative or non-motorized transport options; utilizing reduced and zero-emission operation technologies;

and increasing participation in reliable high-quality carbon offsetting schemes."

But many of the new initiatives that promote 'zero-carbon' or 'carbon-neutral' tourism businesses need critical examination because they may just be marketing gimmicks. For instance, *The Guardian* (UK) announced in January that Per Aquum, the brand behind some of the world's most luxurious resorts, was the owner of the first 'zero-carbon' five-star beach resort designed by architects in London. The developers of the resort, due to open in 2008, claim the project will have no negative environmental impact and will be totally self-sufficient, using only energy from the sun and wind and producing little waste or carbon emissions. "The only drawback, environmentally speaking, is its location-thousands of fuel-guzzling miles away in Nungwi, Zanzibar," cautioned *The Guardian.*

Six Senses Resorts and Spas, a Bangkok-based luxury hotel chain with properties in Thailand, Vietnam and the Maldives is now specialized in 'carbon-cutting getaways' for millionaires who do not want their "vacation dampened by global warming guilt". Apart from introducing energy-saving innovations at the luxurious island resorts, all visitors are required to pay a tax for their flight, which goes into a carbon offset fund. The project owners say the fund will be spent on renewable energy projects for villages in Sri Lanka and India, thus, offsetting among the poor the carbon emissions caused by jets transporting the rich to their holiday destination. Yet, can Six Senses really be called an environmentally friendly company considering that it consumes exorbitant amounts of water to run their spa facilities, for example?

Controversial Carbon Offsetting and Trading Schemes

A growing number of airlines have included carbon offsetting into the price of tickets. However, there are increasing reports about shady 'think green – see cash' carbon trading businesses that are trying to take advantage of well-intentioned air travellers. When Lufthansa earlier this year was looking for a partner to offer a carbon offsetting scheme to customers, half of the 13 studied companies were considered unreliable. Last year, the activists Timothy Byakola and Chris Lang exposed a Dutch company called Green Seat which promised to invest airline passengers' carbon offset contributions in climate friendly projects in poor countries. For the paltry sum of US$28, one would be able to cover the costs of planting 66 trees to 'compensate' for the CO_2

emissions of a return flight from Frankfurt to Kampala. But looking closer at one of these projects, in Mount Elgon National Park in Uganda, the activists found that local people were harassed and even driven from their land to pave the way for the tree plantations. Green Seat has since stopped selling carbon credits from Mount Elgon – because of the problems there. Earlier this year, farmers cut down half-a-million of the project's trees and planted crops and fruit trees on the land. Carbon trading that enables companies and consumers to buy themselves out of responsibility are highly controversial. It "dispossesses ordinary people in the South of their lands and futures without resulting in appreciable progress toward alternative energy systems," argues Larry Lohmann of the UK-based The Corner House, who has coedited the book 'Carbon Trading: A Critical Conversation on Climate Change, Privatization and Power'. "Tradable rights to pollute are handed out to Northern industry, allowing them to continue to profit from business as usual. At the same time, Northern polluters are encouraged to invest in supposedly carbon-saving projects in the South, very few of which are actually helping to halt dependence on fossil fuels."

Linking Climate Change and 'pro-poor' Tourism

If the goal is to effectively decrease greenhouse gas emissions in the travel and tourism sector, there seems to be no way around curbing the growth of the industry. It thus would make sense if governments rethink tourism as a development solution and offer alternatives to tourism in order to at least reduce the over-dependency on this industry in developing countries. But whenever such proposals come up, the tourism world is quick to argue that tourism is a top industry in the battle against world poverty. The UNWTO has declared the global tourism sector offers solutions to the "twin challenges of Climate Change and Poverty" in response to UN Secretary General Ban Kimoon's call for action on Climate to be taken in close coordination with global action on Poverty Alleviation & the Millennium Development Goals. A major aspect of UNWTO's submission to the Bali Climate Summit in December 2007 will be to demonstrate that the agency "is committed to ensuring that this coherence is applied to the tourism sector generally and particularly in regard to the world's poorest countries, for whom tourism is a driver of jobs, livelihoods, exports and competitiveness".

The focus on tourism as a viable foreign exchange earner for poor countries has always been rebuffed by critical analysts due to tourism's high leakages, for example. But tourism's benefits become an even more questionable affair in today's carbon-constrained world as Becken convincingly illustrates in her case study on Fiji tourism. She concludes that "eco-efficiency of tourism is possibly low when the total of greenhouse gas emissions are weighted against the economic benefits for Fiji, especially when about 60 per cent of tourism foreign exchange leak out of Fiji."

The argument of tourism as a poverty alleviation strategy is even more doubtful in view of the increasing foreign takeovers of tourism businesses as a result of globalization and liberalization. To stay with the case of Fiji, investment statistics show that 94 per cent of the 132 tourism projects put into operation between 1988 and 2000 were foreign owned. That means less tourism revenue trickles down to the local economy, but Fiji residents, including those who do not participate in the tourist trade at all, have to bear the high costs of tourism's energy use, greenhouse gas emissions and other environmental impacts. According to Becken, tourism within Fiji contributes at least 7.4 per cent to national energy use and CO^2 emissions, and if international air travel to and from Fiji is included, tourism makes up almost 30 per cent of national totals! Hence, tourism must be considered a burden to the poor, not a panacea!

What's Next?

We can certainly expect more heated debates on climate change and tourism in the coming months. Of special interest will be the outcome of the UNWTO's 2nd International Conference on Climate Change and Tourism to be held in Davos, Switzerland, from 1-3 October 2007. It aims to continue and deepen the discussions that started in Djerba 2003 with a focus on adaptation and mitigation needs and policy options. The results of the Davos conference will then be submitted to the Tourism Ministerial Summit on Climate Change, to be held in London, United Kingdom, on 13 November 2007, and to the UNWTO General Assembly in Cartagena de Indias, Colombia, 23-29 November 2007. After that the UNWTO is intent to show its presence at the Bali Climate Summit in December.

Also important to mention is the Pacific Asia Travel Association (PATA) initiative to mobilize influential travel and tourism industry leaders to sign on to a cross-sector industry response to climate change. In this context, it is preparing for a major event 'CEO Challenge 2008:

Confronting Climate Change' to be held in Bangkok on 29-30 April 2008. The ambitious goal for the 'CEO Challenge' is to create a single platform and action plan, fully engaging tourism ministers and heads of tourist boards, CEOs of airlines and airports, CEOs of leading international hotel groups, major tour operators and other key industry stakeholders.

Also in April next year, the aviation industry will convene its third Aviation and Environment Summit in Geneva.

It is urgent that civic movements concerned with climate change issues monitor and respond to these ongoing activities because travel and tourism is one of the world's most omnipotent industries, not only because of its size and growth but also as a driver of globalization and trade liberalization. Existing campaign networks such as Third World Network or the UK Working Group on Climate Change and Development that includes the New Economics Foundation (nef), Friends of the Earth (FoE), Greenpeace, Oxfam and WWF, should pay more attention to the problems of tourism-related climate change issues in their action plans and help lobby industry, governments, and intergovernmental agencies to take more decisive steps to curb relentless tourism expansion that exacerbates the climate change crisis.

More cooperative efforts to combat the negative impacts of climate change should be made by the academic community, development aid agencies and NGOs that are specifically concerned with tourism development. The Indian NGO Equations (Equitable Tourism Options) made a good start when it released a 'Call for Action on Climate Change, Biodiversity and Tourism' on occasion of the International Biodiversity Day on 22 May 2007'. Among other things, it called on the tourism industry to come up with an *authentic* response to climate change. "We recognize that [effective measures] may require a significant transformation of current forms of mass tourism and we urge a serious engagement on this issue to reduce tourism's climate change footprint," says the statement. Furthermore, Equations demands "climate justice" by phasing out unsustainable growth strategies. It states, "The responsibility of seeking viable and sustainable solutions to avert the climate crisis must take into account particularly the plight of the most vulnerable communities around the world."

7

Nature Tourism: Strategies Nature Based Tourism Strategy

Introduction

Nature based tourism is one of Australia and the world's fastest growing tourism markets, as residents and visitors go to natural and cultural areas and sites to experience beautiful landscapes, flora and fauna and our European and Indigenous culture. In the ACT, even without significant promotion, visitation to natural areas and cultural sites is steadily growing.

Nature based tourism is tourism focusing on visitation to natural or near natural area, including recreation, visits to European and Indigenous cultural sites and simple sightseeing. As a nature based tourism destination the ACT is unique within Australia and possibly the world. Compared to a national average of 8% for land designated as parks and reserves, 53% of the ACT is made up of either national park or nature reserves with a further 10% of the Territory composed of plantation forests. Given this wealth, the ACT's natural areas represent significant recreation and tourism resources. Indeed, experiences of unspoiled natural environments, unique landscapes and wildlife, as well as significant Indigenous and European heritage and cultural resources, offer considerable potential to contribute to the Territory's tourism promotion and positioning.

Canberra's high quality urban environment also provides an opportunity for the ACT to develop an image as a diverse and healthy leisure destination. The Bush Capital's open spaces, parks, walking and cycling trails as well as close proximity to substantial and significant nature parks and reserves provide a wide range of opportunities for Canberrans and visitors to relax, recuperate and revitalise.

This Strategy sets out the ACT Government's directions and priorities for the further development of nature based tourism in the territory. The Strategy has been developed as one component of the ACT Tourism Master Plan. Ongoing community involvement in both experiencing our wonderful assets and in working with the Government in refining and developing the Strategy is actively sought.

Why an ACT Nature Based Tourism Strategy?

Nature based tourism can deliver a range of environmental, social and economic benefits to the ACT community, including:

- Increased community and visitor environmental awareness and understanding;
- Promotion of environmental and cultural values;
- Generation revenue for the conservation and management of natural and cultural heritage;
- Greater community and visitor enjoyment of natural and cultural sites and facilities; and
- Employment opportunities, utilising local knowledge and facilities.

In addition, nature based tourists tend to be high yield tourists, spending more, and staying longer in a destination than general tourists. Importantly, as tourism, and in particular nature based tourism, is essentially about the environment in which we live, work and play the ACT's natural assets also represent significant community resources and recreational opportunities. Many of those visiting the Territory's natural and cultural sites and attractions are and will continue to be Canberra residents and their visiting friends and relatives.

What is Nature Based Tourism?

Nature based tourism can be defined as visitation to natural or near natural areas. This includes ecotourism, adventure tourism, rural tourism, visits to European or Indigenous cultural and heritage sites, and simple sightseeing and recreation. Ecotourism is a niche component of nature based tourism, with a focus on education and interpretation of the natural and cultural environment. The ACT has a wide range of significant nature based tourism assets and resources, including

Namadgi National Park, Tidbinbilla Nature Reserve, Canberra Nature Park, Murrumbidgee River Corridor and Googong Foreshores. Other assets include:

- The Australian National Botanic Gardens;
- The National Aquariums and Australian Wildlife Sanctuary;
- Canberra's city parks and lakes, managed by the ACT Government and the National Capital Authority;
- European and Indigenous cultural heritage sites and objects; and
- Plantation pine and native forests managed by ACT Forests.

Who are the Nature Based Tourists?

We are all nature based tourists. Most of us enjoy getting out into the natural environment, and most of us seek a range of experiences, from wilderness trekking and bush walking through to less demanding activities such as scenic driving and casual visits to nature reserves and parks. Bureau of Tourism Research (BTR) data notes that:

- The appeal of nature based tourism experiences are similar across most age and life cycle groups;
- Educative and interpretive experiences are of similar appeal amongst both sexes and across age and life cycle groups (although people with children are more likely to see learning about nature as important than those without children);
- Nature based and ecotourists tend to be more educated than non-ecotourists and often have higher incomes; and
- As experiences become more physically demanding, more expensive or specialised the nature based tourism market quickly narrows.

Thus there is no single nature based tourism market, rather a range of markets and market segments that flow into one another as the tourists seek a range of experiences. These experiences range from what can be described as 'hard' nature based such as wilderness trekking and bush walking through to less demanding or 'soft' nature based activities such as scenic driving, and casual visits to nature reserves and parks. Many visitors to natural and cultural heritage sites are Canberra residents-families and friends wishing to simply experience nature and culture.

Plantation Forests

Approximately 10% of the Territory is plantation pine and other forests managed by ACT Forests. About 1.1 m residents and visitors come to the forests each year. These areas are managed as multiple purpose forests, being both commercial forest and available for a wide range of recreational activities. Of the 26,900 hectares managed by ACT Forests, about 16,000 hectares is pine plantation. The remainder comprises nature reserves, native vegetation corridors, water bodies and streams and over 1200km of forest roadway.

The range of activities available in these areas is much wider than in the national parks and nature reserve areas, and includes car rallies, paint ball, sled dog trials, horse riding, cycling, orienteering and off-lead areas for dogs. ACT Forests offer a range of activities including bush walks, fishing and camping. The forests also contain a diversity of European and Aboriginal heritage sites, as well as several arboreta and the largest cork oak plantation in the southern hemisphere. The less restricted use of the forests also reduces any pressure to use the more sensitive natural areas for more intensive activity, for example the FAI Rally of Canberra, a major car rally, is also held in ACT Forests areas.

In contrast to the other states and territories, the ACT's bush parks and forests are relatively close to our urban areas, enabling easy access for both residents and visitors to experience the ACT's natural and cultural heritage.

The Environment Green Evaluation Programme

Balatonfüred managed environment protection as an important mission even before the political –economical changes of '89. But the real progress started only in the nineties. The Self-government created its own Local Order of Environment amongst the first towns in the country, introduced selective waste collection subsided financially by EU after a successful PHARE submission, joined local forces of NGOs interested in environmental issues. As a continuation of this progress the Self-government participated in a large international environmental project led by the Union of Baltic Cities along with Siófok and Lake Balaton Development Coordination Agency.

The goal of the project is to create and introduce an up to date, environment conscious managing system in the participating cities for a sustainable urban environment. Dr. Bóka István, the mayor of Balatonfüred signed the co-financing statement on 26th March 2004. The Kickoff meeting was held in Riga on 13th-14th June, 2005, where the most important steps and the frameworks of cooperation of the three years long project were discussed. Only after this meeting, on 21st July, 2005. The Partnership and Grant Agreement was signed by UBC and Balatonfüred. Yet in Riga on the starting plenary conference the frameworks and the forms of cooperation and the schedule of work were determined.

First of all the preparation of a Baseline Review and then a Strategic Program were decided. After having collected the available necessary local documents and refreshing data Balatonfüred has compiled its Baseline Review. As a part of this work, the SWOT analysis gives a proper starting point for the Strategic Program of the town, as it formulates step by step the strengths to be exploited consciously better in the future, weaknesses we have to eliminate as far as possible, or to reduce their negative effects and the possibilities we are to make the best and the threats which are to avoid. This Strategic Program was compiled following the structure of the BR. In the process of creation of SP the still existing documents (City Developing Concept, Urban Organization Plan, for Public Health, etc.) and the newest developing ideas were highly taken into consideration Evaluation of the present situation (SWOT analysis) Environmental elements

The natural environment of town Balatonfüred belongs to the most beautiful and most precious sites in the country. This beauty has not only aesthetic but a high economic value, as it considerably contributes to the tourist attractiveness of the town itself. Thus protecting and improving the natural environment is a basic interest of the community.

The Koloska valley, the Tamás hill and the Malom valley are the most precious outskirt areas of Balatonfüred. These sites along with the other outings are threatened mostly by two main dangers. The first is building up and fencing (illegally or evading the law) and the illegal waste deposits. Building up and fencing endangers mostly Tamás hill and the other higher areas where the beautiful panorama induces such needs and intentions. Illegal waste deposits have been occurring in decades long on certain places well accessible by cars and lorries, mainly by the roadsides leading out of town.

The Strategic Program is to preserve the natural environment by the following measures: On the non built green areas of Tamás hill total ban of construction is to introduce except those improvement involved in the Strategic Program. It is to acquire the ownership the areas around Jókai lookout tower and the paths leading to the summit. More frequently emptied and more numerous waste containers are to be placed on the most often visited illegal deposits by the roads leading out of the town- The control of these area must be realized by joining forces of official and voluntary environmentalists.

Besides preservation of the natural environment it is to make efforts to a careful and cautious exploitation of these values, as the improving ecotourism, and with raising incomes increase the city welfare. The Strategic Program supports the following improvements: Ecological recreation of the streambed of Malom valley brook and establishment a fee fishing pond above the Dobogóhid section of the brook. Previously or simultaneously The recultivation of the neighbouring dumpsite is to be completed.

A cable lift is to establish on the slopes of Tamás hill. Its incomes are to ensure the costs of a permanent warding of the natural environment. It is a further benefit, that heart patients and disabled people can enjoy the beauty of the panorama. On the still existing forest paths of the northern slopes a system of jogging tracks is to establish. This can also be used as cross country sky courses in winter. Summer bobsleigh course is also supported by the Strategic Program. The excursion centre in the Koloska valley needs a better and easier access and a higher level of services and more comfort. The Strategic Program supports such improvements. Besides this a cautious riverbed recreation on the lower sections of the brook is allowed. On the upper sections it is only the installation of small wooden barrages to retain water what is supported by the SP. The middle section of the brook is to remain in its natural condition. The renovation of the Füredi Kiserd (Small Forest Park) is supported but the old and precious wood stock must be preserved. The Balaton shoreline is to be protected.

Further concrete walls and stoning is allowed only sections where the Shoreline Rehabilitation Plan indicates boat jetties or yacht harbours. Reeds and natural shoreline are to be protected even at that sites. A mobile, floating aquarium and ecological showplace is to be built and placed between Tagore Promenade and the Annabella beach Efforts are to be made for the most detailed mapping of underground mineral carbonic water bases. Further research drillings must be carried out in order to substantiate an improving medicinal spa culture. Constructed environment The three historical centre of the town, Fured Old Village, the Resort Quarter and Aracs historical village core is to preserved and developed according to the traditions.

At a different extent these three areas became city centres by the commerce, catering and services focused here. Further improvement is possible and desirable mostly by the private investments attracted here, but for the preserving renovation of public places financed by municipal and granted funds is also necessary. The "Mainstreet program" aims at the development of the main street of the Old Village besides preserving the picturesque values, strengthen the functions of town centre. The improvement of the historical village centre of Aracs has already commenced. It must be completed by reconstructing the municipality owned buildings into a centre of education, culture and services.

The partly finished renovation of the Resort Quarter is to be extended with the reconstruction of Gyogyter (Medicinal square), and east and westward continuation of the Tagore Promenade. In the eastern section of the littoral zone between the two main beaches on the plot of the Anglers' Association a municipal water sport centre is to be established. This places will afford possibilities for fishing rowing and sailing first of all for the local people. The former Huray –market (once the village football ground in the old times) building up is allowed only with establishments for only cultural and/or entertaining activities.

On the public plots behind it recreational or educational establishments are to be built. Building areas for economical activities which are not desirable in residential districts will be provided primarily by the northern side of Aszof road, towards the dumpsite and on itself the dumpsite after its restoration. The building of the west bypass road is the most important traffic task. Renovation of pavements and urban streets must be continued. The number and the length of bike roads are to be increased. This improvement is desirable primarily in the case of bike roads joining to the Balaton Bike road and leading north out town, thus the background settlements, the stations of wine routes, and the values of nature can get an easy access. The total renovation of the rainfall system is vitally necessary. Humane factor First rank task is to increase the number of birth.

It can be realized by increasing the certainty of existence (creating new places of employment, flat building programs) education and by the financial support for young mothers and newborns We have to protect our fundamentally good education system of the unfavourable effects, spreading from outside. Further cooperation of our primary schools is desirable. In health aspect the conditions of the environmental elements are generally suitable. Occasional air pollution from traffic will be reduced by building bypass roads, and the sporadic water and soil pollution will also diminished by perfecting the sewage system.

The main mortal risk factors are to be reduced by proper and effective health education and by the extension of screening tests. At present only the State and the local Self-government play essential role in social care. It is desirable to establish and support civil organizations with a vocation to such aims and goals. The crime status is rather suitable in the city.

The main figures in crime reports are ceasing year by year. The Self Government, NGOs and enterprises support effectively the work of the Police and other crime pursuing organizations through the Foundation for Property Defence. To counter against drugs and other addictions prevention is the number one tool, and secondly a more effective crime pursual work and a rising social support is to be achieved. The seasonal (autumn, winter) unemployment is a very characteristic and impending factor on city development.

Thus the main goal is to increase the numbers of permanent work places. City function and management The Mayor's Office, which is responsible for city function and management carries out its task profoundly suitable. Its cooperation with the elected city management, the Self-government is also proper. Within the Office the cooperation between the departments must be strengthen.

Regular heads of departments meetings-are to be held, where they report on the achievements and where the tasks for the next period will be shared out. Reinforcement of environmental affairs with minimum one new staff member is absolutely necessary. In the case of public space wards the situation is similar. Employment of an additional staff member is justified as well as the widening of their authority and competence. The clarks' ability of communication in a foreign language are to be improved. Employment of a new civil servant ought to be conditioned by a communicative skill in a foreign language. It is the PROBIO zRT which performs definitely the communal duties of the town in a suitable and a improving way. This company is responsible for collecting, transport and deposit of communal waste on a dumpsite operated by itself. The dumpsite is to be operated until the start up of the regional waste management system including the new dumpsite. Then the old dumpsite must be recultivated and environment friendly activities are to be settled here.

We have to stimulate and increase the selective waste collecting and the in situ composting on the detached estates with a garden. The self-government has to review the whole city function especially the energy supply of the town. It is vitally important to compile an energy concept and an energy action plan. The Self-government and the Mayor's Office are to be committed to be the vanguard promoting the utilization of alternative energy resources. Therefore an action plan must be worked out for the installation of public buildings with solar collectors. The Self-government is to encourage the establishment of small local di- and trigeneration power stations for new public establishments and bigger private buildings.

For the realization of this program a conscious and well prepared project strategy is to be compiled. This is the way to acquire the majority of the necessary financial funds. A local program is to be worked out for the renovation of public and private buildings introducing more efficient heat isolation technologies. Economy The economy of the city is mostly based on summer tourism. This must be changed in two ways. First the tourist period must be widened, and secondly other economical activities must be settled in the town. The extension of tourist season has already begun. The Balaton Congress and Leisure time Centre has built and organises diverse programs, the year round functioning Aqua park opened for the public.

Three four star hotels affording high level services all the year are going to be finished and opened at the end of this year. The still existing older hotels are to be renovated thus joining to the season elongating program. The sport tourism is also improving thanks to the new possibilities by the opening of BCLC and by building new yacht harbours. Former institute offers place for sport events all the year, sailing life is restricted to the period from the late spring until early autumn. Establishment of an ice stadium would give an additional push to the development of sport tourism.

As this establishment needs much energy it is to be built and operate by the most modern and effective energy utilization. The cultural tourism also has got a huge possibility by the opening of BCLC. A new theatre performing all the year around would significantly animate the cultural life in the town. The traditional wine tourism is the only economical activity what is based on agriculture and has significant role in the town. Its quantitative improvement is hardly possible. Further development seems to be possible in the still existing estates, achievements of a better access to the wine route stations and improving better services. Fishing tourism is to be also improved. The Balatonfüredi Horgasz Egyesulet has to get a possibility to build a new jetty and fishing clubhouse, which can afford a proper level of services for guest anglers.

The careful improvement of natural environment mentioned under will also contribute to the prolongation of the tourist season. For the sake of creating new jobs, it is also vital to attract other economical activities in the city. First of all economical, logistic and financial centres are to be settled as they won't spoil the tourist appeal of the town. Different kinds of environment friendly artisan manufactures are also welcome Certain faculties of high school education according to character of the region (environmental, nature protection, hydrobiology or tourism and economy, possibly faculty of law) would animate the local economy and the whole spirit of the town.

Executive Summary

Tourism in Turkey has developed rapidly for the last two decades and it had a profound and irreversible effect on many destination areas. As the demand for new destinations increases, there is an unrelenting pressure for development in order to satisfy the growth of this complex, pervasive industry. Yet the approach of sustainable development does not allow uncontrolled growth and opening of new areas to tourism, where environment and local culture may be negatively affected. On the other hand, eco-tourism allows opening of new areas to tourism and creates new contacts between tourists and local society. Travel agencies who create and/or sell ecotours, with or without awareness, are acting against sustainable tourism development. This research was undertaken in order to explore the attitudes of TURSAB member local travel agencies engaged in eco-tourism towards sustainable tourism development.

Introduction

The growth in alternative forms of tourism has occurred simultaneously with an increased recognition of the need to implement the concept of sustainable development. Ecotourism has been widely assumed to be inherently sustainable, although few attempts have been made to verify this assumption. Ecotourism incorporates environmental and cultural conservation objectives, and emphasizes economic benefits to local communities. Hence, eco-tourism would appear to be, and is increasingly presented as, a tool for sustainable development. However, it also has the potential to be more environmentally damaging than mass tourism since it typically occurs in fragile environments and opens up previously undiscovered destinations to the mass market.

By the late 1980s, a shift in the tourism industry's marketing strategy occurred alongside the emergence of the global environmental movement. In the decade of "green consumerism", critical consumers were soon leading the demand for "environmentally sound" holidays. Tour operators and travel companies began to promote themselves and their products as "environmentally friendly", and a number of companies published ethical and environmental codes of conduct and guidelines for travellers as well as guidelines for self-regulation. Tour companies also started to promote eco-tourism holidays to all corners of the world, to coincide with the inclusion of the environment on the mainstream political agenda. At the same time the tourist hunting industry has expanded dramatically.

Literature Survey

Sustainable Development

In the 1987 Brundtland Report of the World Commission on Environment and Development, sustainable development is defined as the "development that meets the needs of the present without compromising the ability of future generations to meet their own needs" (World Commission on Environment and Development, 1987:43). To meet the needs of the present, the new development has to provide ground on which the basic necessities of all humans and the opportunities for a better life can be satisfied.

Sustainable development is being discussed for the last two decades, mostly among academicians. The core elements of these discussions are:

- The idea that the needs of present and future generations must be considered;
- The need to ensure that renewable and non-renewable resources are conserved, not exhausted;
- The requirement that access to and use of natural resources must take fair account of the needs of all people;
- A recognition that issue of environment and sustainable development must be treated in an integrated manner.

Sustainable Tourism Development

The tourism and recreation industry is at a crossroads in its development. Now as one of the world's largest industries, it is increasingly confronted with arguments about its sustainability and compatibility with environmental protection and community development. Consideration of tourism, the environment, and concepts of sustainability should consider four key challenges: (1) a better understanding of how tourists value and use natural environments; (2) enhancement of the communities dependent on tourism as an industry; (3) identification of the social and environmental impact of tourism; and (4) implementation of systems to manage these impacts. The tourism and recreation industry is confronted with serious and difficult choices about its future. The decisions made now will for decades affect the lifestyles and economic opportunity of residents in tourism destination areas. Many of these decisions are irreversible because once communities lose the character that makes them distinctive and attractive to nonresidents, they have lost their ability to vie for tourist-based income in an increasingly global and competitive market place.

Owen (1993) characterizes sustainable tourism development as:

- Tourism should be one part of a balanced economy.
- The use of tourism environments must allow for long-term preservation and for use of those environments.

- Tourism should respect the character of an area.
- Tourism must provide long-term economic benefits.
- Tourism should be sensitive to the needs of the host population.

Butler suggests the following working definition of sustainable development in the context of tourism: "tourism which is developed and maintained in an area (community, environment) in such a manner and at such a scale that it remains viable over an indefinite period and does not degrade or alter the environment (human and physical) in which it exists to such a degree that it prohibits the successful development and well being of other activities and processes".

The growth in alternative forms of tourism has occurred simultaneously with increased recognition of the need to implement the concept of sustainable development. As with "eco-tourism", "sustainable development" is another environmental catch phrase with no single definition.

On the face of it, no other economic activity would appear to lend itself to sustainable development better than tourism. Alternative forms of tourism that incorporate environmental and cultural conservation objectives with an emphasis on economic benefits to local communities would appear to be a panacea for sustainable development. Because damage to the environment threatens the resource base on which alternative forms of tourism depend, it would be logical to expect all involved in tourism to ensure the protection of these resources. All forms of tourism consume resources such as land and energy. However, when practiced against the standards of its definition, the small scale and dispersed nature of eco-tourism, combined with connotations of sound environmental management, means that it has the potential to consume far less basic resources than other forms of tourism or other developments.

A recent article in the UK Youth Hostel Association's magazine, Triangle, takes up this theme: "Spending your holiday in one of the latest artificial all-weather tropical pleasure domes or in intensely developed but properly managed holiday resorts like Benidorm and Torremolinos can be more environmentally friendly than indulging in trips to remote or fragile areas where tourism is more likely to be environmentally and culturally damaging and puts little or nothing back into managing and protecting the environment" (YHA, 1996).

Quoted in the same article, the popular conservationist David Bellamy comments "Ecotourism is already a dirty word. Hill walking, jungle trekking and all the rest are just as potentially harmful as conventional resort holidays, if not more so. Most of the tourism industry is simply sponging off clean water, fresh air, the natural and cultural environment and is putting nothing back in. But there are praiseworthy exceptions, which not only do not damage the environment, but also actually help to restore it. This is real eco-tourism." (YHA, 1996).

In addition to the potential damage caused locally to tourist destinations, the air transport of tourists to remote areas of the globe seriously undermines the concept of sustainability of the industry as a whole. For example, air travel contributes 2-3 percent of global emissions of fossil fuel derived carbon dioxide, the principal greenhouse gas, as well as nitrogen oxides, which contribute to low-level ozone formation. Paradoxically, nitrogen oxides released at high altitudes also contribute to the thinning of the protective ozone layer over the earth.

Not all of the impacts of tourism are necessarily negative. If development and change are bound to occur in a particular site from some activity or other, tourism may be a far less damaging alternative than many other more polluting industries. The Overseas Development Association (ODA) Manual of Environment Appraisal (1996) provides a checklist to help develop management strategies to minimize negative impacts and maximize positive benefits. Therefore, alternative or other forms of tourism are not necessarily a panacea for sustainable development, unless well planned and well regulated.

In most countries, there usually is no coordination between programs that promote and market tourism and those that manage environment and culture. On the other hand, agencies dealing with the promotion of tourism are not involved with the evaluation of its effects or with advance planning and management of the adverse impacts of tourism through avoidance, mitigation, and compensation strategies.

Ecotourism

The term "eco-tourism" is often assumed largely to alternative tourism that involves international travel by people from rich developed countries to developing countries, as a means of providing much needed foreign exchange for hard-pressed national economies, and earnings for poor rural people. The notion of these interrelated conservation and economic benefits has led to much confusion surrounding the variety of terms currently in use that appear to have similar meanings and aims. These include "alternative tourism", "sustainable tourism", "soft tourism", "special interest tourism", "green tourism", and "eco-tourism". Some of these terms frequently appear to be used interchangeably, while others may be defined in a variety of ways.

In reality, eco-tourism has become widely adopted as a generic term to describe tourism that has, as its primary purpose, an interaction with nature, and that incorporates a desire to minimize negative impacts. Implicit in the term is the assumption that local communities should benefit from tourism and will help to conserve nature in the process. In this study, the term "Ecotourism" will be used to generalize all the other terms, and if a specific section of eco-tourism like wildlife tourism or alternative tourism is explained, then those terms will be used specifically. The terms "eco-tourists" and "ecotours" will be used in this study to summarize the group of tourists and the tours created for them in the name of eco-tourism.

As with the term "eco-tourism", there is similar confusion regarding the term "alternative tourism" that is often used as a generic term encompassing a range of variations such as eco-tourism and green tourism, all of which purport to offer a more benign alternative to conventional mass tourism. Indeed, eco-tourism has been described as "one of the most widely used and abused phrases of the last decade", which it is argued can mean anything to anyone.

A few definitions of "Ecotourism":

"An enlightening nature travel experience that contributes to the conservation of the ecosystem while respecting the integrity of host communities".

"Responsible travel to natural areas, which conserves the environment and improves the welfare of local people".

"Purposeful travel that creates an understanding of cultural and natural history, while safeguarding the integrity of the ecosystem and producing economic benefits that encourage conservation".

Ecotourism can contribute enormously to the management of protected areas. Benefits include foreign exchange revenues, employment opportunities, improving awareness of conservation objectives and stimulation of economic activity. While protected areas are major destinations for eco-tourists, private enterprise is playing an increasing role in the eco-tourism sector.

In addition, eco-tourism is a major vehicle for realizing tangible benefits of conservation for local communities with wildlife populations occurring on their land. However, the benefits accruing to local communities from tourism have so far been overstated. The type and magnitude of the environmental impacts associated with eco-tourism vary with the type of tourist activity pursued. Some impacts are obvious and easily identifiable, while others are indirect and difficult to quantify.

Strategies to manage the impacts arising from eco-tourism may also be direct or indirect. Direct strategies include limiting the total numbers of visitors to an area; dispersing visitors; zoning; using fixed viewing points; and setting guidelines for minimum viewing distances. Indirect strategies are those that aim to modify the behaviour of tourists. One of the most important ways of achieving this is to educate visitors about the potential disturbance they can cause and to provide advice on how to reduce it.

Ecotourism has the potential to be more damaging than mass tourism since they often occur in fragile or unique environments. Small-scale operations in environmentally sensitive locations may eventually turn into much larger and more destructive operations. Ecotourism may simply represent the early stages of the conventional tourist destination life cycle. The life cycle concept essentially revolves around the premise that, unless intervention occurs, tourist destination areas and resources inevitably will become overused and, consequently, will decline. The six stages of the cycle are as follows:

- Exploration (few tourists, poor access and facilities, environment unchanged);
- Involvement (local initiatives, some promotion, increasing numbers);
- Development (many tourists, locals lose control, deterioration of environment);
- Consolidation (tourist numbers exceed local residents, all major chains represented);

- Stagnation (numbers peak, destination falls out of fashion, environmental and social problems);
- Decline or Rejuvenation (or intermediaries).

This cycle has a number of obvious implications for sustainability, based on the consideration of factors such as carrying capacity, local participation, ownership, social and environmental impacts.

Mass tourists may have less impact than eco-tourists, because they tend to limit themselves to well known, easily accessible areas and insulate themselves from the local people. In some instances, the zoning of mass tourism (or enclave tourism) is adopted as a deliberate policy by a host country. For example, tourists in the Maldives are confined to self-contained, purpose built resorts on isolated, often formerly uninhabited islands, in order to avoid a culture clash between bikini-clad tourists and the conservative, Islamic islanders. Bhutan limits the annual foreign tourist entrance to their country to 3,000 pax only.

Ecotourism proved to be a very lucrative sector of the industry, and commercial considerations of marketing the latest "undiscovered" paradise quickly overshadowed any concerns for environmental or cultural degradation. Indeed, the marketing of eco-tourism may well have accelerated social degradation, because more and more previously unknown destinations were discovered and subsequently opened up to mass tourism.

Turkey and Sustainable Tourism Development

Without giving due regard to the underlying principles of eco-tourism, tour operators and even governmental agencies seem to be securing the short-term economic benefits to sell regions or products.

As a developing country, Turkey's choice of pursuing a tourism development strategy is to create opportunities for economic improvement, since it suffers from deficit in the balance of payments. Tourism is also a tool for decreasing unemployment, because it is a labour-intensive industry. Turkey is trying to secure the short-term inflow of the foreign currency by increasing its bed capacity and trying to attract more tourists. Although the industry is centralized as being governed by the ministry, there are not any records available of any act for sustainable tourism development. Some accommodation units and travel agencies to a certain extent, as a tool for revenue generation, only use sustainable tourism. Accommodation units try to decrease the operational costs like usage of sun energy. Some demand less usage of towels. Clearly, the aim of these acts is not to maintain sustainable tourism, but to minimize their costs. Indeed, the travel agencies' main concern is to maximize the total number of tourists to increase their profit. Therefore, the carrying capacity is totally ignored.

Like many other developing country governments, Turkish governments have helped the fast development of tourism without taking into account the factors of local culture and environment. All governmental acts have been related to monetary gains, since Turkey have been used to economic crises during the last decade. Even IMF has expected certain tourism income figures in order to give credits.

Research Methodology

The purpose of the research was to explore the perceptions of and the possible commitments of Turkish travel agencies engaged in eco-tourism to sustainable tourism development. An exploratory study were undertaken since not much was known about the situation at hand, and there were not any information available on how similar problems or research issues have been solved in the past. In other terms, there were not any previously defined theoretical framework and any hypothesis to test, so this research was to develop related subjects and their groupings by content analysis.

In order to address the quality of information obtained about nature tour operators, substantial attention will be given to survey design and administration. The aim of the research was to examine how travel agencies perceive the impacts of their development and to evaluate their level of response to environmental concerns. In order to satisfy these aims, the objective was to obtain rich data. This pointed towards using a qualitative method involving relatively few people. According to Oppenheim (1992) 'the longer, the more difficult and the more open-ended the questions schedule is, the more we should prefer to use interviews.' In the light of this, a decision was made to undertake face-to-face, in-depth interviews.

In order to reach desired information, directors or senior personnel of ten TURSAB member agencies who are engaged in eco-tourism as the unit of analysis were interviewed. Having obtained the booklet of TURSAB listing the agencies as the population frame, the initial intention was to undertake systematic random sampling; however, this method of sampling proved unsatisfactory due to the high number of companies unwilling to participate and the fact that only around one-third of the population were in Istanbul, making the rest impossible to reach regarding the time limits.

The choice of researcher was, therefore, very much decided on by the respondents' willingness to participate, i.e. the first ten agencies in Istanbul to agree. Given the seniority of all the interviewees, this was effectively 'elite interviewing': the individuals are influential and in a position to report on their organizations policies and future plan. Furthermore, 'elites respond well to intelligent, provocative, open-ended questions'.

Among the total population of 362, 135 were located in Istanbul and the rest 227 were located especially where eco-tourism activities took place. A limitation should be noted that the number of agencies rapidly change and figures of 2000 may not be the exact values of today, yet helped us for a fair idea of the population, since links on TURSAB website of the updated lists of agencies did not work during research process.

The research was a cross-sectional study with respect to time horizon, because data were gathered by the interview once, for a period of days.

In-depth, face-to-face interviews with managers of travel agencies engaged in eco-tourism have been used as the data collection method. Other data sources were used during the literature survey such as publications, manuals, archives, journals and related books.

For qualitative data analysis, systematic coding by content analysis was used to analyse the transcripts of the interviews. In this method, the researcher analysed interview answers and prepared a list of subjects. The researcher and one independent sorter categorized these subjects independently. After a discussion between the researcher and the independent sorter, who was a manager of one of the visited travel agencies, a common categorization was agreed upon. For reliability testing, two independent graduate students who have studied research methodology also categorized the subjects.

According to the reliability test, the results of the content analysis came out to be significant.

Findings and Discussions

Types of Tours

According to the segmentation like mass tourism and eco-tourism, travel agencies engaged in eco-tourism also sell tours for the mass market. When the respondents were asked to compare the two types of tours with respect to sustainability, there was a clear dichotomy between the two segments.

At the first glance, special tours and ecotours might be considered more sustainable; their volumes are lower, they are more likely to use local accommodation, local guides and services, and attract more environmentally aware clients. However, a differentiated tour for the mass market may attract eco-tourists as well. On the other hand, some specialist markets are evolving into mass markets, because of the increase in volume and the rapidly changing markets. This shows the danger of using broad statements, as ecotours are more sustainable.

Types of Activities

According to the frequency order derived from the answers of the respondents, the following activities are marketed by the travel agencies: Walking/rambling, alternative water sports, trekking, golf, adventure, cycling, hunting, safari, photographing, mountaineering, rafting, horseback riding, fishing, alternative winter sports, bird watching. Many of the agencies sell more than one type of tours.

Why to Sell Alternative Forms of Tourism?

Travel agencies sell alternative forms of tourism in order to earn more money. Other reasons are to reach the young generation, to increase the variety of products and to enter a new market. Travel agency executives feel that their companies should be considered like markets or small shops in evaluation of any effects of operations, but they forget the fact that they do not sell products of another company like a market, but they produce the ecotours themselves and sell them. Since those tours selling the nature are their products, they are responsible for the positive or negative effects of their products.

These effects may be to the environment, to the local culture or to other aspects related to sustainable tourism. Travel agencies do not seem to accept the fact that some of the activities they make are acting against sustainable tourism by opening new areas to tourism without considering carrying capacity, using the nature as a marketing concept and allowing uncontrolled contact with local culture and tourists.

Sustainable Tourism

Sustainable development is a new subject of concern that many of us are not familiar with. Sustainable tourism development is also new, but it is being discussed in meetings of many international organizations. The first and obviously the main finding was that most of the interviewed senior personnel or managers of travel agencies in Turkey that are engaged in eco-tourism do not even know what sustainability is all about.

Interesting answers on the definition of sustainability, which were totally unrelated to it, reminded the researcher the fact that many of the employees and managers in the tourism industry are uneducated or did not have their education on tourism. This was proved by the respondents' education levels, which were mostly high-school graduates. The most interesting answer for the researcher was: 'Sustainable tourism, should be related to renovations of the hotels, planes it should not be related with travel agencies, we sustain tourism'. No matter the answer is funny or dramatic, but it seemed to be the reality for general knowledge of travel agency executives in Turkey related to sustainability. So, the respondents did not take into consideration the important aspects of sustainability like local culture or environment, since they did not know the term.

Who is More Responsible for Realization of Sustainable Tourism?

Economically, travel agencies feel that any attempt to take steps on sustainable tourism will put them at a commercial disadvantage because of increasing costs. They agree on helping the realization of sustainable tourism only if the tourists accept to pay more. Therefore, they feel that governments are more responsible for imposing restrictions, limiting growth and controlling volumes and so helping sustainable tourism. The result of this study showed that, travel agencies are willing to comply with regulations if governments impose them to the whole sector. Another point that Turkish travel agencies engaged in eco-tourism mentioned is their operations are too small with respect to the whole market to make any influence.

Conclusion and Implications

This study has examined the social, environmental and cultural impacts of alternative tourism activities with regard to the travel agencies in Turkey engaged in eco-tourism. First conclusion is that it has become harder to segment the market into mass tourism and eco-tourism, since the two segments are becoming more integrated into each other and there are products, which cannot be put under a certain category. Second conclusion is that, although these travel agencies sell ecotours and earn money, they believe that government has the major responsibility to ensure sustainable development. The third general conclusion is the fact that most of the travel agency executives has learned the definition of sustainability after the general explanation of the researcher.

It is easy to make an assumption like because travel agencies are small enterprises; their responsible behaviour may have a very small effect on sustainable tourism. Yet, specialist tours take tourists deeper into nature and sensitive local culture, and import the necessary skills instead using local work force.

Environmental policies and sustainable acts have become nothing more than a marketing ploy and a vehicle or eluding regulation. Environmental departments and affiliations with glossy campaigns have arguably become a PR exercise designed to meet the growing awareness in some markets to appear environmentally sound and to attract higher spending tourists. For sustainable tourism to be a marketable concept, tourists themselves have got to really buy on it.

To conclude, the researcher wants to point out that sustainability is mostly considered as an utopia and will probably never be achieved.

8

Compliance of Nature Tour Operators Nature-Based Tourism Enterprises

Background and Context

As the world has entered the new millennium, tourism has been seen as one of the fundamental sectors vital to economic wellbeing in the Pacific region. Despite international catastrophes, such as terrorist attacks, local communities have to find ways to sustain themselves even if there is a decline in tourism travel. The Pacific region is unique and dynamic as a social and cultural environment, and many local communities in Pacific Island countries have seen the benefits from tourism. This makes South Pacific culture a major asset for the tourism industry of each country, but raises the question of how to sustain it and do justice to the people in the far scattered islands of the Pacific Ocean.

The Maori are one group who shares the rich and varied past of the Pacific region. They are Polynesian people who can be considered indigenous to such areas as Aotearoa, New Zealand. The unique cultural heritage of the Maori has generated strong international interest in recent years, thus encouraging cultural tourism.

The Growth of Culture in Tourism

There is no doubt that cultural tourism has been a major factor accounting for the positive rates of growth in most Pacific island countries. Recently, this has lead local people to have a new-found pride and respect for their ethnic background, values, beliefs, food arts, crafts and so forth. For over 100 years, the indigenous Pacific image has been used as a marketing tool for promoting tourism. Images of Pacific island people have been stereotyped as guides, entertainers, carvers, weavers and elements of the natural scenery. The indigenous people were seldom consulted, despite their major role in advertising and marketing for tourism. Once people realized that their image had commercial value for tourism, they began to take increasing control over that image. In so doing, the people have built a viable cultural dimension into their local communities. This has lead to an increase in the number of people wanting to gain a foothold and gain more responsibilities in the cottage industry of community tourism. The Maori have done this through joint ventures with non-Maori and Pacific island organizations setting up cooperative partnerships to tap into various markets. In the process, the Maori have decided to ask whether all of their people have awareness about the necessary skills, training and business opportunities that are available in order to establish and develop future-oriented, community-based tourism ventures to provide for their own people.

A number of criteria were set up in order to have a clearer picture of what the Maori want to achieve and gain as benefits from community-based tourism:

1. Tourism development for Maori and Pacific island people must support the revival and maintenance of the culture and society.
2. The definition and use of the term "culture" in the tourism industry and the community must be the responsibility of the local people.
3. Maintain the culture by establishing and working with organizations dedicated to preserving and teaching language, culture, history, social structure and performing arts.
4. Let the people achieve a visible and authoritative presence in the tourism industry with full, unconditional recognition.

Several actions can support the achievement of a visible, authoritative presence and recognition for the Maori in community-based tourism. First, invest in significant capital assets in the accommodation sector (home stays, lodges, farms, hotels and hotels). This is where most of the permanent career employment in hospitality can be found. Second, give access to and acquire a measure of control over marketing and distribution channels to build autonomy and security for the indigenous presence in New Zealand's community-based tourism. Third, develop viable commercial ventures of heritage trails with the perspective that is cultural and historical for the Maori interpretation of local experiences. Fourth, create a symbol or brand identity representing the cultures of the Pacific that will be seen as supporting the quality of products and services within the larger tourism industry.

Community-based Tourism

One starting point for community-based tourism is to focus on strategic planning in order to maximize the long-term benefits that communities could gain from international tourism. At the same time, people at the local and community levels should be empowered through their boards, local governments and enterprise bodies through capacity building and identification of their strengths in sociocultural and environmental preservation. This can serve as a precondition to making basic changes and aiming at the growth in commercial development. In New Zealand, there are key sections of the Resource Management Act of New Zealand that recognize the impact of culture and traditions of the Maori, as well as the heritage value of sites, buildings, places and areas. The Maori Tourism Development Board was set up as an NGO that provides liaison, information, education and networking opportunities to foster a growing empowerment role for indigenous people in community-based travel and tourism. The aim is to develop closer economic relations in promoting cultural tourism worldwide and exchange cultural understanding among groups from all nations. The Maori Tourism Development Board works to establish positive tourism business relationships with regional and international tourism bodies, rural communities, Maori villages and Marae, Pacific island groups in Auckland, universities, other educational institutions, international organizations and businesses.

The awareness about the strength of culture and identity for the Maori derives in part from the general lack of support from the mainstream New Zealand tourism industry. In fact, even at the local political level there is a division in New Zealand where regional community councils acknowledge that the local village or town is a community, but a Maori village or Marae in the same area is a Maori group (*runanga*), and not subject to the same funding.

Maori find that they must look for other ways to sustain their communities, despite the fact they contribute to what might be termed the "mainstream communities" in rural areas. Although many Maori have been invited to be on rural community tourism boards or organizations, they have the general impression of feeling they are token members.

As a result, Maori have been developing their own Marae and cottage industry for community-based tourism. The Maori Tourism Development Board networks and supports such initiatives with advice and consultation based on the growth of the indigenous perspective. There have been suggestions that networking should extend regionally to the South Pacific Tourism Organization. This could help strengthen the role, funding and policy development from Aotearoa and the collective of Maori *hapu* (sub-tribes) and *iwi* (tribes); thus uniting Maori (people) as Polynesians with cousins in the Pacific islands.

Concluding Points

There are a number of community environmental issues that relate to the social and economic aspects of community-based tourism. For the issue of ecosystems, it is important to maintain native plants, animal and their habitats. This means designing cultural tourism development and overall tourism strategies that are relevant for the village, district or region.

Indigenous people need to be recognized and incorporated into cultural tourism development with a focus on their issues. Likewise, it is important to take pup the issue of the community and how to ensure that cultural tourism has a positive social and economic impact on community values.

The issue of heritage relates to ensuring the long-term protection of the cultural values, including their importance as a resource to provide a positive visitor experience.

The important environmental issues related to community-based tourism include concerns about coastal areas. The main issue is to preserve the natural character of the costal environment when designing cultural tourism products. Another issue concerns managing the landscape and visual amenities that provide local communities with their lifestyle choices and the visitor with a unique cultural and environmental experience. The issue about water is how to maintain or improve the quality of water through local planning services that address soil disturbances, run-offs and any discharge of contaminants. Noise is another environmental issue for community-based tourism and noise management as an effect of tourism relates to the product, people and traffic involved.

The final point to consider is that the development and management of community-based tourism is vitally important and deserves more serious consideration. Where indigenous people are involved, this means that the more affluent tourism players and stakeholders should not give exclusive concern to what works and what they do not want to change. Anyone involved in the tourism business should investigate the local community who live at a tourist site in order to give tourists exposure to the grass roots and the cultural dimension of local society. Otherwise, most tourists never see the cultural dimension of a tourist site or the way of life experienced by local communities.

Environmental Management of Ecotourism

Background and Concepts

Ecotourism can be contrasted to tourism in the general sense of the two terms, and this allows a more focused examination of issues related to environmental management. The first difference is that ecotourism is a non-extractive use of biodiversity. This means that it complements nature conservation. Where it is economically feasible, ecotourism reinforces conservation objectives. It also provides local communities and tour operators with a strong incentive to preserve natural features of the local environment. Nature is thus the basis for ecotourism and conservation is prerequisite for the sustainability of ecotourism. Further, nature or biodiversity conservation is an integral and inseparable part of sustainable development.

Therefore, it should not be viewed as anti-development. Any discussion about the environmental management of ecotourism must have a definition of ecotourism. At least two definitions are generally accepted worldwide. First is the definition from the International Union for the Conservation of Nature (IUCN) as cited by UNEP in 2001. Ecotourism is defined as environmentally responsible travel and visitation to relatively undisturbed natural areas in order to enjoy and appreciate nature (and any accompanying cultural features-both past and present) that promotes conservation, has low negative impact and provides for beneficial and active socioeconomic involvement of the local population.

The second definition is from the International Ecotourism Society. Ecotourism is defined as responsible travel to natural areas that conserves the environment and sustains the wellbeing of local people. From both definitions it can be observed that the ideal ecotourism is environmentally friendly and sustainable. It assumes a class of traveller who is well-educated, enlightened about the environment and committed to the conservation of nature.

Observations About the Ideal and the Reality

However, ecotourism as practiced in many Pacific island countries verges on being unsustainable. It thus requires close monitoring and continuous efforts to mitigate the negative impacts. With these considerations in mind, it is useful to see at what point does the reality in Pacific island countries depart from the ideal of ecotourism. One point of departure is the fact that less discriminating visitors grossly outnumber the number of ecotourists. It is often not easy to tell the difference between the two groups of tourists and the result is that some Pacific island countries are too eager to attract visitors, but are inexperienced in assessing the extent of ethics and etiquette among tourists about ecology, conservation and ecotourism.

A second point of departure is that ecotourism is considered first and foremost as a business enterprise where profits depend on numbers of tourists. Operators are under pressure to satisfy customers who are willing to pay. The result is that the line between environmentally sustainable numbers of tourists (carrying capacity) and levels of visitation considered to be profitable are difficult to define. Many kinds of impact are often less visible and not immediately discernable; the full consequences of these impacts are manifested at a later time. At the same time, there is the tyranny of small numbers. This is many small negative impacts accumulate over time and contribute to a significant, perhaps irreversible, negative trend or outcome. A third point of departure arises from the poor design and inadequate management of ecotourism activities and related infrastructure. One example is the noncompliance with design and building guidelines. Another example is the absence of proper environmental impact assessments.

Impacts and their Management

There are at least four types of direct impacts on the environments of Pacific island countries: (a) waste accumulation and littering; (b) altered natural features (such as reef/coral damage, vegetation damage, soil erosion, vandalism); (c) introduction of non-native plants and animals; and (d) excessive disturbance to wildlife. In order to manage such direct impacts, three different targets for improvement have been identified: tourist behaviour, facilities design and construction and activities design and implementation. In 1993, the Ecotourism Society listed more specific policies, regulations and actions.

A number of related actions can also be taken to manage direct impacts. There can be awareness raising activities, including greater availability of information and guidelines so that tourists have access to the information and clear instructions. Tour guiding that is good and responsible is also important. Any guidelines must include effective application and compliance in order to have sound ecotourism practices. All varieties of stakeholders should be involved: tour operators, tour guide trainers, eco-travel agencies, environmental agencies, environmental NGOs, schools, retail suppliers of outdoor equipment, hiking clubs and consumer societies. In Pacific island countries, there is also a need for awareness that some impacts are indirect. Many environmental impacts are less visible, but have lasting consequences and are often irreversible. Examples include the changing composition of a forest as a result of invasive plant species, declining wildlife population over time, and infrequent or irregular visits by migratory species.

General Picture of the Pacific Environment

Looking at the area of the South Pacific Ocean from a big picture perspective can give a clear view of how the environment is at risk and the extent to which tourism is part of the threat to the environment. The area is comprised of 38 million square kilometres of ocean, with land being less than 2 per cent of that area. The small land area is divided into 22 nations and territories with a great diversity of traditional cultures. There is also a great diversity of species and endemism as a result of species evolution over millions of years in isolation from continental landmasses. In many Pacific islands, up to 80 per cent of the species are native.

The area of the Pacific islands has the most extensive and diverse coral reef system in the world. It is also the location of the healthiest remaining populations of many species that are endangered globally.

The high islands have large areas of original, intact forests that include many species found nowhere else in the world. As of 1998, about 233 areas were under some form of protection, and this is only about 4.5 per cent of the total Pacific land area. The total marine area under protection is unknown. Among various countries, 99 per Easter Island was under protection; 32 per cent of Tuvalu; 15 per cent of the Federated States of Micronesia, 7 per cent of Tonga, 6 per cent of Palau, 4 per cent of Samoa and 2 per cent of Fiji.

It must be noted that at least 50 per cent of the region's biodiversity is at risk. Island ecosystems and certain species are particularly vulnerable. Islands are the location where birds have the highest extinction rate. Human activities that are direct threats include over-harvesting, habitat destruction, uncontrolled waste disposal, proliferation of invasive species, illegal bio-prospecting and destructive trade in live reef fish. In addition, tourism is a significant threat to the environment in island developing countries. According to the world Conservation Union, development is the third major cause of habitat loss. Within the category of development, the top three causes of habitat destruction are industry, human settlements and tourism. Among the indirect effects on the environment, tourism/recreation was the number one threat to the environment.

In the mid-1980s, there were 30 land and marine sites of regional and international significance that were not under any form of protection. However, for the last five years, many Pacific island countries have taken a conservation area approach. At least 12 Pacific island countries, including Samoa and Tonga, have established conservation areas with support from SPREP, the World Wildlife Fund, the Nature Conservancy and Conservation International. A number of Pacific island countries and NGOs have also taken a joint initiative in conservancy to propose a South Pacific Whale Sanctuary, which would be re-submitted to the International Whaling Commission.

Among the future possibilities for conservation and environmental management is the recommendation that Pacific island countries sign the World Heritage Convention so that important cultural and nature areas can be included on the World Heritage List. There is considerable international interest in protecting marine areas of the Pacific region. It could be worthwhile for all Pacific island nations to consider signing the World Heritage Convention. In addition to protecting the environment and cultural heritage, World Heritage listing can be used as a marketing tool.

The Pacific island environment is the foundation for successful ecotourism, but that environment is highly vulnerable and under threat. In order for ecotourism to succeed, it is important to highlight three major implications. First, the natural environment is a total package in which all elements must be maintained and protected, not just small areas or enclaves that are tourist attractions. Second, effective protection can only be achieved in large areas covering entire ecosystems, not just particular species or habitats. Third, ecosystem-based management would cover large areas and require public and local community involvement, especially the integration of economic, social and cultural considerations.

Strategies for Developing Ecotourism

Introduction

The International Year of Ecotourism 2002 has helped heighten the profile of ecotourism, especially with an increase in the number of international meetings and seminars. However, it might be difficult to formulate or implement policies that are attractive for ecotourism and for the strategies needed to implement tourism projects and policies that are ecologically based and sustainable. One difficulty is to know precisely what ecotourism is in order to prepare strategies.

It is clear that ecotourism is a subset of tourism and that it refers to sue of natural/ecological resources and usually entry into sensitive and fragile environments. Many might think ecotourism is the same as nature-based tourism, while others consider that an objective, value free definition is needed. Ultimately, it is the case that people who use the term determine the meaning of the term ecotourism as they intend it.

Ecotourism is, in fact, a very complex tourism product as some agencies and entrepreneurs have discovered. First, not all natural environments are suitable for tourism; second, ecotourists are a special group among the general category of tourists, and some tourists might not adopt an ecological frame of mind for only a small period during their tourist visit. Third, there are basic principles about a tourism attraction that apply even if the tourism resources are not environmentally based. Fourth, the management of ecotourism facilities and locations could become quite demanding and may become isolated geographically in the form of an enclave. Representatives from tourism organizations throughout the South Pacific subregion are probably already aware that commitments to any form of tourism are uneven with considerable variations in the international tourism profile of their country. For the most part, the Pacific islands have a profile described as leisure and recreation based. However, other Pacific island countries do not yet have tourism products that would appeal to tourists from the major source markets. Even in countries where tourism is not well known, some of the critical issues related to ecotourism and the process of strategic planning can be viewed in light of the special circumstances of Pacific island countries. This should assist policy makers who are considering whether ecotourism could be an important component in their set of tourism resources and whether tourism development might be made more sustainable.

Strategic Questions about Ecotourism

It has already been recognized at the global level that just having the requisite resources might not be sufficient to sustain viable experiences or businesses based on ecotourism. There is a range of prerequisite criteria that must be met, and some strategic questions help identify these criteria. The following questions have been identified as important: (a) What has motivated the interest and commitment to developing a strategy for ecotourism? (b) What have been the strongest influences affecting the interest and commitment? (c) Who are the principal participants in ecotourism? (d) Should ecotourism be an independent strategy, or should it be integrated as a component of a broad-based tourism strategy? Policy makers would have their own set of purposes or motivations in each country that accepts a strategy of ecotourism development. It is necessary to clarify what is being planned and why before the overall strategic exercise reaches an advance stage. The purpose that policy makers establish for ecotourism development would directly influence the process and outcomes.

To a great extent, the purpose for a strategy of ecotourism development has been derived from many discussions about the potential of ecotourism. Discussions at international meetings have asserted that small island countries, which may be unable to meet the challenges of conventional mass tourism, might be better suited to ecotourism as a specialized niche market. This message helped create the potential of ecotourism for policy makers concerned abut the negative social effects of mass tourism, the concern about the fragility of ecological resources and a willingness to share cultural and natural resources with discerning visitors who were environmentally and culturally sensitive.

The potential of ecotourism has several additional assumptions to keep in mind. A commitment to ecotourism requires the recognition that the outcome may not give many economic advantages, because the strategy is ecologically-driven, not economically-driven. In addition, ecotourism development presumes a need to involve the local population in the planning and the management. Community-based planning is thus an important component, and perhaps a prerequisite. From an early point in the process, it is also necessary to ask and answer whether ecotourism should be a stand-alone strategy or a sub-strategy within a broad-based tourism strategy. The opinion on balance is that an ecotourism strategy would be a subset of a broad-based tourism strategy, because it is dependent on many components of a general tourism strategy.

Strategic Planning Process

Whether a component of the general tourism strategy or a stand-alone specific ecotourism strategy, there would need to be a systematic process of formulating strategy based on clearly articulated objects, thorough assessment of available resources, an estimation of market demand and the creation of an appropriate quantitative, qualitative and geographical strategy.

Regardless of the scope and scale of the strategic planning process, there are basic similarities based on a thorough step-by-step approach. This approach could be the significant factor for determining how appropriate is the choice of a strategy. Creating a purpose-designed strategic planning process has become fairly standardized, but the key issue is to fine tune and balance the components to fit the circumstances of the agency and the community and address critical issues.

The critical elements of the strategic planning process are prepare the study; do the survey; conduct analysis, synthesis, projections and predictions; formulate the policy and plan; and specify what is the output and the expected outcomes. It is important to keep in mind that no matter how broad or narrow the focus of the plan, it must be integrated with other sectors on the national agenda.

The main steps in the strategic planning process start with setting the objectives and how this is done. The objectives set the vision and often the operational targets for the plan. Equally important is the consultative process involving various stakeholders that should lead up to statements about what everyone expects to accomplish along with statements about the purpose of activities. Since various stakeholders will have different expectations, it is important that objectives be categorized as (a) essential or optional, (b) independent or dependent on achieving other objectives, (c) statements of what is intended, and (d) statements of implementation.

Methods of Resource Assessment

There are many methods and techniques used to assess capabilities and what is suitable from a wide spectrum of resources needed to support tourism development. Simple methods would involve building an information base that includes inventory, categorizing, simple assessment and identification of patterns and linkages.

Assessment of carrying capacity can involve analysis and projections in the early phases of plan formulation as long as the limits and suitability of this method are understood. In recent years, various types of opportunity spectrum methods have been used to assess resources. The eight factors used in the Ecotourism Opportunity Spectrum (ECOS). The significance of each factor will depend on the circumstances of where the ecotourism region and site are located. The intensity of existing or proposed ecotourism development and the nature of the development, whether by an eco-specialist or eco-generalist, would also have an impact on any opportunity for ecotourism development.

The ECOS assessment could be further refined to include other features and criteria, such as: landscape assessments, attractiveness indices, resource status

Frameworks for Geographical Arrangements

Any framework for the geographical arrangements of ecotourism development must be derived systematically in order to protect ecotourism resources, have a balance between development and conservation, concentrate the touristic experience, integrate ecotourism with appropriate related tourism activities, create special enclaves suited to the particular needs of ecotourism, maintain capacity limits for development and access, provide services for ecotourists and create investment confidence. In order to meet all of these criteria, three basic points should serve as the guideline: (a) only certain areas within a tourist region are absolutely necessary for tourism development; (b) strategic planning for tourism goes beyond and rejects the popular belief that all land has equal potential for tourism development (if promoted heavily); and (c) any examples of unstructured tourism development located anywhere have inherent social and ecological problems due to one-dimensional tourism development approaches.

Using a systematic framework for geographical arrangements will show that social and ecological problems could be avoided or reduced; they are not inherent or unavoidable for ecotourism development. There are three basic frameworks or models for the geographical arrangements of an ecotourism region and destination.

Destination Region Model

The destination region model is a simple model for an ecotourism destination. It allows for separating on a geographic basis those areas to be used intensively for tourism activity, regardless of scale. It includes circulation routes, service centres, all of which are separated from the natural environmental resources that need protection or preservation. The natural environmental resources keep their attractiveness for ecotourism, and it is possible to manage and sustain these resources. The four major components of the destination region model.

The Corridor model is characterized by route systems through the ecotourism region in order to provide access to ecotourism resources. While there are many variants to the model, it is best used for conservation areas, wilderness regions and hill country zones. The model has its origin in the principles of the conservation movement. These principles include providing limited access to environmentally sensitive areas, surrounding core areas with buffer zones to provide limited access and restricted support development, nodal points that represent small excised support services, and conserved areas with controlled circulation.

A network of principal routes with supporting secondary routes and trails characterizes the model. The network patterns can include corridor access through the protected region with no detours; targeted trail heads and significant sites as detours from the principal route; and secondary loops through subregions with particular tourist experiences or access to selected sites. The model has geographical referencing for differentiated zones of access. There is controlled access through a series of sub-zones designed to protect the ecology of the core environmental ecotourism zone. In wilderness areas where planners are concerned with both conservation and tourism development, they may differentiate the trail systems according to various criteria.

The Twin Model

The twin model is a hybrid combination of the first two models. Its main characteristic is to provide a base camp at the outer perimeter of the ecotourism region along with most, if not all, essential support services. The idea of "twinning" comes from the match between two components –the base camp and the ecotourism attraction. In some circumstances, the base camp could be an ecotourism attraction in its own right.

Management Regimes

Resources have to be managed in a way that achieves sustainability in order to make ecotourism a realistic development possibility. Various types of management regimes have been developed and advocated. For example, there are protocols and agendas from international organizations such as UNEP and UNCSD; the Rio Agenda 21; the SIDS agenda and United Nations and NGO guidelines. Tourism industry groups such as WTTC and PATA have developed and advocated management regimes as have national tourism organizations and regional tourism organizations. At the same time, research institutes and tourism interest groups have developed and/or advocated systems, principles, values, norms and procedures for management of ecotourism.

Among the management tools and mechanisms that have been developed and advocated are:

- Industry self-regulation as an alternative to government-imposed regulations
- Technical assistance packages from the government
- Industry-based codes of practice for ecotourism operators
- Reward systems for good practices
- Accreditation programmes – whether by government or industry
- Rapid assessment models

- Financial assistance programmes when preferred styles and forms of ecotourism are developed
- Partnership programmes
- Community-based programmes
- Codes of practice for ecotourists about appropriate behaviour.

Each of these management tools and forms has its own characteristic approach and depends on supporting structures and resource requirements. Circumstances may determine which forms are appropriate and whether a combination of forms can be implemented concurrently. Local factors such as politics, culture and economics will have an effect on choice of management regimes and related mechanisms, and this means that tools and mechanisms that work in one case of ecotourism development might not be easily transferred or copied for another case. The main point, therefore, is that a specific purpose-designed management regime would be needed for each new case of ecotourism development.

Concluding Points and Some Questions to Consider

The special circumstances of the island developing countries in the Pacific region raise a set of three questions. First, is ecotourism a viable strategy everywhere in the region? Second, Will national ecotourism strategies be independent and competitive with neighbouring island countries, or will ecotourism strategies be integrated and cooperative across the region? Third, what strategic capacities are needed to support the creation, development and implementation of sustainable strategies for ecotourism development?

Assuming the suitable ecotourism resources are available, there are three important strategic linkages to consider, because they will influence the viability of ecotourism in any region. The three linkages are: (a) between ecotourism resource regions and the ecotourists' country of origin; (b) between ecotourism as a principal attraction and as a companion attraction; and (c) between the prerequisites of tourism and ecotourism.

In terms of ecotourism resource regions, the prevailing evidence is that the most desirable locations are often in developing countries. The ecotourist visitors will be from the main developed countries in North America and Europe, plus Japan. In the countries of the ecotourism resource region, such as the Pacific subregion, targeted areas exploiting ecotourism can create a competitive market edge in the international tourism market, whether or not ecotourism is the main attraction. Moreover, there is evidence that ecotourism is a special form of tourism that depends on the basic requirements of general tourism, including infrastructure, accommodation, transport, support services, information, marketing and trained human resources.

If these three kinds of linkages are kept in mind, then ecotourism might also benefit from being viewed at a regional level. Once attention is at the regional level, another set of questions would have to be addressed: (a) How comparable, competitive and complementary are the ecotourism resources in the Pacific island subregion? (b) How sustainable are the ecotourism resources? (c) How adequate are the support resources? (d) Could there be cooperative, mutual support strategies within and across the region?

If policy makers start thinking about the answers to these four questions, then it would be possible to address the overriding strategic question about the future of ecotourism in the Pacific island subregion. That is, would some type of cooperative ecotourism strategic structure be worthwhile, could it be created and could it be sustained? While the Pacific island countries generally face difficulties of location and logistics, they do have unique natural and cultural resources and the mystique of the south Pacific. This is the starting point for opportunities to bring together and strengthen the resources needed to create ecotourism at the national and regional level.

Development and Management of Community-Based Tourism

Introduction

In early 2001, a team that included the author as a community development specialist had reviewed New Zealand's assistance to Fiji in support of two community-based ecotourism projects. The projects supported by New Zealand were considered as best practices in ecotourism in Fiji and provide the case study for this presentation.

Tourism is the major industry for Fiji and it is a major tourism destination in the Pacific, second only to Hawaii. In 1998, a record number of tourists, about 372,000 people, visited Fiji. The tourism industry has made Fiji a major destination and it is also the largest sector of the economy. However, an average Fijian family gets very limited direct economic benefits from mainstream tourism development. The economic benefits from resort-style tourism development are unevenly distributed. Ecotourism, nature-based and culture-based tourism in rural districts has been seen in terms of the potential to bring economic benefits of tourism to local communities in rural areas.

Ecotourism is considered to have the potential of contributing to protection of natural and cultural values and poverty alleviation in rural areas accessible to main tourist centres; and this is how ecotourism fits into the integrated development strategy. The government of Fiji supports ecotourism ventures that are carefully targeted to maximize economic benefits and minimize negative social impacts.

The government's overall guiding policy document is the *Fiji Tourism Development Plan 1998-2005*, which gives an important role to ecotourism in terms of environmental protection and rural job creation. In 1999, the government approved the *Ecotourism and Village Based Tourism Policy and Strategy for Fiji*. This document defines ecotourism and adds to the definition by mentioning the activities and characteristics considered to be ecotourism ventures.

These include: small scale, low capital ventures; provide activities that let tourists experience nature and indigenous culture; are likely to be owned by local people; ventures likely to be owned and operated by local people; activities based in the village or involving transportation by land or sea; and projects with fewer leakages that large-scale tourism projects.

Over the last ten years, over 70 ecotourism attractions have been developed and ecotourism has become the most important segment of Fiji's tourist industry. At the same time, the Ministry of Tourism (MOT) has become the lead government agency by implementing the policy, plus gaining more attention for taking a greater role in local rural communities.

The Ministry of Tourism has also strengthened its capacity to promote community-based ecotourism and conservation projects. Equally significant, at the regional level the 1998 SPREP Ministerial Meeting endorsed the Action Strategy for Nature Conservation in the Pacific Region 1999-2002, based on the experiences with rural ecotourism development built up in Fiji, as well as other island developing countries.

Case Studies of Fijian Ecotourism Projects Supported by NZODA

The NZODA Fiji Ecotourism Programme started in the late 1980s as an investigation of the remaining important natural forest areas in Fiji. NZODA had become the major supporter of ecotourism development activities as part of piloting integrated projects in two areas: one is the Bouma National Heritage Park on Taveuni, an island just off Vanua Levu, a second is the Koroyanitu National Heritage Park near Lautoka on Viti Levu. The aim of NZODA assistance has been to provide communities in the project with the means to protect their natural environment within the national heritage parks, while achieving sustainable livelihoods based on conserving natural resources and the cultural heritage. The villagers chose ecotourism as the income-generating activity, with a community-based project to be established in each village. The objectives of the projects are: (a) conserve, protect and enhance the area's natural and cultural heritage; (b) develop and maintain first class recreation and tourism assets for local people and overseas visitors to enjoy and create a benefit for Fiji's international tourism image; (c) create local employment and income opportunities for women and men in the local communities; (d) facilitate and strengthen capacity building in the project communities in order to sustain project activities, especially ecotourism management, enterprise management, natural resource conservation, cultural protection and community self-development; and (e) facilitate development and consolidation of linkages from communities to organizations at all levels in order to sustain community projects in the medium-and long-term.

One objective of the team when reviewing New Zealand's assistance to the two projects was to bring a clear vision of market reality to the projects in terms of the ecotourism products being developed and to facilitate the development of community-based tourism enterprises. The team brought skills that could be transferred to counterparts in Fiji, including a clear understanding of the strong link between nature/ heritage conservation and the components of ecotourism.

Tourism Product Development

The two projects in Fiji that have been supported by New Zealand covered six villages. Unique ecotourism products were developed in each village.

(1) At Abaca village, visitors can stay at a lodge or with families. Guides are available for day trekking and there are also self-guided trails to waterfalls and a mountaintop. A visitor centre in the park supports management, provides information and sells souvenir items and handicrafts. Ecotourism at this village has won a number of regional awards.

(2) A new overnight trek operation is run by Navilawa village in partnership with Abaca village and a transport company in Nadi. The village provides accommodation and food, and then visitors take a two-day, one evening trek.

(3) Waitabu village provides a guided snorkelling tour of the marine reserve, Waitabu Marine Park, using traditional bamboo rafts. A travel company acts as a partner. Ecotourism in this park has been added to the Bouma National Heritage Park ecotourism activities.

(4) Vidawa village organizes a guided day-long forest hike through Bouma National Heritage Park, which includes a traditional meal at midday.

(5) The Tavoro Waterfalls is the most well-established and popular ecotourism activity at Bouma National Heritage Park. Visitors can enter the area at their own leisure and use the other available tourist services.

(6) The Lavena coastal walk is the second oldest ecotourism activity at Bouma National Heritage Park. The area involves a walk along the coast to the waterfalls nearby. The community raised funds to build a lodge, which includes accommodation, a restaurant, a handicraft shop and visitor's centre.

Building the Community

The project has focused on building capacity and capability in the areas of ecotour operations and enterprise management. At the time of the review, all communities had the capacity and were successfully operating their ecotourism activities. It was found that some additional assistance would be needed to build greater depth to their capacity, thus enabling the local people to sustain the activities over a longer term.

A second focus was developing the communities' capacity to manage their ecotourism activities as business enterprises. This would increase direct employment and income within the communities and expand the range of options for new locally based livelihoods. The people have already had some training and experience in business operations, but more assistance could build business enterprise capacity further. The extent of the need and the priorities for attention varied among the different communities.

It was observed that the project had strengthened social cohesion and improved the well being of individuals and the community as a whole, although there is variation among the villages. Individuals with particular skills and interests, especially women and youth, have been able to develop non-traditional roles with the support of the community. Ecotourism has provided all of the communities with a new steam of income and this is an incentive for people to stay in the village and manage their own enterprise. Local people have recognized and valued the preservation of their culture and heritage. There is increased awareness of conservation and management of natural resources along with environmental protection. The main challenge is to see how community development can ensure the long-term sustainability of the projects and the communities.

Areas for Building Greater Capacity

Work plans are needed and additional capacity has to be created in some communities to manage the ecotourism activities as well as carry out daily activities and have some spare time. This has been a challenge for the smaller communities in particular. Another challenge for community-based tourism was the conflict between traditional practices and business practices, because this could determine the success or failure of a particular local enterprise. Outside support agencies could help in this area and build linkages with the community enterprise management people.

The communities were in need of more support from and linkages to provincial and national agencies that could act as partners. To meet this challenge, the government needed to improve its capacity by having one national agency with a mandate and capacity to guide participatory community development. At the same time, parts of the government with technical expertise in ecotourism, small business enterprise and environmental management, for example, should be identified and encouraged to help local communities.

Development impacts

The project has had a major positive impact on the natural environment by establishing protected areas. The communities are committed to protection and the provincial authority has received assurances from landowners and the wider community that they would support environmental protection. There have also been direct gains in biodiversity, especially since creation of Koroyanitu National Heritage Park has prevented the spread of commercial logging.

The understanding is now broader, with a stronger commitment to environmental sustainability, especially since communities are aware of the benefits already realized. People have realized that environmental protection is good not only for the tourists, but for the community as well. There is also a national agency to support land conservation and assist landowners to give long-term protection to their land and not open their land to commercial logging. Some physical infrastructure has been upgraded and replaced.

The economic and financial impact can be considered as successful. A new form of income generation has been developed and sustained thus far. New or expanded income generating enterprises based on ecotourism have been established and are operating. There are still some contradictions between the traditional reciprocal economy and the sustainable enterprise management model based on the cash economy. Where the previous cash economy was extractive and degraded or destroyed the environment, the sustainable enterprise management of ecotourism might fit more appropriately with the traditional economy. However, this aspect needs more careful study and community participation to improve understanding.

The aim of creating self-sustaining, community-based ecotourism enterprises is to have a local business activity that can sustain recurrent costs. In some villages, this has occurred and ecotourism has even supported other non-related development activities. Careful monitoring is needed to be sure this will eventually occur in other villages without economic or social complications.

The social impact of the projects relates to the impact of the financial benefits from the projects. Ecotourism has introduced different ways of doing many activities in daily life, as well as added new experiences when ecotourists come to villages. Operating an ecotourism enterprise has crated new roles and challenged existing roles, especially traditional gender roles. Women have gained socially in many ways, but this has also created some conflict in the household. Visitors can disrupt family life as well as community commitments and obligations. The social development process has created both cohesion and conflict, and this is a challenge to traditional village decision-making and dispute settlement. At the same time, the projects have helped to save indigenous knowledge, and the government is documenting this.

Technical assistance in community development would enable local communities to have dialogues, articulate viewpoints and reflect together on what has been changing in the life of the community when a business culture and ecotourism operations are introduced. Training in facilitation and social group interactions can help address the challenges to how the community is organized, leadership issues and governance issues.

Key Issues

The review team noted the achievements in all six villages and ongoing training to strengthen people's capacities for managing and operating ecotourism enterprises. The priority at this stage would be to secure these achievements and make the ecotourism activities self-sustaining in ways appropriate for the local level. The emphasis is now shifting to capacity building of village communities for sustained management and implementation. While ecotourism training would still be included, training that is ecotourism-related would cover community development, sustainable resource management and development and maintenance of ecotourism products.

Financial sustainability is a component in the ultimate aim of self-sustainability, but this also involves long-term financing and management of the system at the national level. Therefore, self-sustainability involves a more complex set of issues relating to localization of management at the local community level, building productive partnerships from the local to the provincial level and establishing supportive links from the local level to the provincial and national level. At the national level the various tourism entities in the government need to establish clear roles and maintain national level partnerships that can assist communities and projects at the local level. Assistance from the national and provincial levels can also help to better establish village ecotourism activities in the cultural context in ways that community enterprises could achieve long-term sustainability. Likewise, the national level is able to set up the legal base and the mechanisms to support communities determined to manage their own lands for conservation of the environment and for protection of the cultural heritage.

Agencies at all levels should be able to work together with communities to manage and monitor the natural and cultural heritage resources. Participatory community development and managing change in communities have been difficult to achieve since ecotourism brings many new concepts, practices and influences to rural communities. Building community awareness and establishing linkages from the local to the provincial and national levels can provide expertise that might intervene to help those who see traditional roles and norms being challenged. Building capacity is the cornerstone of all aspects of the project, and this includes ecotourism operations as well as protection of the environment and cultural heritage; building on enterprise management skills; managing community development dynamics and building confidence in local partnerships.

Lessons Learned

The lessons learned from the review by the team from New Zealand covered five areas.

First, community lessons showed that problems occur when there are conflicts between traditional institutions and the requirements of business management. It is important to be aware that community and landholder interests are often not the same. Working with communities is time consuming, especially because there is a wide range of stakeholders and interested parties concerned with ecotourism.

Second, lessons learned in the area of business management show that often ecotourism projects have not been commercially realistic, so management models have to be more flexible and adaptive to each ecotourism business activity. Ecotourism income is often based on a narrow range of products and services, but there are still many opportunities to expand. Transport and road conditions often limit ecotourism development. There are some regulations that limit certain aspects of ecotourism development.

Third, lessons in conservation show that ecotourism has brought gains in terms of areas that are protected. At the least, ecotourism can highlight the need for conservation and the nature of the benefits that occur.

Fourth, exercises designed to encourage participation by all stakeholders are essential at the start of the project. Gender issues have not been fully addressed and they need to be. Projects will work out satisfactorily when people have common interests.

Fifth, the lessons for donors are as follows: (a) a long time horizon is need for community and business development and financial handouts may send the wrong message to community entrepreneurs. Donors should separate their support for park and ecotourism development from business development.

Conclusions

Global Codes of Ethics for Tourism

Tourism's contribution to mutual understanding and respect between peoples and societies

1. The understanding and promotion of the ethical values common to humanity, with an attitude of tolerance and respect for the diversity of religious, philosophical and moral beliefs, are both the foundation and the consequence of responsible tourism; stakeholders in tourism development and tourists themselves should observe the social and cultural traditions and practices of all peoples, including those of minorities and indigenous peoples and to recognize their worth;
2. Tourism activities should be conducted in harmony with the attributes and traditions of the host regions and countries and in respect for their laws, practices and customs;
3. The host communities, on the one hand, and local professionals, on the other, should acquaint themselves with and respect the tourists who visit them and find out about their lifestyles, tastes and expectations; the education and training imparted to professionals contribute to a hospitable welcome;
4. It is the task of the public authorities to provide protection for tourists and visitors and their belongings; they must pay particular attention to the safety of foreign tourists owing to the particular vulnerability they may have; they should facilitate the introduction of specific means of information, prevention,

security, insurance and assistance consistent with their needs; any attacks, assaults, kidnappings or threats against tourists or workers in the tourism industry, as well as the wilful destruction of tourism facilities or of elements of cultural or natural heritage should be severely condemned and punished in accordance with their respective national laws;

5. When travelling, tourists and visitors should not commit any criminal act or any act considered criminal by the laws of the country visited and abstain from any conduct felt to be offensive or injurious by the local populations, or likely to damage the local environment; they should refrain from all trafficking in illicit drugs, arms, antiques, protected species and products and substances that are dangerous or prohibited by national regulations;
6. Tourists and visitors have the responsibility to acquaint themselves, even before their departure, with the characteristics of the countries they are preparing to visit; they must be aware of the health and security risks inherent in any travel outside their usual environment and behave in such a way as to minimize those risks;

Tourism as a Vehicle for Individual and Collective Fulfilment

1. Tourism, the activity most frequently associated with rest and relaxation, sport and access to culture and nature, should be planned and practised as a privileged means of individual and collective fulfilment; when practised with a sufficiently open mind, it is an irreplaceable factor of self-education, mutual tolerance and for learning about the legitimate differences between peoples and cultures and their diversity;
2. Tourism activities should respect the equality of men and women; they should promote human rights and, more particularly, the individual rights of the most vulnerable groups, notably children, the elderly, the handicapped, ethnic minorities and indigenous peoples;
3. The exploitation of human beings in any form, particularly sexual, especially when applied to children, conflicts with the fundamental aims of tourism and is the negation of tourism; as such, in accordance with international law, it should be

energetically combatted with the cooperation of all the States concerned and penalized without concession by the national legislation of both the countries visited and the countries of the perpetrators of these acts, even when they are carried out abroad;

4. Travel for purposes of religion, health, education and cultural or linguistic exchanges are particularly beneficial forms of tourism, which deserve encouragement;
5. The introduction into curricula of education about the value of tourist exchanges, their economic, social and cultural benefits, and also their risks, should be encouraged;

Tourism, a Factor of Sustainable Development

1. All the stakeholders in tourism development should safeguard the natural environment with a view to achieving sound, continuous and sustainable economic growth geared to satisfying equitably the needs and aspirations of present and future generations;
2. All forms of tourism development that are conducive to saving rare and precious resources, in particular water and energy, as well as avoiding so far as possible waste production, should be given priority and encouraged by national, regional and local public authorities;
3. The staggering in time and space of tourist and visitor flows, particularly those resulting from paid leave and school holidays, and a more even distribution of holidays should be sought so as to reduce the pressure of tourism activity on the environment and enhance its beneficial impact on the tourism industry and the local economy;
4. Tourism infrastructure should be designed and tourism activities programmed in such a way as to protect the natural heritage composed of ecosystems and biodiversity and to preserve endangered species of wildlife; the stakeholders in tourism development, and especially professionals, should agree to the imposition of limitations or constraints on their activities when these are exercised in particularly sensitive areas: desert, polar or high mountain regions, coastal areas, tropical forests

or wetlands, propitious to the creation of nature reserves or protected areas;

5. Nature tourism and ecotourism are recognized as being particularly conducive to enriching and enhancing the standing of tourism, provided they respect the natural heritage and local populations and are in keeping with the carrying capacity of the sites;

Tourism, a User of the Cultural Heritage of Mankind and Contributor to its Enhancement

1. Tourism resources belong to the common heritage of mankind; the communities in whose territories they are situated have particular rights and obligations to them;
2. Tourism policies and activities should be conducted with respect for the artistic, archaeological and cultural heritage, which they should protect and pass on to future generations; particular care should be devoted to preserving and upgrading monuments, shrines and museums as well as archaeological and historic sites which must be widely open to tourist visits; encouragement should be given to public access to privately-owned cultural property and monuments, with respect for the rights of their owners, as well as to religious buildings, without prejudice to normal needs of worship;
3. Financial resources derived from visits to cultural sites and monuments should, at least in part, be used for the upkeep, safeguard, development and embellishment of this heritage;
4. Tourism activity should be planned in such a way as to allow traditional cultural products, crafts and folklore to survive and flourish, rather than causing them to degenerate and become standardized;

Tourism, a Beneficial Activity for Host Countries and Communities

1. Local populations should be associated with tourism activities and share equitably in the economic, social and cultural benefits they generate, and particularly in the creation of direct and indirect jobs resulting from them;
2. Tourism policies should be applied in such a way as to help to raise the standard of living of the populations of the

regions visited and meet their needs; the planning and architectural approach to and operation of tourism resorts and accommodation should aim to integrate them, to the extent possible, in the local economic and social fabric; where skills are equal, priority should be given to local manpower;

3. Special attention should be paid to the specific problems of coastal areas and island territories and to vulnerable rural or mountain regions, for which tourism often represents a rare opportunity for development in the face of the decline of traditional economic activities;
4. Tourism professionals, particularly investors, governed by the regulations laid down by the public authorities, should carry out studies of the impact of their development projects on the environment and natural surroundings; they should also deliver, with the greatest transparency and objectivity, information on their future programmes and their foreseeable repercussions and foster dialogue on their contents with the populations concerned;

Obligations of Stakeholders in Tourism Development

1. Tourism professionals have an obligation to provide tourists with objective and honest information on their places of destination and on the conditions of travel, hospitality and stays; they should ensure that the contractual clauses proposed to their customers are readily understandable as to the nature, price and quality of the services they commit themselves to providing and the financial compensation payable by them in the event of a unilateral breach of contract on their part;
2. Tourism professionals, insofar as it depends on them, should show concern, in cooperation with the public authorities, for the security and safety, accident prevention, health protection and food safety of those who seek their services; likewise, they should ensure the existence of suitable systems of insurance and assistance; they should accept the reporting obligations prescribed by national regulations and pay fair compensation in the event of failure to observe their contractual obligations
3. Tourism professionals, so far as this depends on them, should contribute to the cultural and spiritual fulfilment of tourists and allow them, during their travels, to practise their religions;

4. The public authorities of the generating States and the host countries, in cooperation with the professionals concerned and their associations, should ensure that the necessary mechanisms are in place for the repatriation of tourists in the event of the bankruptcy of the enterprise that organized their travel;
5. Governments have the right – and the duty-especially in a crisis, to inform their nationals of the difficult circumstances, or even the dangers they may encounter during their travels abroad; it is their responsibility however to issue such information without prejudicing in an unjustified or exaggerated manner the tourism industry of the host countries and the interests of their own operators; the contents of travel advisories should therefore be discussed beforehand with the authorities of the host countries and the professionals concerned; recommendations formulated should be strictly proportionate to the gravity of the situations encountered and confined to the geographical areas where the insecurity has arisen; such advisories should be qualified or cancelled as soon as a return to normality permits;
6. The press, and particularly the specialized travel press and the other media, including modern means of electronic communication, should issue honest and balanced information on events and situations that could influence the flow of tourists; they should also provide accurate and reliable information to the consumers of tourism services; the new communication and electronic commerce technologies should also be developed and used for this purpose; as is the case for the media, they should not in any way promote sex tourism;

Right to Tourism

1. The prospect of direct and personal access to the discovery and enjoyment of the planet's resources constitutes a right equally open to all the world's inhabitants; the increasingly extensive participation in national and international tourism should be regarded as one of the best possible expressions of the sustained growth of free time, and obstacles should not be placed in its way;
2. The universal right to tourism must be regarded as the corollary of the right to rest and leisure, including reasonable limitation

of working hours and periodic holidays with pay, guaranteed by Article 24 of the Universal Declaration of Human Rights and Article 7.d of the International Covenant on Economic, Social and Cultural Rights;

3. Social tourism, and in particular associative tourism, which facilitates widespread access to leisure, travel and holidays, should be developed with the support of the public authorities;
4. Family, youth, student and senior tourism and tourism for people with disabilities, should be encouraged and facilitated;

Liberty of Tourist Movements

1. Tourists and visitors should benefit, in compliance with international law and national legislation, from the liberty to move within their countries and from one State to another, in accordance with Article 13 of the Universal Declaration of Human Rights; they should have access to places of transit and stay and to tourism and cultural sites without being subject to excessive formalities or discrimination;
2. Tourists and visitors should have access to all available forms of communication, internal or external; they should benefit from prompt and easy access to local administrative, legal and health services; they should be free to contact the consular representatives of their countries of origin in compliance with the diplomatic conventions in force;
3. Tourists and visitors should benefit from the same rights as the citizens of the country visited concerning the confidentiality of the personal data and information concerning them, especially when these are stored electronically;
4. Administrative procedures relating to border crossings whether they fall within the competence of States or result from international agreements, such as visas or health and customs formalities, should be adapted, so far as possible, so as to facilitate to the maximum freedom of travel and widespread access to international tourism; agreements between groups of countries to harmonize and simplify these procedures should be encouraged; specific taxes and levies penalizing the tourism industry and undermining its competitiveness should be gradually phased out or corrected;

5. So far as the economic situation of the countries from which they come permits, travellers should have access to allowances of convertible currencies needed for their travels;

Rights of the Workers and Entrepreneurs in the Tourism Industry

1. The fundamental rights of salaried and self-employed workers in the tourism industry and related activities, should be guaranteed under the supervision of the national and local administrations, both of their States of origin and of the host countries with particular care, given the specific constraints linked in particular to the seasonality of their activity, the global dimension of their industry and the flexibility often required of them by the nature of their work;
2. Salaried and self-employed workers in the tourism industry and related activities have the right and the duty to acquire appropriate initial and continuous training; they should be given adequate social protection; job insecurity should be limited so far as possible; and a specific status, with particular regard to their social welfare, should be offered to seasonal workers in the sector;
3. Any natural or legal person, provided he, she or it has the necessary abilities and skills, should be entitled to develop a professional activity in the field of tourism under existing national laws; entrepreneurs and investors-especially in the area of small and medium-sized enterprises-should be entitled to free access to the tourism sector with a minimum of legal or administrative restrictions;
4. Exchanges of experience offered to executives and workers, whether salaried or not, from different countries, contributes to foster the development of the world tourism industry; these movements should be facilitated so far as possible in compliance with the applicable national laws and international conventions;
5. As an irreplaceable factor of solidarity in the development and dynamic growth of international exchanges, multinational enterprises of the tourism industry should not exploit the dominant positions they sometimes occupy; they should avoid becoming the vehicles of cultural and social models artificially imposed on the host communities; in exchange for their freedom

to invest and trade which should be fully recognized, they should involve themselves in local development, avoiding, by the excessive repatriation of their profits or their induced imports, a reduction of their contribution to the economies in which they are established;

6. Partnership and the establishment of balanced relations between enterprises of generating and receiving countries contribute to the sustainable development of tourism and an equitable distribution of the benefits of its growth;

Implementation of the Principles of the Global Code of Ethics for Tourism

1. The public and private stakeholders in tourism development should cooperate in the implementation of these principles and monitor their effective application;
2. The stakeholders in tourism development should recognize the role of international institutions, among which the World Tourism Organization ranks first, and non-governmental organizations with competence in the field of tourism promotion and development, the protection of human rights, the environment or health, with due respect for the general principles of international law;
3. The same stakeholders should demonstrate their intention to refer any disputes concerning the application or interpretation of the Global Code of Ethics for Tourism for conciliation to an impartial third body known as the World Committee on Tourism Ethics.

TIES Global Ecotourism Fact Sheet

Size of Global Tourism

- As the largest business sector in the world economy, the Travel & Tourism industry is responsible for over 230 million jobs and over 10% of the gross domestic product worldwide.
- In 2006, Travel & Tourism (consumption, investment, government spending and exports) is expected to grow 4.6% and total US$6.5 trillion.
- If tourism were a country, it would have the 2nd largest economy, surpassed only by U.S.

- In over 150 countries (four out of five), tourism is one of five top export earners. In 60 countries, tourism is the number one export.

Global Growth of Tourism

- 1950: 25 million tourist arrivals.
- 1990's: Tourism grew globally at 7% per year.
- 2004: 760 million tourism arrivals corresponded to a 10% global growth.
- 2005: The number of international tourist arrivals recorded worldwide grew by 5.5% and exceeded 800 million for the first time ever.
- 2020: Global tourism is forecast to reach 1.56 billion international arrivals.
- Importance to Tourism in Developing Countries:
- Tourism is a principle "export" (foreign exchange earner) for 83% of developing countries, and the leading export for 1/3 of poorest countries.
- For the world's 40 poorest countries, tourism is the second most important source of foreign exchange, after oil.
- Over last decade, tourism has been "the only large sector of international trade in services where poor countries have consistently posted a surplus."
- International tourism in developing countries is increasing by 9.5% a year compared to 4.6% worldwide.
- Tourism 'appears to be one of the few economic sectors able to guide a number of developing countries to higher levels of prosperity and for some to leave behind their least-developed country status."
- Negative Impacts of Tourism
- There are 109 countries with coral reefs. In 90 of them reefs are being damaged by cruise ship anchors and sewage, by tourists breaking off chunks of coral, and by commercial harvesting for sale to tourists.
- Cruise ships in the Caribbean are estimated to produce more than 70,000 tons of waste each year.

- An average 18-hole golf course soaks up at least 525,000 gallons of water a day-enough to supply the irrigation needs of 100 Malaysian farmers.

Fact Sheet: Global Ecotourism

Ecotourism: "Responsible travel to natural areas that conserves the environment and improves the welfare of local people" (TIES, 1990).

Since surveys rarely ask either travellers or businesses specifically about ecotourism, precise statistics are difficult to determine. Ecotourism is frequently lumped together with nature tourism and other forms of 'experiential' or 'alternative' tourism. These figures represent TIES best effort to put together an accurate assessment of the strength of ecotourism, particularly since 2000.

Size of Global Ecotourism

- Beginning in 1990s, ecotourism has been growing 20%-34% per year.
- In 2004, ecotourism/nature tourism was growing globally 3 times faster than the tourism industry as a whole.
- Nature tourism is growing at 10%-12% per annum in the international market.
- Sun-and-sand resort tourism has now "matured as a market" and its growth is projected to remain flat. In contrast, "experiential" tourism—which encompasses ecotourism, nature, heritage, cultural, and soft adventure tourism, as well as sub-sectors such as rural and community tourism—is among the sectors expected to grow most quickly over the next two decades.
- United Nations Environment Programme (UNEP) and Conservation International have indicated that most of tourism's expansion is occurring in and around the world's remaining natural areas.
- Sustainable tourism could grow to 25% of the world's travel market within six years, taking the value of the sector to £250 billion (US$473.6 billion) a year.
- Analysts predict a growth in eco-resorts and hotels, and a boom in nature tourism — a sector already growing at 20% a year — and suggest early converts to sustainable tourism will make market gains.

Economics of Ecotourism vs. Mass Tourism

- In Dominica, in the Caribbean, "stay over" tourists using small, nature-based lodges spent 18 times more than cruise passengers spend while visiting the island.
- In Komodo National Park in Indonesia, independent travellers spend nearly US$100 locally per visit; package holidaymakers spend only half this. In contrast, cruise-ship arrivals spend an average three cents in the local economy.
- 80% of money for all-inclusive package tours goes to airlines, hotels, and other international companies. Eco-lodges hire and purchase locally, and sometimes put as much as 95% of money into the local economy.
- The daily expenditure of cultural tourists (over €70/US$90) is higher than visitors on a touring holiday (€52/US$67), beach holiday (€48/US$62), city break (€42/$US$54) or rural trip.

Consumer Demand

- More than two-thirds of U.S. and Australian travellers, and 90% of British tourists, consider active protection of the environment and support of local communities to be part of a hotel's responsibility.

TIES Global Ecotourism Fact Sheet

- In Europe: 20%-30% of§ travellers are aware of needs & values of sustainable tourism. 10%-20% of§ travellers look for 'green' options. 5%-10% of§ travellers demand 'green' holidays.
- In Germany, 65% (39 million) of travellers expect environmental quality; 42% (25 million) "think that it is particularly important to find environmentally-friendly accommodation."
- Nearly half of those surveyed in Britain said they would be more likely to go with a "company that had a written code to guarantee good working conditions, protect the environment and support local charities in the tourist destination... [E]thical tourism will rightly be a big issue in the new millennium."
- A survey of U.S., British, and Australian travellers revealed that 70% would pay up to $150 more for a two-week stay in a hotel with a "responsible environmental attitude.

- In a U.K. survey, 87% of travellers said their holiday should not damage the environment; 39% said they were prepared to pay 5% extra for ethical guarantees.
- 53% of American travellers say their travel experience is enhanced when they learn as much as possible about local customs and culture.
- 95% of Swiss tourists consider respect for local culture to be highly important when choosing a holiday.
- Nearly a third (46 million) of U.S. travellers buy specifically from companies that donate part of their proceeds to charities. In Europe, where there is a strong and growing sustainable tourism movement, these figures are even higher.

Profile of Ecotourists in Europe

- Experienced travellers.
- Higher education.
- Higher income bracket.
- Age: middle-age to elderly.
- Opinion leaders.
- Ask & tell their friends & colleagues about trip.
- Are the most important source of trip information xxxiv.

9

Promoting Tourism in Rural America

Introduction

This revision of *Promoting Tourism in Rural America* covers the major issues in rural tourism including agritourism, cultural/heritage tourism, ecotourism, planning, marketing, economic impact and more. It provides web links to more than *fifty* full-text "how to" information guides, manuals, and handbooks for assisting local officials, communities, and citizens involved in tourism development and includes a section of resources organizations.

The reader may also access additional tourism resources including success stories/case studies, funding and assistance programs, and statistical information located on the Rural Information Centre's Tourism Resource page at

This source guide was revised and updated by Patricia LaCaille John November 2004.

Rural Information Centre Publication Series Number 60, Revised Edition. Last Modified: May 22, 2008

Tourism Development Overview

Advantages and Disadvantages of Tourism Development

The pros and cons of tourism development in rural America are varied. Tourism provides income and diversification to rural communities. Most of the dollars generated from outside visitors stay within the local economy.

In addition to gains from direct sales to visitors, many indirect benefits are realized from tourism. Visitors contribute to the tax revenues collected and can influence the quality of life by financing community facilities such as swimming pools, golf courses, restaurants, and shopping facilities. Community events intended for tourists, also attract local residents. Many potential industries prefer locations that provide high quality services and recreational resources. If the community is a pleasant place, the visitors may become a permanent resident.

Tourism offers other indirect benefits. For example, the need to provide services to tourists creates new jobs in the community. Although they may not be high paying employment opportunities, these jobs satisfy the need of students and dual-earning families for part-time or seasonal employment.

On the other hand, developing and maintaining the tourist industry in a community requires added costs and puts pressure on public services. The cost of surveys, impact analysis, promotions, insurance, fund raising, and operations are some points to consider.

Managing Resources Requires Planning

Advanced planning maximizes the advantages and minimizes the disadvantages of developing rural tourism.

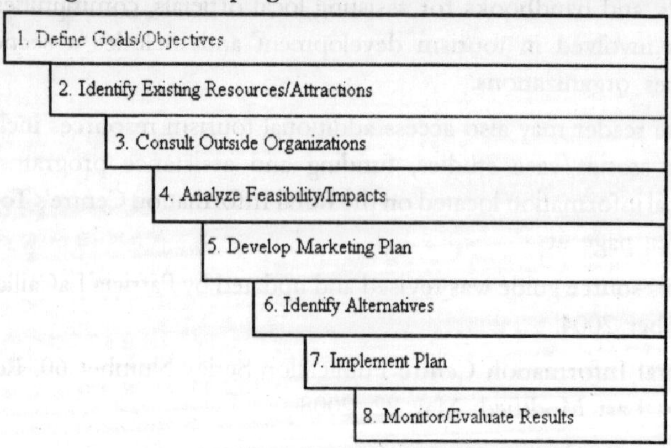

Steps in Planning and Developing Tourism

Tips and Technologies

Many communities can develop tourism into a major industry using these techniques:

- Understand the potential for tourism development.
- Inform and educate the community to create support.
- Secure investments for public and private sources.
- Manage natural, human, and financial resources.
- Build an image for the community.

Where to Start

Leaders must first assess the potential for tourism in the community. What businesses serve travellers and how much additional revenue will it generate? Are these enough services to satisfy the potential demands? What are the goals and objectives of the community? Talk about tourism with other members of the community. Tourism requires support, and one way to gain support is by informing and educating the citizenry. Introduce the idea to the Chamber of Commerce, at civic clubs, at city council, or at other community organization meetings. The community and its leaders can broaden support for tourism by securing financial commitments from public and private sources.

Existing Resources

Managing natural, human and financial resources is an important component of tourism development. Most communities have existing resources and attractions that can draw visitors, such as:

- natural settings.
- scenery.
- parks and recreations.
- historical identity.
- cultural identity.
- ethnic identity.
- volunteers.
- students.
- retirees.
- events.
- festivals.
- fairs.
- shops.
- hotels.

- local industries.
- art galleries.

What Does Your Community Have to Offer?

Conduct an inventory of the things that your community has to offer to tourists. Describe each type of attraction in terms of quality and quantity. Separate them by "core elements" (primary reasons tourist are attracted) and "secondary elements" (supporting resources; those that contribute positively to the tourists' travel experience). Look ahead at the resources that might be enhanced or used more fully.

Surveys and Models

Surveys and models are used in the process of tourism planning to determine:

- Community attitudes toward tourism.
- Recreational use value and demand.
- Tourism patterns.
- Travel costs.
- Economic impacts.

Types of survey methods include telephone interviews, questionnaires, and mall interviews.

Telephone interview are low in cost, and provide a quick turnaround. In order to simplify the responses, the interviewer offers a minimum number of choices to each question in the survey. The interviewer also sends a letter before the call is made to state the date and time of the survey and ask the customer's cooperation.

Questionnaires can be used to identify the different types of tourists, or market segments. The surveyor lists responses that can be checked off by the visitor. This type of response is easy to tabulate. The survey may include questions that ask:

- Where does the visitor live?
- What attracts the visitor to the community?
- How does the visitor find out about tourist attractions?
- What type of businesses/facilities does the visitor use?
- What kinds of accommodations/services are needed?

The survey tests the questionnaire to determine the typical responses and to modify the questions.

Face-to-face interviews are useful if visual aids are necessary, for instance, in evaluating what promotional materials are pleasing to the consumer. These interviews are conducted at a central location, such as in a shopping mall.

Developing a Marketing Plan

An important step in tourism planning is determining target market segments. Experts begin by defining the market areas that will draw the most visitors. They then divide the market into trip length categories. Finally, they define the clientele that will be attracted to the community. Use the chart below as a guide:

Geographic Market Areas

Day Trips

- short — within 50 miles.
- long — up to 200 miles.

Pass Through Visits

- day visits.
- overnight stays.

Overnight Trips

- weekends.
- vacations.

Outdoor Recreation Activities

- Water Recreations.
- Camping, Hiking, Bicycling.
- Hunting.
- Winter Sports.
- Horseback Riding.
- Picnicking.
- Hang Gliding, Ballooning.
- Nature Study.
- Photography, Painting.

Entertainments

- Cultural Heritage.
- Historic sites.
- Events.
- Fairs, Festivals.
- Shopping.
- Picnicking.

Other Travel Purposes

- Visit Friends & Relatives.
- Business.

When the expert has determined the market segments, leaders of the community are ready to make a written marketing plan. This plan helps them to see the best combination of marketing strategies, prices, places and promotions to use. Which characteristics are unique to the community? Using the plan, the leaders are able to develop a theme that ties the community's businesses and services together.

It is important to involve all facets of the community in the decision making process. Remember that everyone and everything the visitor has contact with projects and promotes something about the community.

Keep your promotional messages short and targeted to the community theme. Use your theme to promote your community:

- on brochures, billboards, posters.
- ont-shirts, hats, stickers, coupons.
- at demonstrations, contests, the library.
- for public announcements on television, radio or community calendars.

10

Emerging Dimensions in Tourism: India Specific

Introduction

We have discussed in the previous units in detail, that tourism industry is one of the major segments of the Indian economy. It is a major contributor to foreign exchange earnings provides employment to millions directly and indirectly and acts as a vehicle for infrastructure development. Recognising the importance of the tourism industry, the Government of India has taken many policy measures such as Tourism Policy 1982, Tourism Plan of Action 1992 and Tourism Policy 1997. Through these policies, the government called for effective coordination of public and private participation to achieve synergy in the development of tourism. These plans identified new forms of tourism products for taking advantage of the emerging markets. Business tourism, health tourism, rural tourism, pilgrim tourism, adventure tourism, and sustainable tourism are some of the new products devised for changing demand. Let us study these emerging dimensions in the tourism sector.

Objectives

After studying this unit you will be able to achieve following objectives:

- Understand emerging trends in tourism.
- Learn about new products and old traditional tourism products.
- Know the importance of sustainable tourism development.
- Understand the concept of nature tourism.
- Develop environmental consciousness.

- Develop skills to locate important tourist destinations on the map.
- Know that tourism can be an instrumental for developing secularism and national integration and universal brotherhood.

Emerging Dimensions

Tourism will expand greatly in future mainly due to the revolution that is taking place on both the demand and supply side. The changing population structure, improvement in living standard, more disposable income, fewer working hours and long leisure time, better educated people, ageing population and more curious youth in developing the countries, all will fuel the tourism industry growth. The arrival of a large number of customers, better educated and more sophisticated, will compel the tourist industry to launch new products and brands and re-invents traditional markets. The established traditional destinations founded on sun-sea-sand products will have to re-engineer their products. They must diversify and improve the criteria for destinations and qualities of their traditional offers. Alongside beach tourism, the tourism sector will register a steady development of new products based on natural rural business, leisure and art and culture. Thus the study of new markets and emerging markets and necessity of diversified products are the basis of our strategy, which can enhance and sustain, existing and capture new markets. Let us discuss some of the new tourism products.

Spiritual Tourism

Globally people are increasingly mentally disturbed and looking for solace in spiritual reading, meditation and moments of divine ecstasy. Our country has been known as the seat of spiritualism and India's cosmopolitan nature is best reflected in its pilgrim centres. Religion is the lifeblood for followers of major religion and sects. Hinduism, Islam, Buddhism, Jainism, Zoroastrianism and Christianity have lived here for centuries. The visible outpouring of religious fervour is witnessed in the architecturally lavish temples, mosques, monasteries and Churches spreads across the length and breadth of the country. India is not only known as a place rich in its culture with varied attractions but also for many places of worship, present itself as embodiments of compassion where one get peace of mind.

Thus India has been respected as a destination for spiritual tourism for domestic and international tourists. Spiritual tourism is also termed as religious heritage tourism. It includes all the religions mentioned above; religious places associated with, emotional attachment to these centres and infrastructure facilities for the tourists. This can also be referred to as pilgrimage tourism, as clients are not looking for luxury but arduous journeys to meet the divine goal or simple life.

The essence of spiritual tourism is inner feeling through love. Love should not be rationed on the basis of caste, creed and economic status or intellectual attainment of the recipient. Religions come into existence for the purpose of regulating human life; what are common to all of them are the principles of love. Thus through religious tourism there is a sincere effort to bring better understanding among various communities, nations and thus foster global unity.

Hinduism is one of the oldest religions of India. Over 5000 years of religious history created wonderful temples and survived through ages all over India. The most popular spiritual tours are those that are centred on holy Ganges River. Badrinath, Kedarnath, Haridwar, Gangotri, Yamunotri, Allahabad, Varanasi. Jaganath temple at Puri, Bhubaneshwar, Konark in Orissa, Mata Vaishnodevi of Jammu and Kashmir, are some of the important pilgrim centres in north India. There are many spiritual sites in South India as well which dates back beyond the 10th century.

Rameshwaram, Mahabalipuram, Madurai Meenakshi temple in Tamil Nadu and Tirupati in Andhra Pradesh are some pilgrim centres. Every year millions of tourists, both domestic and international, visit these places. India is special to Buddhists all over the world and India is the destination for pilgrimage because Buddhism emerged in India. The country is dotted with places that are associated with the life and times of Gutham Buddha; Lumbini-the birthplace of Buddha, Saranath where Buddha delivered his first sermon, Buddha Gaya where lord Buddha attained enlightenment and Vaishali where he delivered his last sermon and announced his nirvana.

Sikhism also emerged in India. The Golden Temple in Amritsar, the Hemkund Sahib, and Gurunanak Devji Gurudwara at Manikaran, which is also known for its hot water springs with healing properties, the holy city of Patna Sahib and Anandpur Sahib are important for Sikhs. The Jain temples of Dilwara and Mount Abu in Rajasthan, the Gomateswara temple at Karnataka, draw thousands of Jain followers. Even small communities like the Bahais have their own Lotus Temple at Delhi.

The Sultanate and Mughal empires built many historical monuments and mosques during their reign, all over the country. Red Fort, Fatehapur Sikri, Jama Masjid, Taj Mahal, Charminar etc., bear testimony to the blend of the Indian and Islam traditions of architecture. The followers of Islam have many mosques and shrines of Sufi Saints, like Moin-Uddin Chisti and Nizamuddin Aulia. For Christians, spiritual tours to Goa among other place like Mumbai and Kolkata are must. Among the most popular sites in Goa is the church of Our Lady of Rosary, the Rachel Seminary, and Church of Bom Jesus.

In addition to pilgrim centres there are personalities like the Satya Sai Baba, Osho, Shirdhi and others. This shows that spirituality and religion in India is a serious pursuit. The State Governments concerned, charitable trusts, temple trusts have made elaborate arrangements for accommodation, transport and ritual ceremonies. These organizations are also running hospitals, educational institutes, ashrams, meditation centres which benefit local community. More than 500 religious places have been identified and efforts are being made to develop these centres by Central and State Governments with private participation.

Adventure Tourism

Youth tourism has been identified as one of the largest segments of global and domestic tourism. The young travellers are primarily experience seekers, collecting, enquiring unique experiences. Adventure and risk have a special role to play in the behaviour and attitudes of young travellers. The growing number of young travellers is being fuelled by a number of factors such as increased participation in higher education, falling level of youth unemployment, increased travel budget through parental contribution, search for an even more exciting and unique experience and cheaper long distance travel.

Youth and adventure tourism appears to have considerable growth potential. The rising income in some major potential source markets such as the Central and Eastern Europe, Asia and Latin America, combined with the lower travel cost, growing student populations around the world particularly in developing countries, has fuelled the demand. India: a heaven for adventure tourism India has been an attraction for travellers from all over the world. Though in the field of international tourism, the segment of adventure tourism in India is getting only a fraction of such traffic. The trend has been showing an increased movement year after year with the development of facilities and greater awareness about adventure tourism options. Indian tourism offers both international and domestic adventurers a wide choice of adventures. Water sports, elephant safari, skiing, yachting, hail-skiing, gliding, sailing, tribal tours, orchid tours, scaling the high peaks of Himalayas, trekking to the valley of flowers, riding the waves in rapids, and camel safari in the deserts are breath taking opportunities for nature enthusias. Laddakh, the Garwal hills, the Himachal hills, Darjeeling, Goa, Lakshadweep, Andaman and Nicobar, Jaisalmer and wildlife sanctuaries and reserves are some of the places that offer adventure tourism. Himalayas are the centre of India's main adventure activities as well as outdoor recreational tourism. Our rivers, backwaters, Indian Ocean, Arabian Sea and deserts are unique attractions for the various branches of adventure. Trekking holds out the greatest potential in terms of numbers. It requires little infrastructure and carries its benefits to remote hills and mountain regions. Many of them are economically poor and backward. For our own youth it also helps in inculcating a spirit of adventure, respect for nature.

Indian Mountaineering Federation, Ministry of Tourism and State Governments are trying to improve trekking facilities and ensure safety and protection of travellers. The Institute of Mountaineering also organises courses for guides to train them in basic rock climbing safety procedures, environmental knowledge, and flora and fauna conservation. The major trek heads in the Himalayan region include Kashmir valley, Kirshwasser Zanskar, Ladhak, Lahul and Spiti, Champa and Manali, etc., Trekking in the Himalayas is a quite enjoyable. Let us now discuss some important adventure activities.

Mountaineering Expedition

This is the first and foremost activity in the Himalayas. In India, the expeditions are controlled and regulated by Indian Mountaineering Federation, which is the nodal body. Foreign expedition groups have to request the Indian Mountaineering Foundation (IMF) to book the required peak and IMF confirms the peak, by charging the royalty depending upon the number of persons and height of peak. Ministry of Defence, Home Ministry, of External Affairs are also involved in this process.

River Rafting

The Himalayan river's offer River rafting that run through the beautiful terrains, sandy white beaches, boulder studded rapids, river confluences, deep gorges, and some revered temples and towns. White-water sports are popular in Rishikesh, Manali, Zanskar Teesta, Beas, Central Ministry of Tourism has great extremely extended support to import inflatable rafts, canoes, kayaks, and accessories to boost water sports. Lakshadweep and Andaman have been promoted for scuba diving and wind surfing.

Water Sports

To boost water sports, water skiing and sailing both in seas and lakes, and river facilities has been provided. Chilka Lake in Orissa, Kollam in Kerala, Bhopal Lake in Madhya Pradesh, Dal Lake in Kashmir are some of the places where facilities have been provided for water sports. In Himachal hills Heli-skiing is also being promoted in season. The Garwal Mandal Vikas Nigam provides regular skiing courses during the season. It can be said that India is a new destination for adventure tourism. The Ministry of tourism, The Himalayan Task Force and Himalayan Tourism and Adventure Tourism Board (HMTAB) meet every year to discuss conservation, promotion for Himalayan tourism, and conservation of ecology.

Nature Tourism

In search of new tourism products, travellers and suppliers are today seeking to reshape the meaning of nature as a tourism attraction. Modern nature based tourism focuses on experiencing flora and fauna in natural settings. The nature based tourism related to nature, its attractiveness so that the visitors experience it in its natural settings. Ecotourism takes into account unspoiled natural and sociocultural attraction. Today the term nature tourism is often used synonymously with eco-tourism. Today nature tourism is the fastest growing segment of the tourism sector. It comprises around 40-60% of all international tourism. Diversity of India is to be seen not only in its people, culture, religions, language and life style, the diversity starts in the land itself. The snowbourd peaks of the Himalayas, tropical rain forests, and hot deserts and breathtaking beautiful coasts. Each diverse geographical region generates a different picture and exploring them provides a unique experience. Now all these are packaged for tourists to provide eco-friendly holidays in India.

Wildlife

The diversity of wild life in India is as rich as that of its flora and fauna. The great wealth of Indian wildlife can be imagined with the sight of majestic elephants, the dance of peacocks, the camel strides, the roar of tigers, at unparalleled acts of beauty. Watching birds and animals in their natural habitat is an experience in itself. The vastness of wild life and wilderness is India unparallel in the world. All these account for the immense opportunities for wild life tourism in India.

The immense heritage of wild life in India comprises 80 national parks and another whopping 441 wild life sanctuaries including bird sanctuaries. These reserves and forest areas are spread across the breadth and length right form the foot hills of Himalayan, the Jim Corbet National park to six national parks in Andaman, from Ranthambhor national park in Rajasthan to Hazaribag wild life sanctuary in Bihar. India also boasts of the unique ecosystem at Sunderbans which is a UNESCO world heritage site and home to the largest number of tigers in the world. The Himalayan region is renowned for being the national habitat for a variety of wild life, elephants, snow leopards, deer, panther, wild buffalos, wild ass, one horned rhinoceros, porcupine, snow leopards, etc. The Kaziranga Game Sanctuary is ideal habitat for the rhino that the nature lovers and environmentalists are fascinated by.

The great Indian bustard and the black buck of Kerera sanctuary attract a lot of tourists. The Madhav National Park (Shivpuri Park) is another rich habitat for the wild life. The royal animal, tiger happens to be symbol of strength and speed. Amongst the best-known tiger reserves in India is Bandhawgarh in Madhya Pradesh. It is also known as the crown in the wild life heritage of India.

The variety of birds in India is enormous. Several hundred species of bird can be spotted across India. Indian wild life has its share of native birds along with migratory birds. The region of Andaman is home to rare species of birds like Narcondum hornbills, Nicobar pigeons and megaspores. The Himalayan region is well known as the natural habitat for the pheasant griffon, vulture and ravens. Dudhuwa wild life reserve, Keoladeao, Ghana national park, the Bharatpur bird sanctuary in Rajasthan is home to indigenous and migratory water birds. These bird sanctuaries are attracting tourists from far and wide.

Fishing and Angling

Among the amazing array of nature tours offered in India are those that offer angling and fishing. The waters of Indian subcontinent are mind-blowing grounds for the nature sports. The adventures settings range form the majestic Himalayan valleys, snow fed streams and high altitude lakes and wide coastal stretches of the Arabia Seas and Bay of Bengal. Amidst the beautiful hills of the Himalayas is tented accommodation along the river beds, excellent option for adventure holidays in India. The Cauvery fishing lodge near Mysore, the hill stations of Munnar, and streams and lakes of Kerala and Kashmir are a paradise for anglers.

Hill Stations

At heights that range from 600 m to 3500m above sea level, most of the hill resorts of India are tourist destination in India. The hill stations add to the nature tour of India with majestic mountains and ravishing rivers. Mountain ranges of Shimla, Kullu Manali, Dalhousie, Palampur in Himachal Pradesh, Nainital-Almora-Kausani in Kumaon hills of Uttar Pradesh, Pachmarhi in Madhya Pradesh, Darjeeling are important for their snow-dusted peaks, lakes, parks and hot springs. The waterfalls, sulphur bath and all provide such an experience, which will linger in one's mind.

Green heavens are on not only in the forest but the Islands are also a source of the best eco-tourism destinations. The tourism activities in Lakshadweep bring you close to nature. Andamans that are covered with rainforest, ringed by coral reefs, marine life, swimming and sunbathing are good experiences.

We are promoting tourism but while promoting tourism in eco-sensitive areas the emphasis is to control the volume of tourists so that the fragile balance of the area is not disturbed. The whole objective of nature tourism is to have purposeful travel to natural areas. Taking special note of this very objective of the eco-tourism while utilising the economic opportunities we should ensure conservation of natural resources. People travel to those areas, which enlightens, educates and entertains them. The new changed concept of nature tourism revives the tired source of the eco-tourism. It also provides basic economic upliftment to local people and other stakeholders who are directly dependent on this natural heritage. This strong relationship is targeted throughout eco-tourism.

Government Initiatives

Ministry of Tourism formulated eco-tourism guidelines for regulated and sustainable tourism. Tour operators operating in the fragile zones have adopted the (American Society of travel Agents) eco-practices for eco-tourism practices. These are:-

- Leave only foot prints, take photographs, but do not take away from natural areas and heritage monuments.
- Encourage local culture.
- Respect local traditions.
- Help in the conservation efforts.
- Do not buy products made of endangered plants and animals.
- Try to respect natural habitats and support those products which promote the cause of environment and protection Ecotourism.
- Madhav National Park.
- Andaman & Nicobar Island.
- Bharatpur.
- World heritage site.
- Narcondum hornbills.
- Munnar.
- Kanha.
- Shivpuri.
- Sunderbans.
- Bird sanctuary.
- Angling.
- Wild life sanctuary.

Rural Tourism

Rural tourism has been identified as one of the priority areas for development of Indian tourism. Rural tourism experience should be attractive to the tourists and sustainable for the host community. The Ninth Plan identified basic objectives of rural tourism as:-

- Improve the quality of life of rural people.
- Provide good experience to the tourist.
- Maintain the quality of environment.

Indian villages have the potential for tourism development. With attractive and unique traditional way of life, rich culture, nature, crafts, folk-lore and livelihood of Indian villages are a promising destination for the tourist. It also provides tourism facilities in terms of accessibility, accommodation, sanitation and security. Rural tourism can be used as a means to:-

- Improve the well being of the rural poor.
- Empower the rural people.
- Empower the women.
- Enhance the rural infrastructure.
- Participate in decision-making and implementing tourism policies.
- Interaction with the outside world.
- Improve the social condition of lower sections of the society.
- Protection of culture, heritage, and nature.

To tap the immense opportunities, coordinated actives of all agencies involved in the development are required. A carefully planned and properly implemented development will definitely benefit the community economically and improve the quality of life in the villages. The success of such development depends upon the people's participation at grass root level for the development of tourist facilities and for creating a tourist friendly atmosphere. Development of rural tourism is fast and trade in hotels and restaurants is growing rapidly. Increase in the share of earnings through rural tourism will no doubt; provide an attractive means of livelihood to the poor rural community. It increases the purchasing power at all levels of community and strengthens the rural economy. Development of infrastructure facilities such as rail, electricity, water, health and sanitation will definitely improve the quality of life.

Government Initiatives

Central Government and State Governments have been encouraging rural handicrafts and fairs and festivals that have direct impact on preservation of heritage and culture of rural India. It also draws tourists from all over the world. Regional fairs, festivals help the growth of tourism, provide a ready market for the handicrafts, alternative income to the community, and facilitate regional interaction within the country. The state governments have been monitoring closely the ecological relationship, sociocultural impact and conducting feasibility studies before selecting tourist sites. The state governments also ensure that: Tourism-

- Does not cause the tension for the host community.
- No adverse impact on the resources.
- Psychological satisfaction for the tourist.
- The large inflow of tourists would not put a stress on the local system.

- Local community should not be deprived of basic facilities for the benefits of tourist.
- The rural tourism does not disrupt the rhythm of community life.

Thus the Central Government and State Governments have taken various steps for the promotion of tourism and attainment of the goal of sustainable tourism development.

Sustainable Tourism

The concept of sustainability means that mankind must live within the capacity of the environment that supports. Sustainable development has been defined briefly as "that which meets the needs of the present without compromising the ability of future generations to meet their own needs".

The definition brings out certain important aspects of sustainable tourism:-

- Conservation and enhancement of resources for the future generation.
- Protection of biological diversity.
- Equity within and between generations.
- Integration of environmental, social and economic considerations.

The concept of sustainable development is all about conservation and stewardship of resources for the future. The support for ecologically sustainable development emerging strongly in the tourism sector, as it is the logical way of balancing environmental concerns with growth and development of the industry. Environmental problems facing the world today are of such magnitude that urgent actions have to be taken at the highest levels to counter this fatal degradation. But it is not just enough for government organisations to work towards sustainable development. Every individual, every neighbourhood, and every community has to contribute in every away possible to get close to the goal. Since the earth summit, the concept of sustainable development has been placed firmly on the global agenda. This issue is assuming great significance in the development of tourism in India also.

Tourism activities depend upon nature and natural heritage, it is essential to ensure that tourism development is ecologically sustainable –ecological process must not be neglected. Similarly tourism offers real experience of unique culture of the country. Hence the development should ensure that social and cultural sustainable tourism development compatible with the culture and values of the local people. The World Tourism Organization (WTO) defined sustainable tourism development as "that which meets the needs of present tourist and host regions while protecting and enhancing opportunities for the future. It is envisaged as leading to the management of all resources in such a way that economic, social and aesthetic needs can be fulfilled while maintaining cultural integrity, essential for ecological process, biological diversity and life supporting system".

Thus tourism has to be human and adapted to the needs of the tourist, respond to the needs of the local communities, be socioeconomic and culturally well planned and environmentally sound. The tourism must offer products that are operated in harmony with the local environment, community attitudes and culture so that they become permanent beneficiaries and not the victims of tourism. The basic cultural identity of these local people should not be adversely affected. Sustainability also ensures economically sustainable-development process in the efficient management of resources and such management to ensure that the resource supports the future as well as the present generation.

Thus sustainable tourism aims to:-

- Improve the quality of life of people.
- Provide good experience to the tourists.
- Maintain the quality of environment that is essential for both tourists and the local community.

Tourism can be one of the effective tools for building a prosperous community economically, socially and culturally. It must be environmentally sustainable and based on the sustenance of the natural and cultural base. Each destination should examine whether it has adequate attractions and facilities for tourism and there is a potential for tourism generating markets to be open to exploitation. The carrying capacity is the central principle in environmental protection and sustainable tourism development. It determines the maximum use of any place without causing negative effects on resources on community, economy and culture. Thus tourism has to be environmentally sustainable in both natural and cultural environment

Basic Guidelines for achieving sustainable tourism The following are certain guidelines that have to be followed to achieve sustainable tourism:

- A general tourism policy incorporating sustainable tourism objectives at national regional and local level should be followed.
- Targets established for the planning, development and operation of tourism involving various government departments, public and private sector companies, community groups and experts could provide widest possible safeguards for success.
- Primary consideration should be given to the protection of natural and cultural assets.
- All tourism participants will follow ethical and sound behavioural and conservative rules regarding nature, culture, economy, and community value system.
- The distribution of tourism development project should be rationed on the basis of equity.
- Public awareness of benefits tourism and how to mitigate its negative impacts should be pursued.
- Local people would be encouraged to assume leadership roles in planning and development.

In the Tourism Policy, 1982 the guidelines in Ecotourism have attempted to achieve sustainability in tourism. It indicates that the key players in the ecotourism are Central Government and state governments, local authorities, developers, operators, visitors and local community. Each of them has to be sensitive to the environment and local traditions and follow the guidelines for successfully development of sustainable tourism.

Summary

Tourism industry is one of the major segments of our economy, it contributes major part of foreign exchange and generates employment and helps infrastructure development. Government of India has formulated policies to boost the tourism industry. Tourism will expand greatly in future mainly due to the great revolutions that are taking place in demand and supply.

Thus the study is a critical issue in tourism industry. And new product development and innovation is essential for survival. Health tourism in India is promoted as high-tech healing destinations, which provide world-class treatment at low cost, incorporating the Indian system of medicine-ayurveda, naturopathy, unani, sidha and allopathy. India is the seat of spiritualism. It is the confluence of different religions: Hinduism Sikhism, Islam, Christianity, and Jainism, etc. The followers of religion built many lavish temples, mosques, monasteries and churches across the country.

These are attracting both domestic and international tourists. In India, adventure tourism and nature tourism have been identified as the largest segment of global and domestic tourism. The geographical diversity makes India as a heaven for adventurers. MICE tourism is a fast emerging sector; especially after the liberalization of the Indian economy and Indian tourism industry is equipped with all facilities to welcome business tourists. Sustainable tourism is a new concept, which says that the tourism development should meet the needs of the present without compromising the ability of future generation to meet their needs.

Key Words

The various key words which are mentioned in this lesson are:

- Yam
- Dhyana
- Samadhi
- Niyam
- Asana
- Pranayama
- Prathyahara
- Arduous
- Exotic
- Ecstasy
- Fervour
- Rejuvenation
- Expertise
- Therapy
- Multi specialty
- Preventive health care.

Bibliography

Andrew, N; Flanagan, S & Ruddy, J: *Tourism Destination Planning*, Dublin, Dublin Institute of Technology, 2002.

Apostolopous, Y and Leivadi, S: *Sociology of Tourism, The: Theoretical And Empirical Investigations*, London, Retailed, 1996.

Ashworth, G J and Dietvorst, A G J: *Tourism and Spatial Transformations: Implications For Policy and Plan*, Wallingford, CAB International, 1995.

Ashworth, Greg and Larkham, P J: *Building a New Heritage: Tourism, Culture & Identity in the New Europe*, London, Routledge,1994.

Baum, Tom: *We're all Going on a Summer Holiday: Images of Tourism Past and Person*, Buckingham, University of Buckingham, 1995.

Beeho, A & Prentice, R: *Conceptualising The Experiences of Heritage Tourists*, 1997.

Beeton, Sue:: *Film-Induced Tourism*, Clevedon, Channel View, 2005.

Belie et al.: *Tourism and the Inner City: An Evaluation of / Impact of Grant Assist*, London, HMSO, 1990.

Benefice, Brian G, and Cooper, Chris: *Geography of Travel and Tourism*, The, London, Heinemann, 1987.

Bolshevism, Germy: *Coping with Tourists: European Reactions to Mass Tourism*, Oxford, Berghahn Books, 1995.

Boniface, Priscilla and Fowler, Peter: *Heritage and Tourism: In the Global Village*, London, Retailed, 1993.

Bosselman, Fred P: *In The Wake of the Tourist: Managing Special Places in Eight Countries*, Washington, DC, Conservation Foundation, The, 1978.

Briguglio, L and Vella, Leslie: *Competitiveness of the Maltese Islands in Mediterranean in Tourism*, Chichester, John Wiley, 1995.

Brown, Dona: *Inventing New England: Regional Tourism in the Nineteenth Century*, Washington DC, Smithsonian Institution, 1995.

Brunt, Paul: *Market Research in Travel and Tourism*, Oxford, Butterworth Heinemann, 1997.

Burkart, A and Medlik, S: *Management of Tourism*, The, London, Heinemann, 1975.

Chambers, Erve: *Native Tours: The Anthropology of Travel and Tourism*, Prospect Heights, Waveland Press, 2000.

Chandler, Harry and Carter, John: *Chandler's Travels: A Tour of the Life of Harry Chandler*, London, Quiller Press, 1985.

Clark, Colin: *Tourist Services and Guidance: Heritage and Information*, Strasbourg, Council of Europe Press, 1989.

Coccosis, Harry and Nijkamp, Peter: *Sustainable Tourism Development*, Aldershot, Avebury, 1995.

Cohen, Erik: *Towards a Sociology of International Tourism*, 1972.

Dann, Graham M S: *Language of Tourism*, The, Wallingford, CAB International, 1996.

Davidson, R and Maitland, R: *Tourism Destinations, London*, Hodder and Stoughton, 1997.

Davidson, Rob: *Travel and Tourism in Europe*, Harlow, Addison Wesley Longman, 1998.

Ecotec: *Calderdale: Tourism Impact Study*, Calderdale, ECOTEC/Calderdale Council, 1990.

Edensor, Tim: *Tourists at the Taj*, London, Retailed, 1998.

Edgell, David L: *International Tourism Policy, New York*, Van Nostrand and Reinhold, 1990.

Elliott, James: *Tourism: Politics and Public Sector Management*, London, Retailed, 1997.

Fairgrieve, James: *Geography in School*, London, University of London Press, 1926.

Foster, Douglas: *Travel and Tourism Management*, London, Macmillan Educational, 1985.

Frechtling, Douglas C: *Practical Tourism Forecasting*, Oxford, Butterworth Heinemann, 1996.

Gamble, P. R: *The Educational challenge for Hospitality and Tourism Studies*, Tourism Management, 13, 1992.

Ghimire, Krishna: *The Native Tourist*: Mass Tourism within Developing Regions, London, Earthscan, 2001.

Goeldner, C. R: *The Evaluation of Tourism as an Industry and a Discipline, Paper Presented to*, International Conference for Tourism Educators, Guildford, University of Surrey, 1988.

Gunn, Clare and Var, Turgut: *Tourism Planning*, London, Retailed, 2002.

Hall, C Michael *Tourism Planning: Policies, Processes and relationships*, Harlow, Prentice Hall, 2000.

Hall, Colin and Jenkins, John: *Tourism and Public Policy*, London, Retailed, 1995.

Hall, Colin Michael: *Tourism and Politics*: Policy, Power, & Place, Chichester, Wiley, 1994.

Harrison, Lyndon: *Tourism Means Jobs*, Chester, Lyndon Harrison, 1996.

Harron, S and Weiler, B: *Ethnic Tourism*, Belhaven/Wiley, 1992.

Inkpen, G: *Information Technology for Travel and Tourism*, Harlow, Addison Wesley Longman, 1998.

Inskeep, Edward *National and Regal Tourism Planing*: Methodologies & Case Studies, London, Routledge/WTO, 1994.

Irwin, William *The New Niagara: Tourism, Technology, And the Landscape of Niagara Fal*, University Park, PA, University of Pennsylvania, 1996.

Jack, G and Phipps, A: *Tourism and Intercultural Exchange: Why Tourism Matters*, Clevedon, Channel View, 2005.

Jakle, John: *Tourist, The: Travel in Twentieth Century North America*, University of North Nebraska, 1985.

Jennings, Gayle: *Tourism Research*, Chichester, Wiley, 2001.

Judd, D R: *Promoting Tourism* in US Cities, 1995.

Karski, A: *Urban Tourism* - A Key to Urban Regeneration?, 1990.

Kotler, Philip et al: *Marketing Places: Attracting Investment, Industry & Tourism etc*, New York, free press, 1993.

Labarge, Margaret Wade: *Medieval Travellers: The Rich and Restless*, London, Hamish Hamilton, 1982.

Laws, Eric: *Tourist Destination Management: Issues, Analysis & Policies*, London, Routledge, 1995.

Leed, Eric J: *Mind of the Traveller, The: From Gilgamesh to Global Tourism*, New York, 1991.

MacCannell, Dean: *Tourist, The: A New Theory of the Leisure Class*, London, Macmillan, 1976.

Machin, Alan: *Retracing the Steps: Tourism as Education, Janus*, Fin, ATLAS / FUNTS, 2001.

Opperman, Martin and Chon, Kye-Sung: *Tourism in Developing Countries, London*, International Thomson Business Press, 1997.

Patullo, Polly: *Last Resorts: The Cost of Tourism in the Caribbean*, London, Cassell, 1996.

Pearce, Douglas: *Tourism Today: A Geographical Analysis*, Harlow, Longman, 1995.

Pearce, P L: *Social Psychology Of Tourist Behaviour*, The, Oxford, Pergamon, 1982.

Peters, M: *International Tourism*, London, Hutchinson, 1969.

Ringer, Greg: *Destinations: Cultural Landscapes of Tourism*, London, Routledge, 1998.

Ritchie, Brent: *Managing Educational Tourism*, Clevedon, Channel View, 2003.

Robinson, H: *Geography of Tourism*, A, London, Macdonald and Evans, 1976.

Robinson, M, Evans, E & Chalazion, P: *Tourism and Cultural Change, Sunderland*, Business Education Publishers Ltd, 1996.

Rogers, H Anthea and Slinn, Judy A: *Tourism: Management of Facilities*, London, Pitman: M & E, 1993.

Schwaninger, M: *Trends in Leisure and Tourism for 2000 - 2010*, Prentice Hall, 1989.

Scottish Tourist Board: *Visitor Attractions: A Development Guide*, Edinburgh, Scottish Tourist Board, 1991.

Seaton, A V et al: *Tourism: The state of the Art*, Chichester, John Wiley, 1994.

Shaw, G and Williams, A: *Tourism and Tourism Spaces*, London, Sage, 2004.

Stevens, Terry: *Island Tourism*: Malta, , WTO, 1993.

Trench, R: *Travellers in Britain*, London, Aurum, 1990.

Tribe, John *Corporate Strategy for Tourism, London*, International Thomson Business Press, 1997.

Urry, John: *Tourist Gaze*, The, London, Sage, 1990.

Van den Berg et al: *Urban Tourism: Performance and Strategies in Eight European Cities*, Aldershot, Avebury, 1995.

Van Harssel, Jan: *Tourism: An Exploration*, New York, Prentice Hall, 1994.

Veal, A: *Leisure and Tourism*: Policy and Planning, Wallingford, CABI, 2001.

Wahab, S A: *Tourism Management*, Tourism International Press, 1975.

Walle, Alfred H: *Cultural Tourism*: A Strategic Focus, Boulder, Co, Westview Press, 1998.

Wilkinson, Paul: *Tourism Policy and Planning: As Studies from the Caribbean*, Elmsford New York, Cognizant Communications Corporation, 1997.

Yale, Pat: *From Tourist Attractions to Heritage Tourism*, Huntingdon, Elm, 1991.

Zarkia, Cornelia: *Philoxenia: Receiving Tourists*-but *not Guests-on a Greek Island*, Oxford, Berghahn Books, 1996.

Index

□□□